THE
PLAYWRIGHT'S
Process

THE PLAYWRIGHT'S

Process

Learning the Craft from
Today's Leading Dramatists

Buzz McLaughlin

BACK STAGE BOOKS
AN IMPRINT OF WATSON-GUPTILL PUBLICATIONS
New York

For Kris

Copyright © 1997 by Buzz McLaughlin
All Rights Reserved

First published in 1997 in the United States by Back Stage Books, an
imprint of Watson-Guptill Publications, a division of BPI
Communications, Inc., 770 Broadway, New York, N.Y. 10003-9595

Library of Congress Cataloging-in-Publication Data
McLaughlin, Buzz, 1944-
    The playwright's process : learning the craft from today's
leading dramatists / Buzz McLaughlin
      p.   cm.
    Includes index.
    ISBN 0-8230-8833-2 (alk. paper)
    1. Playwriting. 2. Dramatists, American—20th century—
Interviews. I. Title.
PN1661.M35 1997
808.2—dc21   97-7977
                                   CIP

Manufactured in the United States of America

Editor: Dale Ramsey
Designer: Jay Anning
Production manager: Ellen Greene

3 4 5 / 01

CONTENTS

11
BEGINNING THE REWRITING PROCESS   216

12
THE ONGOING DEVELOPMENT PROCESS   238

ACKNOWLEDGMENTS

As is always the case, a book gets published with the help of many people. For me the list is a long one and stretches back over three decades of working in the theater and teaching playwriting.

My first thanks must go to the hundreds of students I've had in classes and workshops over the years. How best to tackle the task of writing a good play has been the singular goal in my teaching, and most of the discoveries made in this often elusive arena have come from the give and take that's constantly occurred between us. Everything presented in this book has gone through exhaustive testing and refinement in the classroom, and I'm forever indebted to this large group of people.

I am also greatly indebted to the Dramatists Guild for the extensive interview series I've conducted under their auspices and which is so much a part of this book. And, of course, that indebtedness extends to the playwrights themselves for their willingness to share how they work in such detail. The fruits of these sessions are made available thanks to the generosity of these gifted writers and the organization that represents them. Specifically, I thank Jason Milligan for originally envisioning and then setting up the interview series at the Guild; Gary Bonasorte and Scott Segal for administering the bulk of the sessions; and Dana Singer, associate director of the Guild, for her support and guidance. I'm also grateful to McCarter Theatre and to their literary manager, Janice Paran, for the opportunity to interview Athol Fugard in Princeton.

Special thanks must go to Drew University for granting me the time and financial support to undertake and complete this project; to Playwrights Theatre of New Jersey for the numerous opportunities they've given me to work with new plays in a professional setting; to The New Harmony Project for the many years of my participation in its ongoing developmental work with new scripts; and to all the theaters and directors who have done my plays for the privilege of experiencing what it means to be a produced playwright.

Thanks are due to my play agent, Bruce Ostler, for taking the book manuscript to the Fifi Oscard Agency, and to Fifi for her enthusiastic support.

I am especially grateful to my friend Dale Ramsey, editor of Back Stage Books, for his early belief in the book and his invaluable suggestions and expertise in preparing the manuscript for publication.

Most importantly, I thank Kris, my wife, for giving of her time and talents in her typically selfless way to see this project through with me. This book is really one of our team efforts, although I did actually write the words. Without her collaboration, however, it never would have happened, as is the case with every meaningful endeavor of my life for the last thirty years.

INTRODUCTION

The word *playwright* suggests that plays are *wrought* rather than written, much as wheels were once made by wheelwrights. It suggests that raw materials must be shaped and formed into a working whole by following precise specifications. All parts must serve as a function of the finished piece. And like the wheel, the play must have a hub, a center, which distributes the load evenly. It must spin freely. It must have perfect balance. If a wheel is made wrong, it will quickly fall apart once running on the roadway. If a play is made wrong, it will quickly fall apart once running on the stage.

This book is intended as a basic guide for anyone considering "making" a play. It leads you through the process of (1) formulating an idea with dramatic potential; (2) creating characters who can bring that idea to life; (3) designing a sound structural framework; (4) getting it all down on the page; and (5) testing and launching the play once written.

Throughout, each step is illuminated by the comments and advice offered by the many established playwrights I've interviewed:

Edward Albee	Emily Mann
Lee Blessing	Terrence McNally
Horton Foote	Arthur Miller
Athol Fugard	Marsha Norman
John Guare	John Patrick Shanley
Tina Howe	Wendy Wasserstein
David Ives	Michael Weller
Romulus Linney	Lanford Wilson

Drawing heavily from transcripts of these sessions—most of which took place at the Dramatists Guild headquarters in New York City before audiences of member playwrights—*The Playwright's Process* utilizes over two hundred and fifty quotes from these proven masters of the craft as they explain in their own words why they write their plays the way they do.

What is unique here is that, in a deliberate effort to deal exclusively with process, all the interviews were conducted using the same series of questions asked in the same basic sequence. Because of this, as you work through the book you'll encounter numerous and personal responses to each specific aspect of the craft. Not surprisingly, the dramatists involved proved without exception to be thoughtful, generous people eager to share what they've learned over the course of their extraordinary careers. Their in-depth and personal accounts of how they work and what they've learned shed a rare and bright light on the often difficult endeavor of constructing a play that works.

The book is designed, then, to serve as a support system for you, the writer, as you navigate the often murky waters to get to that first readable draft and beyond. Its single goal is to help you "wright" your plays so they'll run brilliantly and for a long time.

The basis for what is presented here, in addition to the wisdom gleaned from the interviews, comes from my own accumulated insights gained as a playwright, as founder and artistic director of Playwrights Theatre of New Jersey, a professional company working exclusively with new American plays, and also from over twenty years of teaching playwriting at universities and in professional workshops around the country. A good portion of my career has been spent working closely with emerging and established writers as they've tested their new plays, uncovering what worked and what didn't through readings, workshops, and productions. Over the years I've analyzed and dissected hundreds of plays and helped playwrights redesign and reshape their scripts.

What I've discovered is that most people usually approach the writing of a play with little or no grasp of the basic principles of the craft. As a result, their work remains on the shelf or, to put it more bluntly, on the reject stack in literary managers' offices. I can't count the times my theater has rejected a play because, although the writer definitely had talent, he or she had no sense of the essential dramatic ingredients that have to be operating from page one.

We're just coming out of an era when—and this seems to be especially true for playwriting—the rigorous teaching of *craft* has not been considered a logical and necessary first step. Instead, from the start of a student's training, personal exploration and complete liberation from all time-honored "rules" of dramatic writing have been the norm. To me, therefore, it's not surprising that the majority of new plays being written today never see production. Several decades of an anti-craft mentality have flooded the market with plays that simply do not work on the stage. Sadly, thousands of these failed works keep on being written every year.

The fact is that there are a few simple principles of the craft which in one way or another need to be respected in all dramatic writing, principles which have been in place and functioning beautifully for twenty-five hundred years. A playwright ignores them at his or her peril. Without exception, every good play I've read or seen—whether written by an established, successful playwright or a student in a beginning course—has somehow incorporated the basic tenets successfully. There simply is no way around them if you hope to write successfully for the stage.

As the following pages show, the prominent playwrights I've interviewed confirm these assertions. And although their approaches to the craft vary, what has emerged from my discussions with them is that they all incorporate the same basic principles of dramatic writing whether they're fully conscious of it or not. For most of them, the application of these basics has become so automatic, instinctive, and "programmed" into their brains that they sometimes have difficulty talking about the very elements that make their own plays come so beautifully to life. But unquestionably in every case—no matter the specific process employed—the same basic components are being applied.

The good news is that these essential tenets are not difficult to grasp and are relatively easy to incorporate into your work. In fact, the writing of a play—especially during a person's first few efforts—becomes infinitely more enjoyable and ultimately more successful when the basic principles are consciously applied in a systematic way. As you write more plays these underpinnings will become more automatic, as they are with the playwrights I've talked to—more like driving a car, something you do without thinking about *how* you do it.

This book takes into account these basics of the craft from the very early thinking stages through the writing of a finished draft. It moves you through a simple, logical progression of working on a play, showing how the raw materials you draw from must be shaped into dramatic form and how, as your work unfolds, it must be constantly analyzed and tested to ensure that basic tenets are not being violated (or, if they are, that the writer is aware of it so that the necessary compensations can be made). It offers a simple process of thinking and constructing so that what you end up writing turns out to be a play that has "legs."

The difficulty with teaching a beginning course in playwriting or writing a book about it is determining where to start. *All* the basics are important. You should have a working knowledge of just about everything as you start—why one character has to function as the central figure before the preliminary structure can be created; how the dominant need of this central character drives the play and helps guide in-depth character exploration; how the "event" of the play—the central character struggling with his or her dilemma—and its resolution ultimately determines what you're saying; why a first draft can't really be attempted until you have some mastery of the techniques of good dialogue writing; and so forth. There are many aspects of the craft that in one way or another must be utilized each step of the way.

To deal with this, I've arranged the book as much as possible to present concepts, principles, and techniques in an accumulative fashion so that as new information and procedures are introduced you can work them into what you already have under control. However, because it's important early on to gain a working knowledge of the standard playwriting format and to develop your skill at writing dialogue and physical action, I suggest you begin working with Chapter 8 ("Working in the Standard Format") and Chapter 9 ("Bringing It to Life") at the same time you're working through Chapters 1 through 7. Chapters 10 through 12, covering the evolution of the script—on writing the first and subsequent drafts and the eventual development of the play—should be saved for last.

The book, then, is designed to put you through a rigorous training program. My hope is that through using it you'll gain a strong grasp of the basic craft and the process involved in creating a structurally sound play. Obviously, it can't enlarge upon your God-given gift for writing. My hope is, however, that by using this book your work will stand a better chance of eventually coming to life on the boards and that you can indeed call yourself a playwright in the full sense of the word.

FORMULATING YOUR DRAMATIC IDEA

A play's got to be a dramatic event, not a lyrical event. It's not music, it's not poetry, it's not dance, it's not narrative—it's dramatic. . . it's about conflict. It's about forces coming together.

—ROMULUS LINNEY

"The hardest thing about writing is getting from nothing to the first draft."

Every successful, experienced playwright I know agrees with this statement. They accept it as fact, but have managed to find a way of pushing through the writing process. The initial chapters of this book are designed to ease you out of the starting gate well positioned and in good form as you begin the journey to your first draft. It probably won't make the work any less strenuous, but it will provide you with a proven approach to launching the writing of your next play.

The first consideration as you begin work on a play is to come up with a workable idea to write about, something that will easily hold all the basic dramatic ingredients. It doesn't matter what length play you're planning to write. In fact, at this beginning point that shouldn't really be a concern. Your task is to find that seed of an idea that can grow into a brilliant play.

Finding that idea isn't always easy, and there are innumerable places to look for it. But even before you begin the search, you need to know what you're looking for. You have to have a clear sense of the dramatic potential of ideas as they present themselves. You need to know how to put them to the test. This, then, is the obvious place to start the process: Learning *what to look for* in an idea.

This chapter presents a brief overview of the basic dramatic ingredients present in all successful plays, no matter the style or length. It's probably the most important discussion in the entire book, in that it strips everything down to the bare essentials—a preliminary engineering lesson in how plays are supposed to function. This will arm you with the basic criteria necessary to test the potential of the ideas as they come to you. You want to know:

- Will this idea work as a play?

- Does it have the basic dramatic ingredients to sustain itself?

- Will it form the solid foundation needed to support what I'll be building on top of it?

As we proceed, it will be important for you to keep in perspective what this initial discussion is attempting to do. It is definitely *not* intended to rigidly confine your thinking or to stifle your creative juices regarding your ideas for possible plays. I encourage you to explore and try things, to keep an open mind, and to stay flexible. What follows is meant to bolster your expertise in testing potential ideas early on, so that you can at least get a sense of whether or not something has promise.

My primary reason for writing this book is that I've read hundreds of plays, many by extremely gifted writers, that do not work. In almost every case it's clear that the writer did not conduct some sort of preliminary analysis of the central idea. It's as if the entire script had been written blindly, without regard to basic dramatic principles—perhaps in the hope that, in some mysterious way, everything would simply fall into place.

The sad truth is that this rarely, if ever, happens. People spend hundreds of hours, often slaving a year or more over a manuscript which, having little chance of coming to life on the stage, is doomed to sit on a shelf. Like the carpenter who builds a house on sand, many writers build their plays with little or no regard to the essential dramatic underpinnings that plays need in order to work.

I ask you to be patient as you begin. I feel, with every new play I write, the urge to start with the first scene and get those characters talking. And that can be a wonderful exercise to get inner currents flowing and ideas popping. However, be aware that such early exploratory work, exciting as it may be, needs to be identified for what it is. Remember that before you actually start writing the play itself it is critical that you make an initial effort to chart your course. Things may change as you go along (and probably will), but by doing some preliminary thinking and planning, you'll at least be prepared for departure.

In one way or another, all the playwrights I've interviewed for this book report that they do chart their course. They've accepted it as just one of the necessary steps in the process.

More than likely, you already have in your head an idea you think might make a great play. Later on, we'll take a close look at where ideas come from and where to search for them. For now, keep in mind your most promising hunch, even if it's just a shred of an idea. The best way to use this book is to actually apply what I'm talking about to your work.

A Few Initial Guidelines

If you are setting out to write your first or one of your first plays, consider the following preliminary suggestions. They may appear to be somewhat restrictive and limiting, but keep in mind that they're intended to guide you into this business of writing plays without becoming completely overwhelmed. Although you have to put your heart and soul into any play you write, you can't get around the fact that your early efforts are also your learning pieces.

- Aim for a short, or one-act, play of around twenty to forty script pages or less. Writing a few "short short" plays of five to ten pages is also a good place to start. And I suggest that you stay with the short form for your first several efforts. Just as students of prose fiction are urged to write several short stories before attempting a novel, I urge you not to attempt overly long and ambitious projects your first few times out. Obviously, this dictates that you consider ideas which are not overly complicated. You'll be surprised at how simple a dramatic idea can make a wonderful play.

- Try to limit the number of characters to two or three. Generally, the more characters you introduce, the more complicated the writing of your play becomes, much like the degree of difficulty confronted in juggling the more balls you try to keep in the air. The greater the number of vivid personalities thrown in the mix, the more intricate become the human interactions and the plot mechanisms. Keep in mind that many brilliant full-length plays (usually 75 to 100 script pages) have only three or four characters. This economy allows you to focus more clearly and confidently on the dramatic heart of the play, and this is especially important in your early efforts.

• When considering the characters, also be aware that in most cases you'll have an easier time of it if the central character and at least one other major character share a part of their past, or *backstory*, together. Characters who already know each other and have shared important life experiences almost always open up a richer and deeper dramatic field in which to set your play. Obviously, there are exceptions to this; for example, Edward Albee's classic one-act, *The Zoo Story*, is a meeting between two strangers on a park bench. But most great plays involve characters who share a long history. A conflict between a parent and child, brother and sister, husband and wife, or two old friends has a special potency because of their long-standing relationship and memories of closeness and past conflicts.

• Choose an idea set in the present time—that is, a contemporary story, taking place in the general "now." It's possible to dip into the past if you know it intimately and are more comfortable with a bygone setting for a specific idea, but, generally, the present is the least complicated time frame to write in. I urge you not to dive too far into the past (or blast off into the future), especially when the time you're considering is unfamiliar to you. That would bring up a whole new set of demands— namely research—which we'll get to later on.

• Write your play in the realistic style. Have your characters be real, believable people and put them in a real, believable place. The tone of the play should approximate real life. As restrictive as this may seem, I urge you to avoid fantasy, allegory, and highly stylized approaches in your early efforts, for as soon as you introduce unrealistic elements there's an automatic tendency to throw out all the rules and make up new ones as you go along. This can work beautifully if you understand the dramatic conventions you are departing from and know what you're getting yourself into. But if you don't, you can get very lost very quickly.

- Try to visualize your play as one continuous scene in one setting. More often than not, beginning playwrights think they need four, five, or six scenes to tell their story when, in fact, it is in scene five or six that the real play is to be found. Everything else is backstory, which leads up to the actual dramatic event. Keep the story simple and direct. Go right to the heart of it and stay there.

- It's generally easier to tackle and sustain a serious, dramatic idea than an overtly comic one. The motivations driving characters and the mechanisms of plot are usually more clear-cut and direct in serious ideas, and therefore they tend to be more manageable. Good comedies and farces are a delight, but the more effortless they appear, the more tricky they are to write. Of course, I am not suggesting that you avoid humor. Your characters will determine whether there are potentially funny, even hilarious moments or scenes in your play. But the *initial idea* should be basically serious in intent.

Writing good plays is not easy. It's a craft that must be learned and acquired over time. Keeping the foregoing guidelines in mind as you begin will help you select a project you'll be able to manage as you start applying the tools of the trade. You'll stand a much better chance of keeping things under control and of gaining a working knowledge of the basic building blocks of all successful plays.

The Basic Dramatic Ingredients

The first step in the process is to scrutinize potential ideas as they come to you to see if they have the potential to become good plays. And to do this, you have to know what to look for. All good plays—short and long, one-act and full-length, comedies and farces, tragedies and dramas, and everything in between—have the same basic dramatic ingredients whether the playwright is conscious of them or not:

1. *One central, or pivotal, character.*

2. The central character has a strong *inner need* or desire that must be satisfied.

3. The central character's need or desire is being thwarted, setting up *conflict* and an intensifying dilemma.

4. A *resolution* of the conflict/dilemma is somehow achieved, leaving the central character a different person at the end of the play.

That's it. One central character struggling with a strong need which is being thwarted but who manages, in one way or another, to resolve that need by the end of the play, leaving him or her a changed person.

There are infinite variations on this, but all successful plays have these basics firmly in place in some fundamental way. Sometimes they're carefully and skillfully camouflaged or partially hidden from view, but they're there.

It can be expressed even more simply:

Central Character → Conflict/Dilemma → Resolution

This is a basic *structural* truth. When you strip away the elements that make each play unique—the use of language, theatricality, character personalities, humor, specifics of plot and setting—you're left with this basic *structure*. That's why it's dramatic writing and not another form of fiction, like the novel or the short story.

Plays are more akin to music, in that there is always forward movement—action played out in time. There is always conflict and turmoil, a working through of the central character's dilemma.

Arthur Miller explains: "There are two forces always working. One is working against the other . . . and the business of the play is to explore that conflict and resolve it."

John Guare says that he asks himself: "Do I have a good argument going on? Do I have a character who believes in something and a character who believes in exactly the opposite? It all starts with a disagreement."

Or, as **Marsha Norman** puts it: "When you go to the theater you want to know who the main character is, and you want to be able to see what they want, see what's against them, and see whether they get it or not. Then you want to go home."

A brief word here about screenplays: Also inherently dramatic, film scripts operate in much the same way as plays, but with a visual rather than a verbal focus. Much of what is said in this book about basic dramatic structure can be applied to the writing of a screenplay as well as a play, although the focus here is definitely on writing for the stage. And there are important and obvious differences, such as length of scenes, settings, rhythm and pace, dominance of the camera's eye over dialogue, and so on. But all good movies, like all good plays, contain the same structural basics.

This progression—central character → conflict/dilemma → resolution—which is the play's overall structural shape, is often called the *motor* or the *thrust* of the play.

"It's about finding the motor," **Emily Mann** explains, ". . . finding out what keeps it moving, what propels the play, what keeps it going forward actively."

We don't really sense the structure in performance, when, we hope, the language and specific actions of the characters effectively cover it over and sweep us away. It's like watching a car pass by on a highway: You see the color, make, model, and the people inside, you hear the tires on the pavement, but you never think of the motor propeling it all down the road.

However, should that motor break down, everything comes grinding to a halt, the hood is propped open, and you stand there staring at that dark, greasy mass of iron. If you know something about engines, you stand a good chance of getting the car running again. It may take some time, but you'll probably find the problem and be able to fix it. Likewise, if you're staring at a play that doesn't work and you know something about its motor, you'll probably be able to put your finger on the problem.

Some years back, at my own theater, I functioned as the chief mechanic, or *dramaturg* (also spelled *dramaturge*), helping playwrights get their scripts' motor running smoothly. For your own work, you need to become the mechanic, or at least a part of you does. Otherwise, you won't know how to fix your plays, let alone know how to build them effectively from scratch. It's essential, then, that you permanently install in your playwright's head the basics of dramatic structure. To help accomplish that, let's take a closer look at each of the ingredients we have listed above.

The Central Character

It's critical that your thinking focus on *one* central character. Probably the single biggest problem I've run up against over the years as a teacher and dramaturg is that people can't decide who their plays are about. I find myself reading ten, twenty, thirty pages into a script wanting to know who I'm supposed to be attaching myself to and identifying with, and I don't have a clue. Sadly, I too often still don't know by the end of the play.

The point is that *audiences* demand to know which character they're supposed to be watching and listening to more than the others and what his or her problem is. They demand a focus. They need to know up front who the play is about and then to engage with that central character as the dilemma is wrestled with. If they don't get this focus, they don't know how to listen to the play or engage with the story as it begins to unfold. They don't have the information needed to position themselves properly to make sense of what's being thrown at them. When the central character is not identified early on, audiences fall asleep or get that tingling feeling in their legs signaling an intense desire to leave the theater.

Arthur Miller says: "I'm better off if the central character's there to start with. It will more likely work out. If he or she's not there, I'm going to run into trouble sooner or later." And the trouble he's talking about is a lack of focus—the same lack of focus the audience ultimately experiences when a central character is not clearly discernible.

Of course, other characters play a critical role in the development of the central character's dilemma. That's what sparks conflict, and conflict is what plays thrive on. All these other characters must be fully realized; they may even end up with as many or more lines than your central character. They should have their own needs and desires and, consequently, their own conflicts and dilemmas. The more human and complex you make these characters, the more powerful and exciting their confrontations are with your central figure. However, as you begin working with your idea it's crucial that your thinking focus on that one focal, pivotal character. This is the structural spine of the play.

As **David Ives** explains:

> I figure out who is in the play, what the basic thrust of the play is, and, if I don't find that the main character has some sort of powerful objective, the idea probably isn't ready yet. The main character is, after all, the person whose problem or objective runs the action.

The Central Character's Need

The reason most people write plays is that they believe they have something important to say. Whatever that something involves, it's the central character's primary need, want, or desire that serves as the framework for dealing with the issue. Because of this, the central character is sometimes referred to as the *point-of-view character,* for the author's ideas are being conveyed through the character's struggle and the way the struggle is resolved. So the need of the central character, in a very real sense, is really what your play is about.

Dramatically speaking, what's important is that the need be deep-seated and compelling, something the central character *must* satisfy or fulfill. It is what drives that person, pushes him into conflict, or propels her to an inevitable end. "People have to want something," **Horton Foote** explains, "and I don't mean in an overt way or necessarily in a social way, wanting to change the world or something like that. But a *want.*"

Lanford Wilson concurs: "Usually you can't write ten lines without someone wanting something. Even if you don't know it."

John Guare relates:

> I learned about play*wrighting* from the jackets of show albums because I always noticed that the first or second song in any musical was the "want" song—"All I want is a room somewhere." I want. I want. And then I realized that, in a sense, that was no different from page one of *The Three Sisters*: "I want to get to Moscow." King Lear says, "I want to give my property to my three daughters." There is always this searching at the beginning. And this operates much more powerfully in a play than any other form. I think there's a connection between *The Three Sisters* and even a play like *Waiting for Godot*: "I want to get to Moscow" and "I want the man with the answers to arrive." In both cases the wants are not fulfilled. And the failure of that expectation creates the dramatic energy and is extraordinary. When I'm writing and looking at that material, that raw clay I'm creating, I look for the *want* in it.

Arthur Miller says that for his tragic heroes, this has to be "an unstoppable emotion. It cannot be derailed, it cannot be stopped." In Miller's classic drama *Death of a Salesman,* for example, Willy Loman has an intense inner need for self-acceptance and a justification for his life. It comes from deep inside him, from his own insecurities, his fears and buried feelings of guilt. It is this inner force in Willy which drives the action of the play.

Or look at John Proctor, in Miller's *The Crucible*. Here is a man with a compelling inner need to be forgiven in the eyes of his God. This need propels him into a confrontation which leads to the ultimate crossroads—choosing death and forgiveness, or life and perpetual guilt.

Often the need is so submerged that the central character is unable to acknowledge it or recognize the degree to which it is shaping and driving him or her into an intensifying dilemma. Instead, the need manifests itself in surface desires, such as a person's lust for sex, money, or power. Underneath Willy Loman's desire for success for his favorite son or for his own recognition as a salesman is a deeper, unfulfilled need that motivates the behavior we witness on the stage. Miller says: "I gravitate toward people who are aspiring even wrongly to some spiritual engagement and are being held down to the earth by the situation or by part of their nature."

As **Michael Weller** explains:

> I think that drama, as opposed to storytelling, is what Aristotle
> said: It's an action. You're imitating an action, which is a
> person who decides there's something he wants and he gets off
> his ass and goes for it. Now that thing he wants might not be
> what he *really* wants, or he might discover when he gets it that
> that isn't what he wanted at all, but I think drama does break
> down into being people going after something.

Romulus Linney, in describing what separates a play from other forms
of fiction, says: "A play is a piece of action; it's something that rushes by,
like life. It should have that kind of vibrancy to it, that kind of rush, and
that kind of presence. It shouldn't be delicate."

What's important here is that this inner need, however it manifests
itself, is the fuel that keeps the motor of the play running. It's what gives
the play its forward motion. It's what hooks an audience and keeps them
with you. They identify with the central character because they recognize
his need, even if he doesn't. They become emotionally involved and will-
ingly commit the time it takes to see how he's able to deal with the obstacles before him as he struggles to satisfy his need.

"The audience is always waiting to see what will happen," **Marsha
Norman** says. "That is the drama—whether the central character is
going to get what he or she wants or not."

The Conflict/Dilemma

Now that you have a central character with a strong, compelling inner
need which must be satisfied, you must invent ways in which that need is
frustrated and thwarted. **Marsha Norman** says:

> In all really successful plays, there is a protagonist who wants
> something, and then there are obstacles. And those obstacles
> may be people or inabilities or circumstances beyond their
> control or the gods—they could be anything.

Lee Blessing says that he asks himself the following questions:

> If this is the guy's central problem, then how does he want to
> solve it, and where does he go, and who are the people he
> encounters, and what are the things that get in his way, and
> what are the various shifts he tries to get someplace?

The answers to these kinds of questions, of course, will become the action of your play—the actual plot that your pivotal character, in interaction with other characters, works through onstage. In other words, the play itself is your central character's conflict/dilemma as it manifests itself in action.

Moreover, the action you're going to dramatize is the *culmination* of the dilemma—that is, the final struggle before a resolution is found. There may be a long, involved history of the central character's problem, but your play should focus on the specific events surrounding his or her final confrontation with it.

There are two ways a central character's dominant need is frustrated or thwarted, thereby creating the play's conflict/dilemma. First, the character is often his (or her) own worst enemy and is, in a very real sense, at war with himself. He chases after the wrong things; he thinks he has all the answers; his pride blinds him to the truth; his ambition leads him into trouble; his inferiority complex leaves him helpless, and so on. The second way to set up obstacles is through introducing other characters who, in one way or another, block your central character from fulfilling his need.

These barriers from within and without are what make plays come to life. The word, again, is *conflict.* Your job is to put your central character into hand-to-hand combat (verbally and at times literally) with himself and other characters as he struggles to fulfill his need and resolve his dilemma.

In speaking of how she wrote her 1983 Pulitzer Prize–winning play *'night, Mother,* **Marsha Norman** recalled her thinking process when choosing to pit mother against suicidal daughter: "I only wanted to do it in the most direct fashion. Here's a person who wants this, here's a person who doesn't want that person to do that. Let 'em go and see what happens." The conflict is clear-cut: Before the action begins, the daughter, Jesse, has made up her mind to kill herself, and the play dramatizes Mama's attempt to talk her out of it. Norman adds: "If there isn't heightened conflict nobody will want to do it. We have a lot of non-heightened conflict in life. What we go to the theater for, I think, is to see extreme versions of the things that trouble us on a moment-to-moment basis."

As you begin thinking about possible ideas, remember that in most cases the more intimate the relationship the central character has with the other characters, the more potent the resulting conflict. This is why most great plays are set within the family unit. In *'night Mother,* for example, that Jesse and Mama have lived together for years and know each other's habits and routines down to the smallest and most inconsequential detail is what gives the play its intensity.

Also keep in mind that the stronger the need of your central character, the more compelling and desperate you can make it, the stronger your potential for conflict. Likewise, the stronger you can make other characters' needs and desires, which should in some way oppose those of your central character, the stronger the potential for conflict. Your goal should be to have, either directly or under the surface, some sense of conflict present constantly.

Nothing is more deadly than a play that ticks along minute after minute with no conflict manifesting itself in some way. (I should say nothing is more deadly than a play that ticks along *page after page* with no conflict. Because chances are that such a script will never make it to the stage!)

As you begin inventing and building on each initial seed of an idea, try to follow this rule: *Add not a single component into the mix which cannot contribute to your central character's dilemma, further the conflict, or intensify his or her struggle.* Always find some way, even if indirectly, for each and every element you throw into the pot—be it other characters, setting, the central character's inner psychological makeup, major or minor twists of plot, and so on—to propel the play forward and heighten the dramatic impact. At this early stage of the process, you want to be sure that every piece of your material has the potential for enhancing conflict.

The Resolution

Plays, in a very real sense, are like taking a trip, and a trip always involves arriving at a destination, a final stopping place. Although the audience members remain in their seats, their minds and emotions should be on a journey with your characters. As **Athol Fugard** puts it: "You literally, without any interruption, are going to ask an audience to join you at the start of an experience and to travel through time with you until you reach a conclusion."

And as with any trip, as opposed to open-ended wandering, the audience *expects* eventually to arrive at a destination. They want to feel that they're being taken to an interesting new place, and when they arrive they want to know it, to recognize it, to sense that the journey has ended.

"I think the end is the play, and that's what you're looking for," **Arthur Miller** explains. "Until you've got that end . . . it's not a play."

Wendy Wasserstein says basically the same thing: "I start writing the play when I have an idea where the play is going to *arc* to, or land on.

Then I know that, in fact, it's a play, that it's starting somewhere and going somewhere."

Marsha Norman explains:

> I used to have the idea that you could just start to write and see what happens. Now I find that doesn't work out so well. . . . If you set out on a Sunday afternoon for a drive—you're just going to see what happens and where you wind up—you could have an extraordinary day. But the odds are not good. You could get really lost, you could run out of gas, you could get tired of talking to the person who's in the car with you. On the other hand, if you set out on a Sunday afternoon and you decide you are going to Niagara Falls, there's already a structure to the day. There's something at stake: "Will you get there or not? Will it be interesting or not? What does it mean to go there?" Once you have a destination, lots of things come into focus for you as a writer—and as a car passenger as well. So now I would never begin to write without an end.

David Ives says it this way:

> I never start writing anything until I know what the end is. That is probably the one definite condition I have, and I don't think I've ever changed an ending that I started out with. If I know that I have to go to Buffalo, I can go by way of Alaska, but I'm still going to Buffalo. But if I just set out on the road with no destination in mind, I quickly return home with nothing."

What's being said here, of course, is that you'll have trouble planning your play without having at least some idea of how your central character's dilemma is resolved and how his (or her) struggle has changed him, how different he is at the end of the play from the way he was at the beginning. Every choice you make along the way will be influenced by where you want your play to land.

This is not to say that what you come up with in this preliminary thinking can never change. Of course it can, and often does, as you progress with a project.

As **John Guare** points out:

> You have some sort of sketched-up resolution that you're going to go to. But you can't commit to it. You should leave every

door open so the play doesn't become too schematic. Because if it does, it won't surprise you and you don't have to take any detours in the course of writing it.

The important thing is that all good plays have a strong sense of closure, a feeling that the story is finished, the tale spun. Audiences want this. They need it to make sense of what they've just witnessed. Your goal should always be to leave the play in the audience's lap, so to speak, so they can pick it up whole and walk out of the theater with it. This can't happen unless you hand it to them with authority and leave them something to think about. You do this by *resolving* the central character's dilemma. It can be happy or sad, but it must be resolved.

Not resolving the dilemma leaves an audience stranded and frustrated and, at times, angry. Provoking audience frustration and anger is sometimes important at the end of plays, but this is not the way to accomplish it. Ignoring resolution is one of the most effective ways to get the audience to dismiss your play altogether and tell their friends to stay away. The problem is that after you've whetted their appetite for some sort of final destination, you've then denied them the fun of arriving.

Imagine this: You find yourself stranded on a beach without food or water and with one dollar in your shorts. It's a hot July day, and you've been walking for hours. You see an ice cream stand in the distance, manage to find the energy to get over to it, and with your dollar purchase a double-decker peach and raspberry swirl on a wafer cone. Then, ready to devour this indescribable treat, you trip on a piece of driftwood and send the ice cream spinning off the cone into the sand. Major frustration. Don't do this to an audience.

Although it's much too early to come up with precise resolutions, it is essential that you give serious thought now as to how your central character's conflict might be resolved and how he or she is changed at the end. For it is through the way you resolve the dramatic dilemma that you communicate your own beliefs about the issues being dealt with in the play. It's the way playwrights speak to an audience, the way they get across their message, the way they can make powerful statements about the world they live in and get people to listen.

This is why, when asked if he has the ending in mind, however vague, before committing to writing the first draft of something, **John Guare** says, "I'd better, or there's no sense in starting."

In your preliminary thinking about resolution, you should constantly ask yourself two simple questions: First, do I honestly believe the message that is communicated by resolving my play this way? If you don't, change it or discard it as a possibility. If you don't believe what your play is going to say and believe it passionately, why write it in the first place?

And second, is my central character truly changed by the end of the play? Is there a readily perceived difference in his or her outlook toward the world, inner self, or both? Has that character arrived at a new place emotionally or spiritually? "The whole thing ought to add up," **Arthur Miller** explains. "You ought to be in a different space by the end of the play than when you entered at the beginning of it."

In musing over possible resolutions, be tough on yourself. If there is little or no perceived change in your central figure, you must do some rethinking. Don't charge ahead without a genuine sense that you have a character who's going to be "put through the ringer" and come out meaningfully changed. You'll avoid one of the common mistakes writers make. Remember that plays *never* work without this change taking place.

Good plays well performed have the potential for being our most potent form of communication. The immediacy and power of brilliant live performance coupled with a well-written script can leave people profoundly moved. It can change lives and instill entirely new ways of looking at human interaction or social issues.

Consider again Miller's *The Crucible*. John Proctor is ultimately faced with the choice of death and redemption, or life and loss of self-respect. Miller's message is clear and powerful. Proctor chooses redemption. It all happens on the final page. Everything earlier has led up to his staring at a piece of paper he has just signed his name to. Then he rips up the paper, is led out to the gallows, and the audience is left stunned. Miller has communicated a precise and awesome message in a powerful way, for he knew his destination. His play comes to closure, and his central character's dilemma is resolved.

Considering up front what your destination is, in a sense, the most important of all the early steps. What *do* you want to say? What *do* you want to leave in the hearts and minds of your audience? It's all there in how you resolve your play.

Putting Your Ideas to the Test

The first step in the process, then, is to analyze and test your idea, to measure it against the basic dramatic ingredients and see if it holds up, or appears to have the potential of holding up when further developed. Your idea must have one central character with a compelling inner need that is being frustrated by his or her own mistakes and by other characters with opposing needs or desires. From this conflict develops a dilemma which must ultimately be resolved. It is critical that your idea incorporate these ingredients before you commit to going much further with it.

This is the time to be tough on yourself. Take a close, hard look at each play idea you have and determine if it's fully formed enough to pass this test. If it isn't, either file it away for the time being and let it percolate longer, or keep working with it, exploring fresh approaches until you sense that the pieces are in place.

Burn these basic ingredients into your brain. As you proceed through the process of writing your play, you'll run into surprises and hidden turns which you can't anticipate at this point. That's normal. But with the basic building blocks at your disposal, you can stay in control and do your adjusting, rethinking, and reshaping with an awareness of what you're doing—namely, writing a play that will work dramatically.

2

STATING YOUR DRAMATIC PREMISE

I think anybody who takes the trouble to write what we refer to as a
serious play is holding a mirror up to people, saying: "Look, this is
the way you behave, this is who you are. If you don't like it, why
don't you change?" To hold a mirror up to people, to communicate.

—EDWARD ALBEE

Your next step in formulating an idea is to focus your thinking more deliberately on what you'll ultimately be communicating to your audience. As discussed in Chapter 1, how you resolve your central character's dilemma determines what message you're putting across. And what you have to say is the most important consideration of all. It's the real reason you're writing your play in the first place.

A current popular theory used in the teaching of creative writing insists that the writer should never consciously consider theme or message during the writing process. I've had people get upset and even walk out of my workshops when I say it's important to give some thought up front as to what will be the primary communication of a play. I try to tell them their open-ended approach may work for poetry or fiction (although I doubt it), but when developing an idea for a play, it's almost impossible to proceed successfully without giving at least some thought to what you're trying to say.

In one way or another, nearly all the playwrights I've interviewed agree with this. The simple fact is that in gathering the basic materials necessary to construct the framework for a play you have to think about your ending or resolution, and by so doing you're automatically dealing with the primary communication to your audience. To avoid thinking about theme or message, therefore, is to avoid thinking about how you're going to put your play together structurally. And to do that is to beg for frustration.

Write It Out

Because of the interrelatedness of theme and structure, it's important early on in the process to attempt to put down on paper—as accurately as you can—what you think you're trying to say with your idea, to state simply and clearly the primary, universal truth you ultimately want to communicate. In playwriting this statement is called the *dramatic premise*. It's the theme or message of your play as you see it now. Don't worry that you'll be locking yourself in by thinking about this so early on—you won't be. It's simply a preliminary exploration, an initial probing to help get your mind and heart activated and focussed.

It must be stated at the outset that there are writers who don't work this way and who instead discover their premise as they write their plays. Their focus is on a problem they want to solve. For example, **John Patrick Shanley** explains:

> I have always been amazed at writers who start from theme. I don't know how they do it. It's a way that definitely happens, there are people who do this. They have a theme, an abstract idea that they feel passionate about, and they write a play to the purpose of dramatizing that theme. I don't do that. I'm starting from a place of character and extreme specificity of emotion, and I'm trying to state the problem that I'm currently involved with. As fast as I can, I put what is at stake up at the beginning of the play and get to a place as quickly as possible where I don't know the answers. So I am not writing about something where I'm saying: "I know something, and I'm going to tell you about it"; I am saying: "Brothers and sisters, I have brought you to this place because I'm in terrible trouble

and I don't know what to do. And this is the situation, and now I'm going to try and work it out right in front of you."

Shanley also stresses, however, that he hasn't always worked this way. Over the years he has developed a strong grasp of structure and the ability to shape his plays as he's working on them.

We'll cover more on the importance of preparation later. What's important here is that even writers like Shanley start with a strong focus, a clearly defined problem they want to tackle. They may not, at the start, be consciously aware of the solution to the problem they're dealing with, but they have developed the skills necessary to keep their play on track as it's being written. For those in the early stages of their playwriting career, giving serious thought up front to dramatic premise is the best way to gain a grasp of how plays work structurally. And gaining this grasp is essential.

Any discussion of dramatic premise and its importance to playwrights must acknowledge a debt to Lajos Egri, who first applied the term to playwriting in the early 1940s. The first section of his book *The Art of Dramatic Writing* is generally considered the classic analysis of premise as it applies to writing for the theater, and the discussion that follows has its roots in Egri's approach. In my opinion he got it right, and although some of his examples seem outdated today, the truth of his argument stands.

Let's look again at Miller's *Death of a Salesman.* Although different people will come away with different reactions, one overriding truth seems to hit everyone in a powerful way: Looking for fulfillment, both materially and spiritually, in worldly success leads to disillusionment. Willy Loman's need to succeed (and have his sons succeed) as the world has defined it traps him into a downward spiral that ultimately destroys him. This basic truth is implanted in our hearts and minds as we walk out of the theater.

The premise of Miller's *The Crucible* is just as straightforward: Honor and integrity conquer sin and evil. John Proctor does not sell out. At the end of the play, we're left with a powerful sense of this man's integration as a person and of his liberation from guilt. The idea here is that people can and do rise to the occasion, even if their only reward is death. Miller's dramatic premise functions personally for the central character and communally for the society in which the play is set. Proctor has found peace and the witch hunt will now end.

Notice that both plays' dramatic premises are stated with an *active* verb linking the two parts: "Looking for fulfillment in worldly success *leads to* disillusionment" and "Honor and integrity *conquer* sin and evil." It's always important to state your dramatic premise in this fashion, so that you can sense its forward movement, which will reflect the forward movement of your play.

Probably the most common active verb in dramatic premises is "leads to." Something *leads to* something else. Other strong verbs on which a premise might hinge are "encourages," "destroys," "defies," and "defeats."

Lajos Egri offers the following examples of premises for four Shakespeare plays. Again, different people may state the dramatic premises of these plays in different ways, but the basic messages contained in them would have to be the same:

Macbeth — Ruthless ambition leads to its own destruction.

Romeo and Juliet — Great love defies even death.

Othello — Jealousy destroys itself and the object of its love.

King Lear — Unfounded suspicion leads to disaster.

The important point here is that, although there are obvious variations on how these can be stated, each captures the basic, essential communication we're left with at the end of the plays.

Take a close look at some of your all-time favorite plays. Ask yourself: What is the playwright really saying and how does he or she go about communicating it? Analyze the plays in terms of their basic dramatic ingredients, focusing in on the central character's main dilemma and how it's resolved. Then try to write out the dramatic premise for each one. Taking the time to do this will sharpen your critical thinking skills as a playwright and help you with analyzing your own ideas.

Now take a look at your play-in-the-making and write out your own dramatic premise. It all boils down, literally, to filling in the blanks:

_____ leads to _____.

Keep it short and to the point—no clutter or embellishments. And don't worry if it seems overly basic or obvious. It should be fundamental and clear. Writing out your dramatic premise is just for you, an essential tool, like a plumb line to a carpenter. The audience will never see or hear it directly when your work is done, but the finished product will testify to its good use during construction.

Take care not to formulate an inert statement of fact, such as "Adultery is bad," or "Worldly success is hollow." These statements just sit there; they suggest neither a progression nor that the play is going to take you to a destination. Remember, you aren't about to write an essay here. You're going to write a living, breathing piece for the theater that centers on a character struggling to resolve a dilemma. So keep your premise *dramatic*. Instill it with forward motion, and have it tell you that your play is going to be about conflict.

Coming up with a simple dramatic premise stated in active terms isn't always easy. But it's such an essential step that you should force yourself to write it out. You'll find yourself having to ask some hard questions about what you're really trying to say. And although you may not feel entirely comfortable with your initial efforts, remember that what you're really doing is sharpening your focus on the dramatic essence of your play in terms of your central character's struggle—how he or she resolves it—and what it's going to mean for anyone watching this on a stage. As suggested earlier, skipping this step at this point will only short-circuit your thinking and decision-making in the playwriting process.

As with all this early work in formulating your idea, your dramatic premise may change. The discoveries you'll make as you move through the process may very well shift your focus. You may find that your play is really about something different from what you now think it is, and it will become clear when and if your premise is no longer functioning for you. The point is that if you don't formulate one to start off with, you won't have anything with which to gauge the hundreds of ideas and possibilities that will constantly be presenting themselves as you move deeper into the project. Every choice you make as you proceed will be determined ultimately by your dramatic premise. If a more appropriate premise does begin to present itself, it's because you had the first one there to show you the way to the better one.

Take some time to mull all this over for a while. Challenge yourself to discover what it is you really stand for and how this play is going to speak to some aspect of that. Then put it down in writing in the form of a dramatic premise. You won't be locking yourself into anything. Rather, it will help guide you to that part of yourself and your belief system that will fuel the writing of your play.

Horton Foote puts it beautifully:

> There has to be a point where you understand that what you
> have to say is different from what anybody else would say. And
> the quicker you understand that and begin to get in touch with
> what you really have to say, the richer your writing will be.

In other words, know your dramatic premise.

Flexibility Is the Key

When you're ready to write your play, I suggest you put your written dramatic premise up somewhere in clear view of your workspace. It will serve as a constant reminder of why you're sitting there slaving over those pages. Then, when you get stuck or feel that a scene is wandering aimlessly and going nowhere, you can stop and meditate on that simple, clear statement. Force yourself to ask: "How does what I'm writing today contribute to the dramatic premise?" If you can't answer the question (which is usually the case when you've written yourself into a dead end), go back until you find where the scene is still on track and start over from there.

In describing the writing process for his 1980 Pulitzer Prize–winning play *Talley's Folly*, for example, **Lanford Wilson** explains:

> I said: What this play is about is that you must be willing to
> risk everything you have in order to get what you want. And I
> wrote that down and put it above the typewriter, and
> everything that didn't apply to that in some way went bye-bye.

On the other hand, if you finish a scene and love what's happened on the pages but it seems to be heading off in a new direction, one that seemingly has nothing to do with your stated dramatic premise, take a deep breath and keep going with the new material until it either plays itself out or finds its way back to the main thrust of the play. If the new direction persists and continues to bear exciting new pages, look again at your dramatic premise and consider adjusting it to fit more accurately where the play is now heading. Think about alternatives. Try to figure out what your subconscious is telling you.

The key here is flexibility. Plays are not written in one sitting and are rarely written in a hundred. The process is one of constant discovery— thousands of tiny choices being made every day, usually on a hunch or mere whim. It's not a science, but messy and uncertain. In the final analysis, it's a mystery how a finished script eventually gets written.

The more you work with your idea and the further you get into the actual writing of the play, the clearer your thinking will become. Your initial premise may very well need adjustment. You may have to throw it out altogether for something entirely new that more precisely captures what you want to say with the play.

As **Tina Howe** points out: "You have these impulses that make you start a play, but often the heart of the play has nothing to do with what those ideas were that made you begin it in the first place." Writing a play is like removing layers of paint off a wall in an old house—you keep uncovering things that couldn't be seen until you removed the layer on top. It's a constant uncovering and revealing process. And with every layer uncovered, your dramatic premise has to be looked at anew.

Believe It Passionately

Playwrights, like all artists, create their works because they have something they feel compelled to communicate. As you ponder your initial dramatic premise, remember that what you come up with should be something you feel passionately about, something you believe in and can get emotional over.

"Nobody should write unless there is something crying to be said," **Edward Albee** says. "There's absolutely no reason to write—no reason to waste your own time as a writer, no reason to waste an audience's time—unless you're trying to change the world."

Romulus Linney puts it this way: "It should make you cry, it should excite you, it should get you feeling very strange and funny and goosebumpy and all that."

As much as the specific circumstances of your play allow, your dramatic premise should represent who you are and what you stand for. Therefore, don't be afraid to state it boldly. You have to believe it and be willing to defend it. If you're afraid of what your friends or family or anyone else will think of your dramatic premise, you might not be ready to write that play.

As **Horton Foote** says: "My gut instinct tells me that the first person you have to please is yourself, and if you are passionate about it and can find a way to really relate to what you know and feel, then you will find an audience."

And **John Guare** points out: "The premise of a play can be very, very small. It doesn't have to be the most clever or momentous thing in the world. It just has to be something that releases you emotionally."

You want to focus on deeply held truths about life that you, the playwright, want to communicate—otherwise, why should you bother? To *be* a playwright? No good. To make money? There are much better ways. To delineate certain political or historical events? Become a journalist. Sure, there's Cecil B. DeMille's famous line: "If you want to send a message, use Western Union." He was talking, of course, about a heavyhanded peddling of ideologies. This is not what dramatic premise is.

Playwrights from the earliest days of drama were poets and philosophers and, above all, prophets of their times who wanted to convey the truth as they saw it; they cared deeply about life and their fellow humans. Having these motives, too, will fuel you with a passionate drive to get your ideas out there.

Romulus Linney captures this beautifully when he says:

> A good play to me is a play that challenges an audience's assumptions. It says: "You think you know something about this, but I'm going to show you something else. I have other ideas about it." And it's kind of tough and thorny and bristly, and it upsets people, and it gets people talking back and forth, and they get to carrying on, and so forth. . . . A great play—how many are there, maybe fifty?—is a play that completely changes your assumptions about life, so that when you go out and face the world again you look at everything completely differently.

Again, don't be fooled by the general nature of the dramatic premise. Remember that this is a condensation—a crystallization—of what your play idea is about. It isn't meant to be specific. Rather, it's meant to help you focus your thinking as you work through the process. It will constantly guide you back to the true heart of the play. And, like the heart beating inside a person, it's what gives your play a pulsing center, a force from which and to which everything flows.

The dramatic premise is never stated outright in the play itself, but rises out of it. The audience is left with a sense of it as they leave the theater. The play has taken them on a journey and let them off in a new place. They can feel that they've been changed in some way, but are unable to put into words exactly how. But that's as it should be. Plays are meant to be *experienced* and *felt*. Thus the dramatic premise speaks to the audience's emotions and hearts more vividly than to their conscious minds. This is what makes the theater such a potentially powerful form of communication. And your dramatic premise is, ultimately, what you're communicating.

The Personal Statement

Here is an exercise in premise hunting. Keeping all the above thoughts in mind, try this as a way to uncover your premise: Sit down alone and start free-associating on paper your very private, personal thoughts on the thematic subject area you know you want to write about. Don't restrict yourself in any way as to what you put down. Describe how you *feel* about the issues involved. Get angry if you feel angry. Get sad if you feel sad. Give your emotions full play. Express in words everything you can think of on the topic and be one hundred percent honest with yourself as you do it.

"Words are living things, and they suggest other words," **Arthur Miller** says. "And until you put the word down, you don't get the suggestion that's in the previous word." In writing your personal statement, come up with at least a page or two, pouring it forth, and then put it away for at least twenty-four hours without dwelling on it, editing it, or rewriting it in any way. Getting a little distance from what you've just written is critical.

Putting your raw feelings down on paper helps your brain focus more precisely on what it is you really think and believe. As a result, when you do read through your personal statement again, it will give you a clearer sense of the dramatic premise you really want to work with—of what you, in your heart of hearts, really want to say to your audience. This is what you should always embrace.

Negative and Positive Premises

There are basically two kinds of workable dramatic premises: The first conveys a lesson by showing the negative consequences of a certain mode of behavior or action. It leaves the audience wiser about what *not* to do if they want to avoid the central character's fate: ruthless ambition leads to destruction, jealousy leads to ruin, suspicion leads to disaster, chasing after worldly success leads to disillusionment. The majority of serious plays contain this type of dramatic premise. The best of them are extremely powerful and in performance can affect audiences profoundly.

The other type of dramatic premise takes the reverse approach and illustrates the positive consequences when important discoveries are made and steps are taken to change behavior or action. It communicates to the audience not only what they need to avoid in life, but also what they need to do to make their life more meaningful and fulfilling. The central characters in such plays are put through ordeals, but ultimately they come to realize how they have erred and take at least an initial step in a more positive direction.

Look again at the dramatic premise of *The Crucible*: Honor and integrity conquer sin and evil. Or consider *Who's Afraid of Virginia Woolf?*, in which Martha finally rejects her own destructive behavior and takes tentative steps toward living in reality for the first time in her adult life. These are both powerful plays with a great deal of struggle and turmoil—the former ending in the death of its hero—but both leave the audience with a positive message. The dramatic premise points to something constructive, enriching, and basically uplifting, to a way in which life might be lived more fully.

Don't let this discussion make you anxious about whether your play is going to be a tragedy, tragicomedy, comedy, farce, or anything in between. It doesn't really matter. Your play will be what it will be. Your job, as **Marsha Norman** puts it, is to "worry about the truth of it." What's important is to be aware that all plays have one overriding dramatic premise which is stated either in a negative or positive way.

A Word for the Positive Premise

Personally, I think there is a dearth of good new plays that offer up dramatic premises pointing in a *positive* direction. Most new works I read and see tell me what not to do, what to avoid. They reflect the problems of the world I live in without suggesting, in dramatic terms, what I might personally be able to do to rectify them. They don't shed any light on how to live a fuller, richer life. I walk out of the theater drained, but not fed.

My experience at my own theater, where we're committed to developing new plays with positive dramatic premises, has convinced me that I'm not alone in feeling a desire for something more. When we present a reading or workshop, our audiences fill every seat and stand in the back as well to see unreviewed plays they've never heard of before, often by playwrights unfamiliar to them. People have told me they keep coming back because they're starved for plays that are ultimately life-affirming, that reach for the light, that point to a direction that will help them in some way to pursue peaceful lives. They aren't looking for fairy-tale endings but, rather, for some answers, some meaningful clues about how to live in this complicated, complex age. They're hungry for works of art that, as Leonard Bernstein phrased it, reflect "cosmos in chaos," that don't just present us with the chaos of the world but go a step further and try to make some sense of it. They're looking for plays that touch on the mainsprings of human existence and humanity's spiritual connections.

Obviously, both types of dramatic premise are valid. The great plays of dramatic literature, both classic and modern, prove that. And I'm not suggesting that you consider *only* premises that point in a positive direction. Your play as it evolves will determine which way you should go. Just be aware of the fact that there is both a negative and a positive way to treat dramatically most human issues and problems, and that in this increasingly complex and fast-paced society of ours there appears to be a growing hunger for the latter. Your play can pack a punch either way.

Your dramatic premise is the key to determining which treatment or approach you're going to take as you proceed. That's why it's so important to give serious consideration to how you've stated it.

How the Premise Controls the Play

In *Death of a Salesman,* Arthur Miller chose to have his hero self-destruct. The resolution is affecting and unforgettable. His premise—looking for fulfillment in worldly success leads to disillusionment—is communicated with tremendous punch, for Willy Loman's disillusionment is so intense that it leads to utter despair and death.

Now imagine that Miller, in working on the play, had decided to change his premise to this: Giving up the pursuit of worldly success leads to personal integration and peace. A totally different play! The first half would be similar to the script as we know it, but in the second half some major shifts would take place. Miller would have needed some kind of cathartic moment for Willy, a moment when his eyes and heart are opened to the truth. The resolution would be entirely new, and the audience would be left with a different message.

In this differently premised version, audiences would see that if Willy did not change his ways he would be doomed, but they'd also see the man recognize his error and take some initial steps to rectify his life. This would be a play so different that even the powerful title would have to go.

Obviously, I'm not suggesting that Miller change his wonderful play. However, you can see the power of the dramatic premise and how it determines where your play is going.

I agree with Edward Albee's assertion that form and content co-determine one another. But I don't think you can begin to assemble the building materials for your play—the personalities, the style of the piece, the degree of theatricality, the structural components—until you know what the play is going to be in terms of content. And at the heart of every play's content is the dramatic premise: what it's ultimately communicating to the audience.

LOOKING FOR IDEAS

The plays I've written come from a very hidden place, but within my own experience, my own consciousness.

—ARTHUR MILLER

Knowing *what to look for* in ideas is obviously essential while you're conducting your initial search and testing the possibilities you find. It's like having the proper equipment with you as you prospect for gold. Now you've got to come up with possibilities to put to the test.

Where do ideas come from? What can you do to stimulate your thinking about possible ideas for plays? What pitfalls are to be avoided in your search? How do you know when some thought might be the beginning of a new play? These and related questions are examined in this chapter. Suggestions and advice are offered that will help you uncover possible ideas or at least guide you to the places you're most likely to find them.

That Mysterious Well

How and why ideas for plays suddenly pop into your consciousness, why initial thoughts seemingly appear out of thin air is something of a mystery. It has to do, at least in part, with the way one experiences life as an artist: the tendency to observe behavior—both your own and others—with a degree of detached objectivity, as if you were standing outside looking in. Over time, certain aspects of this observed behavior, coupled with the frequency of its occurrence, trigger the brain to formulate thoughts about how and why people do the things they do. These may be just fragments—small, simple ruminations about something. But sometimes, as they filter through your mind and heart, they may become ideas for development.

No two playwrights will give the same answer as to how ideas materialize or how they know when they've come up with something worth pursuing. **Terrence McNally** says: "Sometimes I have no idea where a play came from, in terms of my unconscious, subconscious—whatever you want to call it. It just springs from my emotional insides."

John Guare agrees: "So much of our writing life happens outside of our conscious life."

Romulus Linney declares: "I try to spend long, empty days where ideas can sort of well up inside of me. I think they need to come up from some kind of a deeper mind than one usually uses."

Edward Albee says that he has never known, with the exception of one play, where his ideas have come from:

> I discover, one day, when I'm going around minding my own business, having a perfectly good time, that I am "with play" . . . that I have been thinking about a play for quite a while and haven't been aware that I've been thinking about it, the unconscious moving to the conscious.

And here's how **Marsha Norman** puts it:

> I think there are some ideas that wait for you . . . in rooms or in the street. . . . You simply have walked into the other room, and it was as though your brain is a sieve and sort of *caught* the idea—didn't think of it consciously. It was just there.

How ideas with potential materialize for you will no doubt be unique. What's important to keep in mind as you begin is that there's an element of mystery involved in the creative process and this is just as true at the start of the journey as it is all along the way.

The Writer's Paradox

The most important single truth to know as you start looking for and considering possible ideas is that every play you write should be set in a world you know extremely well. Good plays, like all good fiction, are built detail on top of detail, minutia on top of minutia. Audiences thrive on specifics about characters, places, and events because these provide the only way they can get inside the play. That's how they are able to relate to the people in that world.

The paradox is that *the more specific and detailed and personal your writing becomes, the more universal will be its appeal.* People will begin to recognize themselves and be able to identify with your characters. This happens because you are giving them access to your play.

It doesn't matter if the audience knows anything about the world of your play. What matters is that *you* do. Then you can write true characters who behave according to the rules of the world they're a part of. Audiences delight in films like *Star Wars* or *Star Trek* because, although they might know absolutely nothing about the ins and outs of space travel, they're watching characters who are entirely familiar with that intergalactic world. Any world where the characters seem real and are behaving in what appears to be a truthful way will be accepted (if not finally applauded) by an audience.

Terrence McNally puts it this way:

> Tell your story, write the people you care about, and if you write them accurately and specifically, other people will be interested in them. I think the biggest way to get in trouble as a playwright—or any kind of writer, perhaps—is to start thinking, "This will be commercial; people will really like this; this will be funny; this will be sad." Instead, tell your story in your own voice. Get the facts together that you remember, that you know.

Athol Fugard tells of how he learned the same thing early on by reading William Faulkner:

> All of my writing life, his passionate regionalism—those stories that are so rooted in one place and in one time, a world of his own imagination which is also a real world—was really an inspiration to me and gave me courage at a point when I was being bombarded with advice to be more general. "You are being far too specific a South African writer," they said. "If you hope to reach audiences in London and America, water it down, don't be so specifically South African." So I ignored that very bad advice and carried on, rooting my stories as passionately as I could in the specifics of one place and one time.

Making the Play's World Your Own

Without question, then, the most exciting and productive place to look for ideas is your own personal life experience. "If an idea is powerful enough," **Romulus Linney** has discovered, "it usually intersects with something that has happened in your past."

This is true for two simple reasons: First, your world is one you know very well. Second, it's what you draw from that world that you're probably going to have strong feelings about. Ideas that eventually make good plays always incorporate both elements—the world of your own experience and your strong feelings about it. As **Emily Mann** attests: "In terms of writing, you get these really specific and amazing things from real life."

Because you have to know intimately the world of your play and the people who populate it, drawing on your own life experience is only logical. It's a world you're completely knowledgable about. You're incapable of taking a false step in this arena, because you know it inside out already. A rich, unique, and vast place to go to look for your ideas, your experience is a place no one else has access to. It's like your own private bank into which you're automatically making deposits every day of your life and from which you're always free to make withdrawals.

As **Athol Fugard** says: "Without any variation, all the plays that lie behind me started with an image, something either seen in the daily business of living my life, something I've heard or overheard, something I read in a newspaper . . . an image that has come to me from life, sometimes my own life, sometimes from lives I've witnessed."

Let's look at a potential idea for a play—a good idea for a play I chose not to write. A family runs a small shoe manufacturing business in northern New Jersey. The father has slaved over the business for thirty some years, building his list of several steady buyers in New York City. He's put everything he's had into it—all his money, time, and energy. His wife has been his silent, supportive partner the entire time. They have one eighteen-year-old son who has recently graduated from high school and two daughters, aged nine and twelve. Recently the business has hit hard times. It's losing money and has been for almost two years. The market for the firm's line of shoes has disappeared.

The father has fallen into a deep depression. His dream has been that one day he'd hand over the business to his son, and he stubbornly holds onto this dream despite the fact that things are getting desperate. His wife, who's been trying to hold the family together, doesn't know what to do next. The play opens on the night of the father's fifty-second birthday. He's out in the factory behind the house, working late. The son, arriving home from a date, announces to his mother that he's leaving for the West Coast to start a new life on his own. He doesn't want anything to do with the shoe business.

Again, this idea has great potential for a play. However, even though it's my idea, I decided not to attempt it because I know nothing about the shoe manufacturing business or the people who populate such a world—the salespeople, the buyers, the inventories, the machinery, the kinds of leather, the designing, the history of the industry, the worries that keep you up at night, and so on. Researching these things was an option, but research is involving, a long-time commitment after which I still might not have felt comfortable with my characters' world. Deep down, I felt I hadn't *lived and breathed* it. It wasn't a part of me, and it would be difficult for me to really know the people who inhabit it.

When asked how he knows when a play idea isn't right for him, **Arthur Miller** explained:

> It's very simple. I only know a little bit. And like anybody else,
> I know certain things very well. And once I get out of that little
> area I know something about in terms of people, I don't know
> it well enough to have any original feelings about it.

It's a rare writer who hasn't started on a play only to discover it's not working. As **Athol Fugard** remarks: "There should be some sort of pregnancy test for playwrights . . . because that would avoid a lot of false starts. I've had those. I thought I was pregnant, but I wasn't."

I've written a number of historical screenplays which involved months and, in one case, years of research before I could attempt going through the process of creating a draft. My favorite of these, written with my wife, Kris, is a love story set in a celibate Shaker community in Kentucky, in 1843. For many years we'd had a deep love for Shaker furniture and design and an ongoing fascination with the whole Shaker "experiment" during the nineteenth century. But it took us a solid year to research our subject thoroughly enough to come up with the basics of the story. We took extended trips to every remaining Shaker village in America, talked to the few Shakers still alive, interviewed all the Shaker historians, explored every aspect of Shaker daily life in the 1840s, combed through published and unpublished documents and music and journals. We think we were given access to every relic and shred of information on the Shakers available to mankind.

The point is that it is possible to consider writing a play set in a world you know nothing or very little about. However, be sure you have a deep connection to it and then be prepared, before you start the process of writing, to dive into that world head first and learn it as well as you know your own world. You must virtually live and breathe your subject and make it a part of yourself. Every scene in my wife's and my screenplay is set in a place we knew actually existed, a restored Shaker village. We knew that every detail in every scene belonged there and was true to the life-style. The broom shop, the kitchen, the dining hall, the barn—all became real places for us, places where we had, in our minds, lived and worked ourselves.

Lanford Wilson, in describing the writing of his play *The Mound Builders* relates: "Halfway through the process I discovered that my characters were archaeologists. And I said, 'Oh, God, no—I don't know anything about archaeology. This is going to take forever.' And so I took about a year off, reading about American Indian archaeology so I'd know how these people talk." On doing research on his characters, Wilson adds: "I think it stimulates me in some way. It puts me in the environment of the characters, puts me in their heads in some way. . . . You're really getting into their lives when you're doing research."

Clearly, the investment of time and money that must be put into the research process in considerable. There's no way to cut corners if you're eventually going to write a truthful play. Therefore, I recommend that you stick to your own past life experience as your subject area, at least for your first few plays and until you've learned the craft well. Your task will be less complicated, for your own world is much more accessible and provides a potentially richer soil from which your play can grow.

Tapping into Your Emotional Reality

Drawing from your own life experience also brings you in touch with strong emotions, the kinds of emotions that make for forceful writing. As discussed in Chapter 2, it's essential that you feel passionately about what you're writing. Good plays speak with a sense of conviction, with an authoritative voice that stems directly from the author's own emotional connections to the material. There's a force that hits you squarely in the heart because the writer is dealing with things of his or her own heart. As **John Patrick Shanley** says: "Plays are a reflection of who we are and what's going on with us."

Romulus Linney goes a step further:

> I've found that the one, common thing that happens over and over is that something in your present life, in your mature life, let us say, intersects in some emotional way with something that happened to you a long time ago that has to do with your very earliest ideas about life. Katherine Anne Porter said that anything of any importance to a writer has happened by the time they're ten years old, and everything else is then learning how to use that. And I agree with that.

And **Lanford Wilson** shares how he taps into this personal emotional reality:

> For instance, Anna, in *Burn This,* describes waking up in this kid's room, and he's been collecting butterflies all day and putting them in alcohol and pinning them to the wall, and they're all beating their bodies against the wall because they've just passed out and haven't really died—he didn't know you're supposed to put a pin in their heads—that happened to me when I was six. I collected butterflies all day and put them in alcohol and pinned them to the wall and woke up at dawn with them all beating their wings. Scared me to death. My grandmother—I was at my grandmother's house—had to go up and let them out. So that came about because Anna was staying in a house overnight, and I was using my grandmother's house as a model for this house. Anna had to stay up in the little boy's room, and the little boy's room is actually my room. And that image from my past came to me.
>
> And I was perfectly aware that it was symbolic. I was totally aware that this butterfly beating her body against the wall would be the character from that moment on. And I don't know if I really had a clear grasp of her grief and her sophistication before that. As I was writing that, I knew exactly who this woman was from my experience—because she was the butterfly.

This drawing from life is a major reason some plays have the power to grab you and hold you until the final curtain. The writer cares deeply about what's being dealt with up there on the stage. Again, **Romulus Linney** puts it well:

The main thing is that trigger that will send you back to something that really upsets you and affects you. . . . You have to care so much about what you're doing. I can't work well unless I care so much about what I'm doing that I don't really concern myself with whether the play's good or not. I hope it will be—I hope I'll be able to be craftsmanlike—but that's not the first consideration. The first consideration is whether I'm crying or laughing, how deeply affected I am by it. . . . To me, writing is a rough, psychic business. There always has to be this sort of shattering emotional connection between myself and the subject, or I can't do it.

Looking back into your life for ideas isn't always easy. You're a product of your own experience, and therefore it's often difficult to see how the past has shaped you. Sometimes you're blocked emotionally from pursuing certain potential idea "mines." People tend to dance around the most potent possibilities because they fear the monsters that might be lurking there. Others gently pry at the lid of these potentially rich mine shafts within themselves but, finding them bolted down tight, are unable to dig out the gold inside. Sometimes they can sense that something big is locked in there but they don't know how to get at it.

What's needed is some system of obtaining full access to these personal idea mines.

Mining Your Experience: An Exercise

There's a simple, ten-minute exercise that I've found helps people to tap into their life experience for ideas. It's freely adapted from Ira Progoff's *At A Journal Workshop* (Dialogue House Library, 1975), which explores in depth the ways people can get in touch with themselves by delving into their personal histories. I recommend the book for anyone interested in this type of self-discovery work.

The exercise Progoff has developed encourages you to focus, specifically, on those events that have had a major role in shaping who you are today. I call my version "the milestone exercise," and I suggest you try it now, as I describe it.

First, take a pencil, a pad of paper, and a kitchen timer and go to a quiet place where there are no distractions, where you won't be disturbed. Sit down and make yourself comfortable. Take a few deep breaths and try to unclutter your mind. As much as possible, ease all your other concerns onto the "back shelf" for the duration of the exercise. This is only going to take ten minutes, so look at it as a little mini-vacation or exploratory probe into your idea mine. Don't go on until you're seated comfortably alone and are relaxed.

When you feel ready, pick up your pad and write your *full* name at the top—no initials. Put your nickname, if you have one, in parentheses after your formal first name(s) and your last name. Then, under your name, write out your date of birth.

Focus in on that name and date for a moment. Don't let your mind short-circuit your concentration. Resist that little voice telling you this is stupid and that you don't need to explore your past for ideas. Just go with it. You have nothing to lose and potentially much to gain.

Look at that name and that date. Try to think of the person behind the name as someone other than yourself. Concentrate on the day he or she came into the world. Focus on the circumstances surrounding the actual birth: the hospital; the mother and the father; their financial position; older siblings, if any; the world at large—what was going on that day, that month, that year.

Now, get ready to set your timer, but first read the following three paragraphs.

For a timed three minutes, and without stopping to ponder or analyze, free-associate through the life of this person and make a list of every important event you can think of. Try to come up with at least thirty. Don't worry about putting them in any order. Just write down a word or phrase that nails down every milestone in your life as it comes to you. Be specific, but don't spend time searching for the right words. You know what they are. Just tack them down.

For example, major experiences of mine that I noted down included the following:

Standing at the Dutch door telling Dad I loved him	Meeting Tyagi
Grandpa's death	My talk with God in the backyard
Dad's arrest for drunk driving	Waving goodbye to the folks at Kildahl Hall
Meeting Kris	Getting the job at UVa
The birth of Keri	The opening of my play *Wings*

And so on. Put them down as they come to you. Don't worry about them making sense to anyone else. This exercise is for *you*. No one else will ever see it. Force yourself to scan your life, back and forth, and as your memory brings them up to the surface, grab them. Write down *everything* that comes to mind. Don't be critical. Don't hesitate. Don't list them chronologically. Remember, you only have three minutes to come up with at least thirty separate milestones. When the timer goes off, *stop.*

Now set the timer for three minutes and make your list.

After the timer sounds and you've stopped, look over the list quickly to be sure you can identify every milestone. Make an adjustment only if a description is unclear. *Don't add to the list.* It's what came to the surface on your initial probe that we want to work with here.

Now set your timer again for three minutes, and on a fresh sheet of paper make a second list of the *eight most significant* milestones from your first list. Go through and select the most important shaping events of your life. Choose only those that have had or continue to have a profound effect upon who you've become as a person.

Again, it's important that you work fast and don't get bogged down. Just list the eight most obvious, major milestones. Be sensitive to the emotional pull each item on the first list gives you. The things that still clutch you, make you angry, or warm your heart. Find the eight moments or specific occurrences in your life that are—for *you* at this time—the most meaningful and significant. If you come up with more than eight, force yourself to eliminate all but the eight most important.

Finish when the timer goes off. Don't continue dwelling on making your second list. Just complete it, even if you're not sure it's one hundred percent accurate.

Finally, on a third sheet of paper, again write your full name, under it your date of birth, and then rewrite the list of the eight milestones in chronological order as they occurred in your life.

Now look at this final list closely. Starting at the top, spend a few moments thinking about each item: the circumstances surrounding them, your feelings at the time, how you feel about them now, the other people involved in them, how you feel about these people now, and so forth. Try to recall the details of the places where your milestone events took place. Try to remember the light, the smells, even the music that was, perhaps, playing in the background. Try to bring each of them back into your consciousness in all its richness and fullness.

Be sure to ignore that voice telling you that no one else could possibly be interested in your life experiences, which are completely unimportant in contrast to the world at large. If you're ever to become a playwright, you have to accept that this list you're holding in your hands is really what counts. It's your own composite emotional, spiritual, experiential makeup that will be the touchstone for everything you write. Your plays may end up disguised and camouflaged, but the bare bones or, rather, the guts of them will be uniquely a part of you and what's shaped you.

My contention is that by going through this exercise faithfully, you've brushed against the seeds for every important play you'll ever write. I'm not suggesting you'll use your milestones directly, though in many cases you'll probably come very close, but rather that they will serve as the springboard for your ideas. Inherent in them are the critical experiences which have shaped how you relate to the world today, all the emotional attitudes you hold, all the problems you live with. These are the things that have made you unique as a human being. It only makes sense that this is the place you should go in mining ideas for your plays.

Don't be fooled if this exercise doesn't immediately spark several terrific ideas. It is meant only to be an exploratory trip into your past to stir things up a bit and get you thinking. Often it takes time for ideas to come to the surface in some useable shape. Sometimes it takes years. Just be confident that you're full of potentially brilliant ideas for plays. Be patient and thorough in musing over possibilities, and then be flexible in adapting your own experience to what's needed for a play.

Dealing Only with Closed Chapters

As possible ideas start presenting themselves, be sure the specific life experience or episode you're drawing on is truly in the *past* and not something you're still right in the middle of emotionally. In other words, deal only with closed chapters.

Twelve years ago I made the mistake of starting a play dealing with something I was currently caught up in emotionally—a complicated and troubled relationship I had with a friend. After writing about forty pages of the first draft, I quit in frustration. It simply wasn't working; I was too close to the material, and my emotions kept getting in the way of my writing. So I put the draft in a box along with several other files from another writing project and put the box on a shelf in the basement furnace room.

Six years pass. One day I'm cleaning out the furnace room, which by now is a disaster of accumulated junk, and come across the box. I'd written across it "old writing files." Curious, I open it and pull out the uncompleted first draft, which I'd totally forgotten about. Reading it, I am amazed at where I'd been emotionally six years earlier, in regard to the characters in the play. That chapter in my life had long since closed. Now I could see clearly what was going on between them and how the play should be written, what it was trying to say. The six years that draft sat forgotten on the shelf had given me the distance I needed to be able to deal productively with the material. I took the file upstairs and in three weeks completed a new draft of the play.

The point is that it's always better to deal with experiences on which you've definitely "closed the book." It's almost impossible to write intelligently and well about a subject you're still tied to emotionally—"you can't see the forest for the trees." You're too close to it.

Marsha Norman goes so far as to say:

> For me, if it happened less than ten years ago, it's too soon to write about it. Ten years is just the proper amount of time for all the ridiculous stuff that you don't want to bore anyone with to fall away, and for the really traumatic experience or that really compelling person or that unforgettable sentence to emerge. These things will remain.

Ten years may be longer than you need to adequately distance yourself emotionally, but the point is clear: If you're considering an idea that's based directly on an unfinished chapter, chances are you should let time bring the overall episode to some kind of emotional conclusion before attempting to use it as material for a play.

And, trust me, the ideas *will* come, whether directly from the life experiences which have shaped you or from stories you hear that you recognize and respond to because of your own uniqueness. Stay positive about this. I never let a student get away with the statement "I want to write so badly, but I can't think of anything exciting to write about." Unfortunately, I hear this more than I'd like. The problem here is either laziness or simply not knowing how to tap into one's personal idea field. Just remember: It's there, waiting to be mined.

Exploring the Whole Idea

Almost without exception, plays are written about culminating, profound events in people's lives. As mentioned in Chapter 1, the conflict/dilemma your central character is struggling with may have a long history and involve many other people. It may be something the character has lived with for years. However, your play should focus on that specific period when the problem is confronted head on for the first time. This quite possibly would include the immediate events leading up to this confrontation, but mainly we want to see the character engage in the significant, decisive battle with his or her dilemma, and we want to witness the final outcome unfold before our eyes.

The Timeline

At this early point in considering ideas, it's often difficult to pinpoint exactly how much your actual play should contain. Sometimes it's useful to sketch out a *timeline* of the central character's dilemma as you conceive it now. This helps give you a frame of reference as you focus in on the central event of the play. Actually chart out chronologically when the first hints of the conflict/dilemma appeared, its progressive stages, dormant periods, times of past flare-ups, and people involved along the way.

To take a simple example, say you're considering an idea about two young women, close friends since grade school, who have just finished their first year of college. They go to different schools but have stayed in close touch with each other. Your central character, Jennifer, went steady with a boy, Tom, for three years in high school and through half her first year of college. Now the other woman, Karen, is starting to date Tom and it's getting serious. Jennifer is having a major problem with this and confronts Karen with it.

The timeline could look something like the diagram on page 55. Your play would focus on the final confrontation—the big dramatic event contained in the idea—but the seeds of the conflict go way back into the relationship between the two women. Everything that went before contributes to this big event and feeds into it, but these past events aren't part of the action of the play itself. Obviously, you can go only so far with this without thoroughly exploring your characters and the relationship they've had (we'll deal with these topics in Chapters 5 and 6). However, charting out a possible backstory for a character's problem, even if it's sketchy and incomplete at first, can help you begin to determine if the "stuff" is there for a good play.

The Play as Iceberg

Another useful way to look at potential ideas is to conceive of your actual play—that is, what is contained in the script—as being like the exposed part of an iceberg, the part above the surface of the water. This is about one-tenth of the actual mass of the iceberg. All the rest is submerged and out of sight; we don't see it, but it's lurking there. Just as sailors in ice-

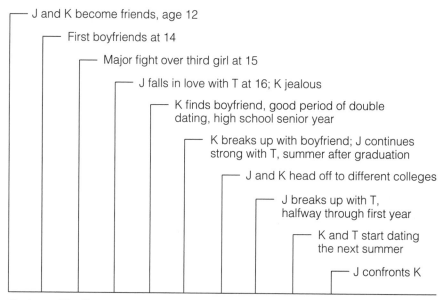

— J and K become friends, age 12

— First boyfriends at 14

— Major fight over third girl at 15

— J falls in love with T at 16; K jealous

— K finds boyfriend, good period of double dating, high school senior year

— K breaks up with boyfriend; J continues strong with T, summer after graduation

— J and K head off to different colleges

— J breaks up with T, halfway through first year

— K and T start dating the next summer

— J confronts K

Backstory Timeline

berg-infested waters must be very aware of this fact, playwrights must know what's under the surface of their plays. If you don't, tragedies can occur. Ships can get wrecked and so can plays.

Terrence McNally tells us that Elaine May, the director of his second play, *Next,* gave him the best advice he ever received when she said: "The dialogue is the tip of the iceberg. Millions of people can write dialogue, that ten percent of the iceberg. Good playwrights know the ninety percent below the water."

When you're looking at ideas, be sure to look at the *whole* idea. Keep in mind that the single dramatic event you're focusing on is just the tip above the surface. It's your job as well to explore thoroughly what's underneath.

The Potential of Settings

Thinking about a specific place or setting will sometimes provide the heat needed to germinate an idea. **Tina Howe,** for example, says that when she starts thinking about a new play, setting is foremost in her mind: "The test I put myself through is trying to come up with a setting I can mine in a theatrical way."

At first this might sound like a superficial way to get things started, but actually it isn't. Settings can be powerful stimuli. A specific place is an environment in itself, with its own atmosphere and mood. You imagine people wandering into it and getting involved with each other. And suddenly those people become interesting. You're attracted to them in this setting because it reminds you of when you. . . .

As **John Patrick Shanley** suggests: "If a room has power for you, if you've felt something there, go back to that room in your memory if you want to write something. Find out what is the emotional geography of that room—which is usually different from what it actually is."

The setting can take you right back to yourself. A good example of how this works is the way I got the initial idea for the play previously mentioned about two friends in conflict. Years ago, my wife Kris, our daughter Keri, and I went on a backpacking trip just outside of Camden, Maine. We spent the night on a high rock ledge overlooking the Atlantic Ocean. The drop-off was significant—maybe 400 feet or more—and so was the view to the east. We were all alone. It was a beautiful place to camp, high up, away from the world, on a piece of rock overlooking the sea. It made me feel secure and at peace.

After we made camp and gathered wood for the fire, I walked to the edge of the rock cliff and sat down. It seemed the perfect spot to lean back and reflect awhile about where I was in my life and where I was going. I looked off toward the ocean for a long time and then my eyes wandered to the rock surface I was sitting on. It was smoothed by millennia of rain and ice and sun. And then my eyes rested on something right in front of me that took my breath away.

There, carved expertly and deeply in the stone at my feet, were the initials "C.L. and H.R." and the date "1925." And I realized I was sharing this rock with two other people who had arrived nearly three-quarters of a century ago. It got me thinking about who they might have been and why they took the time to carve their initials there so beautifully. Was it a couple, two men, or two women? What were they like? They'd left a small piece of themselves up here for me to find. Were they still alive?

That setting has stayed vivid for me for nearly twenty years. It gave me the initial spark for my play about the two friends. I put the characters up there on that ledge, and the play "happened." They find the initials, gaze out at the same view, and look down at the same 400-foot drop-off. I'm convinced the play would never have been written without that setting.

There are so many potent places to set plays—places that reek with mood and family history, where blood and sweat have worn into the woodwork. Think about settings which have affected you profoundly.

Try to bring them into sharp focus, in all their detail. Go to each of them in your mind and linger there for a while. Take a good look around. The beginnings of a great idea could be lurking in the shadows, especially when you connect this special place with something important from your own life experience, something you feel deeply about.

The Use of Occasions

As you consider ideas, keep in mind that setting your story around some special event or occasion will automatically stimulate your powers of invention. The event must be specific for each idea, but it can be drawn from a seemingly endless list: weddings, birthdays, funerals, moving days, trips, visits, major breakthroughs or failures, accidents, engagements, wars, news of pregnancy, and so forth. Plays should be set in special times of people's lives, times of heightened emotions and vulnerability. If you lay the story in which your characters are involved on top of an important event or occasion, you increase the potential dramatic impact of your play. The characters are already primed. Their juices are already being stirred.

John Guare explains: "You want to have an event that's interesting, that the characters want to talk about. With *House of Blue Leaves*, I wanted to write about these people for a long time, but it wasn't until I got that 'envelope' of the Pope coming to New York that everything pulled together."

Major life-changing decisions tend to be made during special times. Breakthroughs in relationships are more likely to take place when people are swept up in an emotionally charged event. At times like weddings and funerals, for instance, emotions are close to the surface. People tend to say things they normally wouldn't and behave in surprising ways. They're more honest, as pretense falls away and true feelings come out. As a result, occasions like these heighten the potential for dramatic interaction.

Events and special occasions are also useful in a structural sense, in that the basic movement of your play can be patterned around the normal way an event plays itself out. For example, if the central occasion is a wedding, numerous possibilities for scenes come to mind: the night before, the morning of, just before the ceremony, the reception, the night after. If your idea needs a number of scenes to work out the drama, you can select them from these various aspects of the overriding event. And it doesn't necessarily matter if the central character is the bride or groom; maybe it is the bride's sister coming into town for the occasion. The point is that you've got a built-in series of events, a framework to lean on for support as you tell your story.

Another example: One of my plays is based loosely on an experience I had in my boyhood home shortly after my widower father's death. The actual setting is the rundown four-room, 130-year-old house my father lived in for forty-seven years in a small southern Minnesota town. It's jammed to the rafters with a lifetime's accumulation of stuff, including furniture, artwork, and a 300-piece woodcarving collection. The occasion for the play is the gathering of the grown children, a son and three daughters, to begin the job of dismantling the house. It's the first week in July, a month after the funeral. All four characters grew up in this house but left town after high school. Their teenage years were difficult because of the father's drinking problem. None of them had been very close to each other since leaving home. The mother had died several years earlier.

For me, this occasion was emotionally potent. Each of the characters brought a lot of baggage to this reunion of siblings. And they didn't have their spouses there to help them through. As they peeled off the layers of what their father left behind, they had no choice but to deal with each other. The occasion had a built-in dramatic element, both structurally and emotionally.

Most important, it was uniquely my story. No one else in the world could have written a play that even remotely resembles the one I wrote, even though the occasion of the post-funeral gathering is commonly used.

Keeping Focused on the Basics

The danger of working from an occasion which is emotionally charged for you personally is that *it* becomes the play. Don't let this happen. The occasion is your framework, the event upon which you lay your central character, his or her need and resulting dilemma, and the working through to resolution. It's always best if the event or occasion merges with and becomes a part of the central figure's struggle, but it should never take over. When it does, your focus upon the basic ingredients and the dramatic premise contained in them will be lost. In other words, the construction of the *drama* should always take precedence over the *event* you've selected as the setting for your story, no matter how potent that event may be.

The predominance of event is, I think, one of the most common mistakes I run across when reading scripts. People feel a strong emotional pull to a personal experience, which usually centers on a specific time, place, and special occasion. They plunge into the writing of their play, submerging themselves in the emotional richness of the experience with all its uniqueness and deep personal connections. In the process, they lose their way. Their focus gets blurred and soon the pages are not taking us anywhere dramatically. We the audience can't attach to the material because the necessary handholds haven't been provided. The story remains diffuse rather than becoming sharply defined. The basic dramatic ingredients aren't there and, as a result, the play—though rich in characters, setting, and especially occasion—does not work.

This could have happened, for example, in the writing of my play with the returning siblings. Being for me so richly layered and emotionally charged, the play could have gone off in many different directions, each one of them interesting. It was essential that I make the choice concerning whose play this was going to be and what the central dilemma would focus on. Once made, that decision determined what went into every scene and how I would use aspects of the occasion to serve the unfolding drama.

Unfortunately, if these essential choices are not made early on, there is no quick fix. The play's been built on sand; the basic structure is faulty. The remedy usually involves tearing the whole house down and starting over. The same materials can be used, but this time the essential dramatic engineering must be applied in the planning and construction. Keep this in mind and perhaps you can save yourself that painful exercise. And believe me, it is painful. I say "perhaps" because sometimes tearing down and rebuilding is just part of the process of discovering who and what your play really is about. Just be aware of this common pitfall as you proceed.

Using Real People as Models

The obvious is always worth mentioning: People are great sources for ideas. All ideas, as they're developed, focus on people and the circumstances they find themselves in. Think of the people you know well and the problems they're facing. If you can strongly identify with their experiences (and most likely you will if they're close to you), perhaps there's a play in there somewhere. Sometimes an interesting personality can trigger an idea by plugging him or her into a set of invented circumstances and asking the right questions: How would this person behave? What would happen to him? What would she learn? How can this person fit into the central character→ conflict/dilemma→ resolution construct?

The key here is that you must know and understand the person you're modeling your central character after. There's little point in using as a model someone who, however powerful and fascinating a personality, tends to mystify you. If you do base a character on such a person, you'll need to create an inner life for him or her that you can relate to. If you don't, more than likely you'll end up with a hollow shell of a character who has very little happening inside emotionally.

As you look for ideas in the people you know, remember that characters usually end up being a blend of two or more actual personalities. Specific traits of different people are put together—for example, the severe emotional problem of one person is combined with the positive, giving nature of another. Such a composite, of course, creates an entirely new personality. So when you find yourself interested in a particular aspect of someone's personality or a specific problem he or she is dealing with, take that one thing and build on it. Combine it with characteristics from other people to invent the character that works for your idea.

Obviously, you don't have to look very far to find an endless supply of interesting and potentially powerful material. Start observing the people around you more closely and think of them—even just pieces of them—as a big part of your idea mine.

It is possible to have ideas triggered from hearing or reading about things that have happened to total strangers, people you've never met. Newspaper stories, usually accompanied by a photograph of someone, can supply the initial spark that eventually ignites into a play. The idea can come from an objective accounting of some stranger's experience. But, of course, you have to make the story your own and give these characters flesh and blood and the breath of life.

When you read something and feel that special tug of recognition and empathy, make note of it for future reference. Some writers clip such stories and put them into an idea file. If you're that kind of person, this might work beautifully for you. You'll be building an inventory of possible ideas. Most of them you'll never use, but one might jump out at you five years from now.

The Myth of Recognition

One consistent problem my beginning students have with modeling characters on people close to them is a fear that their models will recognize themselves in the finished play. Because of this fear, the students tend to steer clear of any idea drawn from their own lives which would automatically involve characters based on real people. They don't want to offend or upset anyone. They're unwilling to risk having a friend or family member see an unflattering portrayal of a character based on him- or herself.

My experience tells me that such fears are largely unwarranted. First, keep in mind that at this early stage—considering possible ideas—most situations and characters will be drawn from your life. You have to accept this as the starting point. You don't have any real choice here; if you want to write good plays, you have to draw, in one way or another, on your own life experience and the people you're close to.

Second, and equally important to keep in mind, is that situations and characters initially drawn from your own life will go through major adjustment and change as the playwriting process unfolds. Without fail, what you think at first is going to be a perfect reconstruction of the real person will, by your second or third draft, be far removed from its model. You have no way of knowing from the outset how this is going to happen, but nine times out of ten, this is the end result.

The writing process has a way of turning characters based on real people into new creations. They take on their own voices and behave in surprising ways. They start telling you what they're going to say and do. Before long, you're forced to leave the models they're based on and allow whole new personalities to emerge. All this is rather mysterious, but it happens every time. It's one of the most wonderful things about writing plays—you end up creating "real" people who didn't exist before. Anyone who has written plays will identify with this.

Another interesting point: People who are the initial models for characters rarely recognize themselves in the finished play. If anything, if you tell them, they're flattered that you found them interesting enough to base a character upon. And if they do see part of themselves in the character, they usually see only the good side. They don't identify with the negative traits, because most people don't admit to themselves that they have them. If they do acknowledge these negative traits, usually they don't have a clue as to how such traits manifest themselves in their behavior. If they did, they'd stop acting that way! As a result, when people see characters based on them do something unpleasant or nasty, they have no way of seeing or making a connection to themselves. Their usual conclusion is that this is where you, the playwright, have used your imagination. In nearly all cases, models for characters simply don't see themselves if portrayed in a less than flattering perspective. You see it and recognize it as theirs, but they won't.

Here's a story that bears this out. When a play of mine was produced in St. Paul, Minnesota, I invited all my relatives living close by to the opening-night performance, including a nephew whom I'd modeled a character after. One important scene in the play involved some painful experiences with his parents' divorce. My sister, who is his mother, was also coming, and as the night approached I must admit I started getting a little anxious. After the performance I asked my nephew and sister what they thought. My nephew said he thought it was "cool" that he could identify so closely with the characters. When I asked if he saw himself in any of the characters he shrugged his shoulders: "Not really." He just could "get into" what they were dealing with. My sister said she was not able to figure out who I'd used as a model for the character based on her son! She could identify all the other people I'd drawn upon except the one closest to her. It was clear she was viewing the play from a totally different perspective and the obvious parallels to her own life were completely missed.

There is the outside possibility that a character modeled on someone close to you will never veer very far from the source. If this happens—and you'll only know this after you've finished writing the play—then you and you alone have to decide what to do. The one time this happened to me, I gave the play to that person to read first. I didn't say anything to him. He read it, recognized himself, bad traits and all, and congratulated me on my honesty. We then proceeded to have an open discussion about our relationship and how we perceived each other. It brought us closer together.

So my advice is: Don't let the fear of recognition short-circuit your idea considerations. Observe your friends and family members. Take advantage of this rich and inexhaustible place to look for your character models and your ideas. Remember, the play you are writing is fiction. Your purpose is not to slander and desecrate those close to you, but to communicate to your audience a dramatic premise you feel passionately about. That you've created characters based on real people is just part of the process of getting there.

Accepting the Risk of Self-Exposure

If you're going to write meaningful, gripping plays, you also have to let go of your private thoughts and secrets and fearlessly deal with them. You can't limit your potential idea mine because you're afraid of what people might think about you as a result of seeing your play. All good writers risk such exposure. It goes with the territory: With few exceptions, such risk is mandatory if your work is going to have real life and punch. To not risk revealing what's going on inside you—the emotional issues you struggle with—is to severely limit yourself as you consider ideas. Instead, I urge you to go right to those problems you wrestle with the most. Put them out on the work table.

As **John Patrick Shanley** says: "Writing a play, to me, is living your life. It's not stepping back from it and writing about it, it's part of your life, it's part of the day that you're in."

Keep in mind the paradox: The more specific, detailed, and personal your writing becomes, the more universal its appeal. Your inner struggles may seem unique to you, and indeed they will have their own little twists and turns, but don't think for a minute that those who witness your play in performance haven't had similar thoughts or urges or experiences. The bottom line is that we're all human beings. Basically, we carry a tremendous amount of the same physical and emotional baggage. As a writer, you're expected to deal with and make sense of this commonly shared inner experience.

So don't shut the very doors that you should be venturing through. Go directly to the source for your material and deal with it honestly. And simply don't worry about it. Take the risk of self-exposure. The more you do so, the more you increase your chances of coming up with ideas that will make wonderful, vibrant plays with something important to say.

Keeping a Journal

Most good courses in creative writing require students to keep a personal writer's journal on a regular basis. The reason for this is that it gets you thinking about and observing life around you and writing down those thoughts and observations. A routine develops, a pattern: The journal writing reinforces your thinking and powers of observation, which in turn reinforce the writing. Your seeing and hearing sharpen, and your mind becomes more alert.

I recommend that you keep such a journal. Most successful writers I know adhere to the practice. "I am an addictive notebook keeper," **Athol Fugard** reveals. "I think of it as sort of the finger exercises of my craft."

Arthur Miller says he has "endless notebooks in which I'm fundamentally talking to myself about trying to lift this or that out of the darkness where it's hiding."

David Ives recounts his habit of jotting down all the ideas that come to him, including the one for "Sure Thing," a one-act that is part of his play *All in the Timing*:

> When I get an idea for a play it goes straight into the notebook. I write down whatever hits me. . . . One day I got this idea while I was standing at a bus stop. I said to somebody, "Does the M14

bus go up this street?" And this person said, "Yes, I mean, no." I thought, "Well, that's kind of interesting. There's a little play here." I started wondering: "What if you wrote a play in which all of the possible things that could happen from asking 'Which way does this bus go?' happened?" Then I asked myself, "How can I limit the play to encompass all of the possible answers?" I also knew that it had to be a love story about two people getting on the bus or not getting on the bus. So I just wrote down this idea that went, as I remember: Two people having all of the possible conversations that can follow from one question.

Terrence McNally says: "I keep a sort of journal. I buy lots of little notebooks for each play, and sometimes I have one page of notes and 300 blank pages, but at least there's a journal called *A Perfect Ganesh* and a journal called *Frankie and Johnnie.*"

And **Horton Foote** declares: "No matter how rudimentary or primitive or unlikely, if an idea comes to me, I keep it in a notebook." Like Arthur Miller, he uses his journal to talk to himself: "I tell myself a story, or I begin to listen to how people might talk. I make little sketches of dialogue."

And so does **David Ives**: "I have a notebook where I keep scenes and dialogue that I overhear. . . . I wrote one down the other day: Two people were talking, and one person said, 'I've got a date tomorrow.' And the other person said, 'Anybody you know?' I wanted to trail those people and see what developed from that."

It doesn't matter what you put down, how long your entries are, or even whether you write in it every day. Just capture the tiny fragments and shreds of ideas as they come to you. **John Guare** says: "I save anything that catches my eye—a thought, something in the paper—I save everything because I can't make that spot decision and say, 'I don't need this now' or 'This will be of use.'"

Try to build a few minutes into your routine to do this kind of writing every day. There's always something to put down, even if it's how boring your day was. It's getting yourself into the habit that's important. Then, when there's something significant to get down, you'll have it. As **Athol Fugard** relates: "I write everyday—a lot of rubbish, sometimes useful stuff . . . and the things I see and the things I hear—the things that my instinct as a writer tells me might be what I'll need or the thing I'll be looking for in five or ten years time—all these things go into that notebook."

Once you get started, you'll discover that certain kinds of observations and thoughts occur frequently. As you go back and read over past entries—something you should do on a regular basis—you'll begin to get a sense of how you perceive the world around you, what you think is important, what turns you off, what turns you on. Keeping a journal is a wonderful way to stay in touch with yourself as you move through your life day by day, week by week, month by month, and over the years provides a reminder of where you've been.

Often, possible ideas for plays jump out at you as you read over old journal pages. As **David Ives** puts it: "When I'm in one of those troughs when I'm not writing anything, or when maybe I've just finished something, I just read the notebook and it tells me what to go to next."

Horton Foote explains: "Sometimes, even three or four years later, I'll go back to a notebook, respond to something, and find that I want to work on it."

It might be a combination of recurring notations that triggers your thinking, or a single small entry. **Athol Fugard** often uses his journal to expand upon a recurring image: "What I find happens is that a period of time passes when that image will resurface in my conscience, and I will examine it and connect a few more thoughts to it, and it will go through a small elaboration and go back into the notebook and disappear again."

The point is that you have the journal to read and reread. And it's your own ongoing personal record of experiences. It'll get you in closer touch with yourself and will, more than likely, prove to be an active and constant source for possible ideas.

Exploring Hunches Through Writing

In your efforts to give more initial shape and substance to an idea, another tool available to you is *exploratory writing.* As my interviews with them have revealed, many of today's major playwrights make this a normal part of the process of "uncovering" their plays. Typically, exploratory writing involves exhaustive testing of various hunches through the actual writing of dialogue scenes.

N. Richard Nash, author of *The Rainmaker* and numerous other plays, once explained to me how he uses this approach. He starts with a simple fragment or shred of conflict, argument, or confrontation between two people—nothing complicated or of any special significance, just something that's in his head. His only requirement is that the two characters always be "screamers"—passionately connected people, and one of them must have a fierce need to satisfy some want. Nash then writes an exploratory conflict scene between these two characters. There's no thought given to dramatic premise or structure; he is just testing a possibility, exploring a hunch by writing it out in dialogue form. Then he puts it away and forgets about it for several weeks.

If, when he looks at it again, it seems promising, he might write one or several more scenes with the same or additional characters, accumulating dialogue material, testing aspects of character, trying out "a bit of this and a bit of that." Sometimes he tries writing a version of the climactic scene if he has that much dramatic shape in mind. Usually, however, there's still no concern for structure and premise.

Only after he has accumulated several such exploratory scenes and finds that the material still excites him will Nash take a closer look at it as a possible play and begin shaping and structuring it in some way. All this happens before he commits to writing a draft of the play.

I asked Nash how many pages he usually accumulates when he does this exploratory work, and in reply he put one hand on the table in front of him, palm up, and the other about four or five inches above it, palm down. When I asked him to be serious, he said he was. This was all his pre-writing process, nothing but an exploratory probing. In other words, he explores a great deal, sometimes hundreds of pages' worth, before he starts putting together the structural elements of an actual play. He uses this approach simply to nail down his ideas, to get the juices flowing and his characters "screaming."

I recommend this type of early exploration if you remember four things:

1. First, you're only playing with an idea, not writing a draft of your play. It's easy to get lost in the sheer volume of material you can accumulate if you're not an N. Richard Nash (a prolific, proven master craftsman who knows all the rules of dramatic construction at the outset). This works wonderfully for him, and it may work for you as well if you don't let it become the end rather than one of several possible means to the end. Always remember that you're exploring a potential idea here, not jumping into the writing of a play.

Arthur Miller describes how he sometimes does similar extensive exploratory work; in the case of one play, he did a thousand pages' worth. When I asked him if this was all just testing his idea, he said: "Yes, looking for the end; that's what it comes down to, really."

2. Don't fall too deeply in love with this preliminary material. As **Horton Foote** warns: "You have to be careful that you don't hypnotize yourself, saying in your neurotic way, 'This is all precious.'" If you have difficulty

throwing material out once it's written, exploratory writing can get you in trouble over and over again. You'll find yourself trying desperately to fit in everything you wrote that seems to work as a scene or an independent argument but really has no business being considered part of the play. It's imperative that once you start writing your actual play, you develop the discipline to reject exploratory material that doesn't belong in it.

"There is a point you have to become a carpenter," **Horton Foote** aptly explains: "a point where I just calm down and cool it and become as objective as I can. I find those moments that are really essential, and I find those that are nonessential, and sometimes it really kills me; I have to cut some of the best writing that I have ever done." So whenever you try exploratory writing I suggest you repeat to yourself daily the old adage: "Words are cheap, words are cheap, words are cheap. . . ."

3. Realize that it's possible to expend so much creative energy in exploring the idea on paper that you lose interest in it before getting to an actual draft of the play. I've seen it happen to many students. In one sense, this is a good thing to discover early on in a project. Running out of gas in the idea-exploration stage indicates that it probably doesn't have enough "stuff" in it to see you through the writing of the play. Better to find this out now than after having struggled halfway through a draft.

4. Finally, keep in mind that many writers use little, if any, exploratory writing at all. Instead, they prepare carefully for writing up-front, clarifying the basic dramatic ingredients, doing character work, designing a preliminary structural framework, and so on, and save the actual writing, with all its surprises and unexpected twists and turns, for when they feel ready to tackle the play itself. Their approach to the process is to save their creative energy, pouring it out only when they feel they're fully prepared.

If you keep the purpose of this early exploratory writing in mind, it may prove to be a great tool. In fact, it may very well loosen you up and help get your writer's brain activated. Using it intelligently and allowing it to function the way it's supposed to may help you uncover ideas and give them initial focus and direction.

The Test of Time

In the end, perhaps the ultimate test of an idea is simply not being able to get it out of your head. One way or another it keeps nudging at you, coaxing you to take it seriously and to commit to working on it. **Marsha Norman** says that when an idea first presents itself she puts it through a process of forgetting, telling herself, "I don't want to write this; it's a crummy idea; it is not an idea I'd be interested in for a long time—go away!" However, she continues: "If in a year it's an idea that's still interesting, that's still puzzling, that still haunts you somehow, then you can maybe go to the next stage with it."

Lee Blessing tends to carry ideas around in his head for months before committing to them. He says: "Hopefully, the process that occurs is that the good ideas stay in my head and the ones that aren't necessary go away."

Athol Fugard explains, "Sometimes it has taken all of twenty, twenty-five years for one image to find the moment in my life when, suddenly, I've felt that the time has come to deal with it—that, over the course of the years, it has acquired enough weight and that I sense that it is full enough for me to take on an actual, daily writing discipline and attempt to translate it into a play."

Many other playwrights have told me how they use time in a similiar way to test the potential of their ideas. It's an automatic process, for your subconscious is at work guiding you to the gold.

If you do not yet have an idea you're burning to write a play about, now's the time to stop and reflect. Think back through the points brought up in this chapter. If you skipped over the milestone exercise, go back and try it. Try writing an exploratory scene or two. Take the time to slowly turn over a few stones and really look at what's underneath. Be sensitive to any small tug on your heart, anything that gives you even a momentary rush of excitement. Ideas for plays don't usually come in one big and perfectly designed package. They start as fragmentary thoughts and feelings, as tiny, fragile observations that have to be nurtured and developed.

As mentioned earlier, students often come to me in utter frustration because they can't come up with an exciting idea. When I sit down with them and start asking specific questions about their lives—what they believe in politically and socially, their spiritual connections, the people that they love, and those they don't love—things start to happen. It's obvious that the "stuff" is there to draw ideas from. It has to be. Each of our lives is too rich and complicated for anyone to come up with a blank screen. It's just a matter of knowing where and how to look.

THE PLAY IDEA WORKSHEET

I tend not to start writing a play until I have a fairly good strategy about how I'm going to take the audience through the experience of an evening.

—Michael Weller

Your next step in developing the idea for your play is to plan—as Michael Weller does—a workable strategy for yourself. Such planning, in one way or another, is a commonly shared procedure among established writers. It involves taking the idea you feel strongest about—even if, at this point, it's just a hunch, a fragment of character or conflict—and getting as many of its essential elements down on paper as you can, so you can examine the idea in a more structured way.

John Patrick Shanley explains how he discovered early in his career the value of this type of initial condensation:

> When I was looking for plots, when I started to get a sense of what plots were, the place I really found them in was fairy tales. Fairy tales really boil away everything but the absolute essentials, and that can be very powerful. It can be very interesting to ask when you're looking at your own play and the story you want to tell: "What can I do away with?"

It's not important at this point to be entirely sure of your idea's dramatic premise or its central character→ conflict/dilemma→ resolution construct. What *is* important is that you sense some real potential and that you can feel a pull on your heart in some significant way.

As you move to this step, remember: Writing a play is a process, and process means moving from one place to another and yet another. It means constant change and adjustment as new information reveals itself. It insists on flexibility, on always being willing to throw out the old and embrace the new, to incorporate an ever-increasing number of discoveries into your creative thinking. Putting your idea down on paper at this early point, therefore, has to be looked at as just another early step that will allow you to move on to other steps and eventually to your first draft.

The intention here is not to lock you into anything, but rather to help clarify your thinking, which will further trigger your imagination.

Getting Down the Basics

The way to get off and running with your idea, shaping it into something that will have solid dramatic possibilities, is to write out the basic dramatic ingredients as you conceive them now. I have drawn up an actual form that I use for this, a worksheet that keeps everything simple and to the point (see page 77). The worksheet consists of eleven entries, as explained here:

PLAY IDEA WORKSHEET

Date: It's a good habit always to date your exploratory work.

Working title: If you cannot think of a preliminary title just yet, write at least a label that, at this point, captures the essence of what you think your play is about. Keep it simple and clear.

Central character: Give him or her a first and last name and write a brief, one-sentence description of the character.

Central character's dominant need: Keep this simple. For instance: "to win the heart of Margaret," "to put her guilt behind her," "to achieve material success."

Other major character(s): Write their names and brief, one-sentence descriptions of them.

Setting: If you know the setting at this point, write a one-sentence description. If you haven't decided on a setting, put down the one that now seems the best.

Occasion: If you know this also, describe it in one brief sentence. Again, make a *choice* here. Put something down.

Major conflict/dilemma as it manifests itself in action: In one sentence, describe how your central character's struggle is manifested in action—that is, tell briefly what happens in the play in terms of the physical and/or emotional conflict that brings the dilemma into focus and forces the central character to respond. Be sure you describe an *action* here—how the central character struggles with his or her dilemma.

Resolution: In one brief sentence, describe how your central character's conflict/dilemma is resolved.

How the central character changes by the end: Write one brief sentence that describes how this person perceives him- or herself and/or the world differently at the end of the play.

Dramatic premise: This is the most important of all. Following the form as discussed in Chapter 2, write one simple sentence, indicating movement and change, that captures what you think now is the primary communication of the play.

Using the worksheet, let's work through a potential idea you can be objective about before you put your own idea through it. This is a simple idea for a short play: Imagine that you, the playwright, read in your local newspaper that an eighteen-year-old boy working the night shift at a filling station in your town was held up at gunpoint by an older man at four in the morning. You know nothing more about the actual incident than the brief report in the paper, but you recognize the story's dramatic possibilities. It raises some enticing questions: What could happen in a situation like that? What could be said between the attendant and the robber? How could the two personalities interact? What would bring someone to the point of robbing a gas station at 4 A.M.? What could be at stake for the attendant? For the robber? Let's consider the worksheet entries:

Date: Don't ignore this. Put the day, month, and year that you're doing the work. Beginnings have a way of taking on major significance, and what you think of now as a simple and quick series of jottings may turn out to be the start of a complicated major effort that takes a long time to complete. More often than not, you'll make use of this early reference as you work your way through a process of constant changes and adjustments. Knowing *when* something was thought of or written down can prove useful.

Working title: Don't spend a lot of time trying to come up with the perfect title. Something as simple as "The Filling Station" or "The Night Robbery" will suffice. Attempt to capture the content and sense of your idea as you conceive it now.

Giving your idea a label, an actual name, is a great help psychologically, because now you have a work in progress rather than just another idea you're knocking around. You've started work on a new play. You have something tangible to refer to, something to write on the tab of the file folder or the cover of a notebook.

Terrence McNally says: "I usually have a title pretty soon. So that's a place to put these notes. I mean, you have to have a title to put the notes under. It's like using a computer; you've got to title everything before you can store it."

Later on, we'll deal with "real" titles and how to come up with them. For now, a good working title is all you need.

Central character: Given your filling station story, you have to make a choice: The central character could be either the boy or the man. So you have to ask yourself which of the two you want the play to focus on and who's going to be left the most changed at the end of the encounter. This in turn makes you stop and think about what the play is going to be about, what primary message you're going to be leaving the audience with—why you're writing this play in the first place. To a degree, you are already considering your dramatic premise when choosing your central character because it's through the working out of his dilemma that you communicate what you want to say.

At this point you have two options. And in choosing either one, you have to dramatize a life-changing experience. The boy could be a bitter, angry young man whose eyes are opened to the desperate lives that some people live; that is, through his interaction with the man, he gains a new understanding of the troubled and downtrodden. Or, withdrawn and afraid of life, he somehow rises to the occasion and forces the man to leave without taking the money, thereby gaining a new, stronger sense of himself.

The man could be at the breaking point and suddenly forced, through his interaction with the boy, to look at what he's doing to himself and to others. Or he could be a hardened criminal and now faced with the choice of killing the boy to get the money and having to decide if it's worth it.

As with all ideas, there are numerous possibilities here. More than one of them, or a combination, should be operating in the play on some level. Making a choice about who is going to be your overall focus may change as you get deeper into the project, but for now you need to "try one on for size" to be able to continue the development process effectively. Otherwise, it would be like trying to drive down two roads at the same time or trying to build two different houses on one building site. You'd lose the ability to shape your play dramatically.

Let's say you consider your options as to what you really want to write about and decide to focus on how a man in the midst of despair and frustration is finally able to come to grips with his problems and himself. In other words, you choose the robber as your central character. You've decided to make him your overall focus as he struggles with his dilemma. This is not to say that the boy isn't critical to the play—obviously, there wouldn't be a play without him. But you've decided to make the man your "hinge" character, your protagonist, your hero.

You've just made a critically important choice, for if you'd chosen the boy, you'd be developing a different play. Later on, after you've explored the idea further, you may discover that indeed the boy is your central character and that it's his dilemma you're really interested in. This happens all the time. So you go back and make the necessary adjustments.

The important point here is that if you're going to proceed, you have to start somewhere. Go with the hunch that seems strongest at the time and see what happens.

Since we've decided to focus on the man, we'd write down on our worksheet something like this: "Harold Davis, 48, a proud but unemployed blue-collar worker, seriously depressed; married, three teenage daughters."

Giving names and ages to your characters as soon as possible immediately makes them *people* rather than abstractions. It gives you something to build on when you start your in-depth character development later on. The rest of the description should hit on the elements of character that you think might have direct bearing on the situation of the play.

Central character's dominant need: "To end the agony of deep-seated depression and sense of failure in life."

Again, this need could be any number of things. What's important is that this is what is fundamentally driving Harold to do what he does. It's what has pushed him to this night and his central action of holding up the gas station.

Other major character(s): "Dave Marshall, 18, defiant, from a middle-class home, no self-confidence or sense of direction in his life."

Your initial thinking about your antagonist (the character most strongly pitted against your central character, the protagonist) should focus on the ways the conflict can be heightened and enriched. In other words, this character should have a dilemma of his own that ties in some way into the play's main event. This will strengthen the play's dramatic underpinnings.

Here Dave finds himself in a situation that will force him to deal directly with a life-threatening problem, represented by Harold. He'll be jarred out of his aimlessness and complacency, and for the first time in his life as a young adult he'll have to take some meaningful action. As the main barrier to Harold's achieving his external goal of robbing the gas station and as the trigger that forces him to face his internal dilemma for the first time, Dave can be given real punch and power as we see him struggling to rise to the occasion. Finding dramatic richness in Dave is critical to the play's ultimate success.

At this early point you need to consider ways in which Dave's personality and background will collide head-on with Harold's at every possible opportunity. Think in terms of the potential for *conflict* based on the characters' age and class differences, specific personality clashes, and so on. Where and how can sparks be generated? Think of Peter and Jerry in Edward Albee's *The Zoo Story*. These two are about as opposite as they come, and Albee's choices contribute tremendously to the play's vitality throughout.

As far as we know from the published news report, Dave and Harold have no shared backstory; they're two strangers meeting in the night. And for our purposes here, that's fine. But imagine how some past relationship, however slight, between a central character and antagonist would give you more material to work with in this early, formative phase of invention. Ask yourself: Is there some way these two could have connected in the past, even indirectly? Could Dave think he recognizes Harold's car? Or is there perhaps something about Harold that reminds Dave of someone? Does interacting with Dave trigger some memory in Harold?

Be careful here: You can't force this. Coincidence is very difficult, if not impossible, to pull off successfully in a play. But you should always make these kinds of probes into character relationships and look for any and every possible point of contact that could exist. Making connections in backstories, if the connections are there to be made, can greatly heighten dramatic impact. Generally speaking, the more intimately connected characters are, the more "stuff" you have to work with.

Everything you throw in at this point won't pan out, of course, but that doesn't matter and shouldn't concern you. Again, remember: At this initial stage, nothing is set in concrete. Many of your early conceptions will change. What's important is that you're aware of why you're putting in what you do.

Setting: "The front office of a filling station." This could be more detailed, obviously, but it's fine for now. Specifics can be added as you uncover what the play requires.

On the other hand, if you "see" a vivid room in all its detail, describe it here. It may help activate your powers of invention.

Occasion: "The night after Harold received his last unemployment check." This could add fuel to Harold's desperation.

Major conflict/dilemma as it manifests itself in action: "Harold demands the money and Dave unexpectedly resists."

What's important to capture here is how your central character's attempt to satisfy his dominant need *manifests itself in action*. The robbery is Harold's desperate attempt, however misguided, to fulfill his need. Dave is the obstacle to the execution of his plan. It doesn't matter that Harold's solution is faulty; this is *his* reality at this time. Life has brought him to this place, he's determined to end his agony, and this is how he's decided to do it. When Dave puts up resistance, the sparks start to fly. Harold *demands,* and—in opposition—Dave *resists.* In putting down the major conflict that occurs in the play, state it in action terms. Don't be vague or philosophical here. Your focus should be on what *happens*— what literally takes place onstage that ultimately forces the central character to come face to face with his dilemma and decide what he's going to do about it.

Resolution: "Faced with shooting Dave to get the money, Harold breaks down and for the first time admits to himself that he's in serious trouble."

This resolution doesn't immediately fulfill all aspects of Harold's need. The resolution of a complex human drama rarely can, especially in a pat or cut-and-dried manner, and that would be neither true to life nor interesting for your audience. In this resolution, certainly, Harold's need isn't fulfilled—not right away. It does, however, represent a critical first step in his being able to deal with his predicament. His depression and pride have been working against him, blinding him to a real solution.

Now he can begin to look at his life more clearly and start putting the pieces back together. It took this event, his encounter with Dave, to get him to this point. He thought he could fulfill his need by robbing the filling station of its cash. Instead, he finds out that the real solution lies in a very different place: inside himself.

How the central character changes by the end: "Harold is a humbled man, no longer blaming the world for his problems."

Your resolution will always answer the question "How is my hero changed?" If it doesn't, something's off track. The way you resolve your play is really only the dramatization of your central character going through a major realization or change in perception. He or she is left a different person as the lights fade because of the resolution, and it's important to clearly see and understand what change it has effected.

Dramatic premise: "Admitting defeat leads to recovery."

You can come up with other premises for the idea we've been considering, but this one comes closest to leaving the audience with its meaning as we've initially conceived it: It's only when a person admits to himself he's got a problem that he can start doing something constructive about it. Many people go through their lives never getting to that point. They live year after year in a haze, talking themselves into the myth that the world is to blame for their misery and not themselves. In terms of Harold, the premise "Admitting defeat leads to recovery" captures this point of view.

Walking this idea through the worksheet gives you a sense of how important it is to secure the basic dramatic essentials early on. You can see how a possible play begins to take shape as you work through it. It forces you to ask the key questions and gets you thinking about the fundamental structure of your play. It goes a long way to turning a relatively abstract series of thoughts into the basic building materials for a workable script. Most importantly, it gets you going.

Terrence McNally says: "Sometimes people sit down to write a play when they're not ready to write it. They stare at the screen for days and get very discouraged." The idea worksheet is intended to help you avoid the agony of staring at that blank screen, sheet of paper, or writing pad.

As you go through this exercise, realize that it's not something that you will always and necessarily go through before writing a play or that established playwrights all apply in a precise way before writing their works. Neither is the worksheet a formula for playwriting success. It's simply a "thinking aid" to help you gain an appreciation for the unseen structural underpinnings of dramatic writing, a way to learn how to build a play out of the ideas you're interested in. At some point, if you keep on writing plays, much of this analysis may become as automatic and unconscious as it is for many of the playwrights interviewed.

Print up Your Worksheets

I suggest that you draw up your own worksheet listing these eleven items *on one page* and making several dozen photocopies. In laying it out, don't leave yourself much room to write out your answers. This will give you a constant reminder to keep things short and to the point when you start using it.

It should look something like this:

PLAY IDEA WORKSHEET

Date: _____

Working title: _____

Central character: _____

_____

Central character's dominant need: _____

_____

Other major character(s): _____

_____

Setting: _____

Occasion: _____

Major conflict/dilemma as it manifests itself in action: _____

_____

Resolution: _____

_____

How the central character changes by the end: _____

_____

Dramatic premise: _____

_____

Analyzing Your Favorite Plays

Before applying the worksheet to your own idea, a good exercise is to put a few of your favorite plays through the paces. It's important that you get comfortable with the thinking process involved in breaking down plays to their bare bones, especially those which have special power for you. It'll help you understand *why* these plays work and what fundamental components they have in common.

Here are worksheets on three of the well-known American plays we've been using as examples:

DEATH OF A SALESMAN

Working title: Miller's original working title was *The Inside of His Head,* which to me makes perfect sense, considering that the play is really dealing with Willy's growing inability to cope with reality.

Central character: Willy Loman, weary traveling salesman in his late 50s.

Central character's dominant need: To be seen as a success in the eyes of his family and the world.

Other major characters: Linda, late 50s, sweet, faithful wife to Willy; Biff, 30, the Lomans' oldest son, a troubled drifter; Happy, 28, the Lomans' other son, following in his father's footsteps.

Setting: The Loman home and yard; the offices of Willy's boss and of Charley, his neighbor; a restaurant; a hotel room; a graveyard.

Occasion: Biff's return home after a long absence.

Major conflict/dilemma as it manifests itself in action: Willy struggles with his family and the outside world, trying to preserve a self-image that is no longer valid.

Resolution: Willy refuses to admit defeat and ends his own life.

How the central character changes by the end: Willy is dead.

Dramatic premise: There's obviously room for variation here. I think the most powerful is "Looking for fulfillment in worldly success ultimately leads to despair." Others might be "Refusing to admit one's own weaknesses and failures leads to despair" or "Pride leads to ruin." No matter how the premise is actually stated, however, the major communication of the play centers on what happens when a man's estimation of himself doesn't measure up to reality.

THE CRUCIBLE

Working title: I don't know what Miller's working title was, but a good guess would be *The Witch Hunt.* Possibly it was *The Crucible*—sometimes, with a little luck, working titles really work!

Central character: John Proctor, mid-30s, a farmer, "powerful of body, even-tempered, and not easily led" (Miller's own description).

Central character's dominant need: To rid himself of the guilt he bears.

Other major characters: Elizabeth, John's gentle, intelligent wife; Abigail Williams, 17, a beautiful orphan girl with an endless capacity for dissembling; Rev. John Hale, nearing 40, a "tight-skinned, eager-eyed intellectual"; Deputy Governor Danforth, etc.

Setting: Parrish's home; Proctor's home and woods; the Salem courthouse; a prison.

Occasion: The Salem, Massachusetts, witch-hunt hysteria of 1692.

Major conflict/dilemma as it manifests itself in action: Proctor fights for his life and honor against the witch hunt hysteria triggered by his adultery with Abigail.

Resolution: To gain his redemption, Proctor chooses the gallows rather than cooperate with the authorities.

How the central character changes by the end: Proctor is freed from his guilt, his integrity and honor restored.

Dramatic premise: Honor and integrity triumph over sin and evil.

WHO'S AFRAID OF VIRGINIA WOOLF?

Working title: Albee reportedly had this title from the start. The story goes that before he wrote the play he found the phrase scrawled on the wall in a Grove Street bar in Greenwich Village and fell in love with it. (Moral: Graffiti may have a useful function after all.)

Central character: Martha, 52, intelligent faculty wife, very discontent. It's important to note that in his interview Albee insists that the play is about all four characters and that he didn't write it thinking of Martha as the central character. However, when analyzed dramaturgically, she clearly emerges as the central figure struggling to fulfull her need. That Albee didn't consciously think this way doesn't change the fact that the play functions as such structurally.

Central character's dominant need: To break free from her illusionary existence and live in the real world.

Other major characters: George, 46, history professor, husband of Martha; Nick, 28, new math professor, self-confident and ambitious; Honey, 26, Nick's wife, naive and innocent.

Setting: Martha and George's campus home.

Occasion: The late-night visit of a new faculty couple.

Major conflict/dilemma as it manifests itself in action: Martha fights George's attempts to hold up the mirror to her.

Resolution: Martha is forced to drop all pretense and accept her true self and the reality around her.

How the central character changes by the end: Martha is living in the real world for the first time in her adult life.

Dramatic premise: Accepting reality opens the door to personal integration.

You may come up with a different way of wording these, but you can see how the worksheet captures what the plays are basically about. Notice how all three deal with a person's private struggle to fulfill a powerful need. All good plays deal with this. The more plays you analyze using the idea worksheet, the more you'll be convinced of this basic truth of the craft.

It's not always easy to fill out a worksheet for a play. You have to become a mechanical engineer of sorts, and it can cause a bit of brain strain. But becoming familiar with this type of analysis by applying it to the best plays you know is worth the effort if you expect to use it on your own ideas effectively. I strongly urge you to keep up the practice of filling out worksheets on plays that move you in some profound way. Developing and maintaining your critical thinking skills in this arena can only sharpen your skills as a playwright.

Tackling Your Own Idea

Now fill out the worksheet on your own idea. Be as concise and brief as possible. All you're trying to do is tack down the basic dramatic ingredients in as simple a way as possible. If you allow yourself to ramble on with any item, you reduce the effectiveness of the exercise. It's imperative that you keep each item to one simple, clear sentence. Then it will be a useful tool. So choose your words carefully. Struggle with it a little until you're able to say exactly what you want to say, but with extreme economy.

Don't worry if you're still unsure about certain items. After all, it's early in the process, and you're just starting to explore your idea. What's important is that you attempt to fill out everything. This gets you started and tells you right away where more invention and thinking are needed.

Don't be timid here. Remember, at this point it's all trial and error, so you want to *try* things and see how they strike you. Fill out several worksheets if necessary. Then choose the one you think comes closest to capturing what you want to work with.

And don't throw away any of these early explorations. You'll be surprised later on how honest they really are. They won't capture everything you'll eventually need to write your play, but they will get down your initial thinking and your first impulses. They can be invaluable if and when you get stuck or lost and are close to going out of your mind writing your first draft. So start a file, and keep them all handy.

When you've finished filling out the worksheet, even if you're not entirely satisfied with it, sit back for a minute and congratulate yourself. You've started work on a new play! Your worksheet is a useful tool that will help you clarify where you're going. Think of it as your preliminary road map as you head further into this adventure and a steady flow of new material presents itself. Because you have kept the worksheet simple, you'll be able to easily adjust it as you make new discoveries along the way. Answers concerning the items you were unsure about will indeed come when the time is right, when enough layers have been peeled off. Eventually, your worksheet may change beyond recognition, but for now you've begun the process that will lead to a finished script.

EXPLORING YOUR CHARACTERS

If you're not really interested in those people, then it's a play no one's going to be very interested in.

—TERRENCE MCNALLY

Coming up with and formulating a workable idea that has passed the initial tests is a major first step in the playwright's process. The play you've conceived of may not be exactly the one you end up writing, but at least you have down on paper a framework, a point of reference, a "strategy," as Michael Weller calls it. Now it's time to expand what you've captured on the worksheet into a bigger and richer dramatic field, to dig deeper into the possibilities you've sketched out and discover what you really have to work with.

The next step in the process, then, is to explore the "stuff" that makes up your idea—the people involved. Who are they, what has shaped them, what makes them do the things they do? Where do their stories really start? What stories do *they* want to tell? This is where the real work begins, work that will largely determine not only what play you'll end up writing, but how alive and dramatically engaging it will be.

When most of the professional playwrights interviewed for this book sit down to write a play, their preliminary work doesn't necessarily include the kind of extensive explorations we'll be discussing in this section. But "professional" is the key word here. Like anyone who's been trained and has become skilled in the craft by years of experience, they've learned how to sit down and begin delineating a character. For them it's become instinctive, almost an automatic process.

However, if you're a beginning playwright, or a playwright whose plays haven't come together the way you'd hoped, the exercises offered here will give you the tools you need for getting to know your characters intimately and thoroughly—an absolutely essential step if you ever hope to write plays that come fully to life.

The Short-Form Biography

The power and richness behind all ideas for plays are the people involved. And you need to care about them, even love them. For this to happen, it's essential that you learn everything about them, their hopes and dreams and fears, their pasts, their secrets.

Your knowledge of your characters has to go way beyond what you now think might be relevant to your immediate story. You have to embrace them as living, breathing human beings with rich, full histories, free from the bondage of your idea.

Edward Albee says playwrights "must invent the life of their characters before the play and after the play, and they should know how a character is going to respond in a situation that will not be in the play." It's only when you know your characters completely from the inside out and from the present back through their lives that your idea has the possibility of taking on exciting dramatic shape and your writing a life of its own.

Each of your major characters, as you think they would be at the start of the play, should now become the subject of a basic sketch in words that I call the *short-form biography*. Don't worry if in this initial exploration your exact starting point is still uncertain. It's too early to be locked into a precise time frame anyway, so just go with your strongest hunch at this point.

The short-form biography involves creating a cursory, beginning picture of who your characters are by looking at them from three different angles:

1. What they look like physically

2. How they relate to and fit into the world around them

3. What's going on inside their heads and hearts

Again, I acknowledge my debt to Lajos Egri, who first presented this basic approach to character exploration in his book *The Art of Dramatic Writing*. The short-form biography is adapted from and expands on the three-part character breakdown Egri calls "the bone structure" of character. It looks something like an overly-thorough job application:

SHORT-FORM BIOGRAPHY

Name: _____

Physical Characteristics

Age: _____ **Date of birth:** _____

Height:_____ **Weight:** _____

Eye color: _____ **Hair color:**_____

Skin color/tone: _____

Posture: _____

Grooming: _____

Vocal quality: _____

General appearance: (indicate degree of attractiveness, elegance or crudeness, sex appeal, "presence," general health, any physical problems or defects, etc.)

External World

I. FAMILY SITUATION

Father: (include age, if alive, or how long ago he died, occupation, any special characteristics, nature of relationship with, etc.)

Mother: (same as for father)

Siblings: (brothers and/or sisters, ages, any special characteristics, nature of relationships with each, etc.)

Other important relatives: (what relation, age, special characteristics, nature of relationship with, etc.)

Family's ability to function: (happy, normal, disruptive, dysfunctional, unusual in some way, etc.)

Marital status: (if not married, describe any significant romantic relationships. If married, how long? Describe spouse in detail, even if not a character in your play; at least fill out a short-form biography for him or her. If divorced, how long? Any special circumstances?)

Children: (include names, ages, nature of relationship with, etc.)

Sex life: (active, dormant, frustrated, specific problems, etc.)

Close friends: (those considered extended family; include names, ages, nature of relationship with)

II. PLACE IN THE COMMUNITY

Occupation: (include how long in the field)

Education: (indicate quality as well as how much)

Economic class: (include annual income)

Political affiliation(s): (this usually goes well beyond a national political party)

Religious affiliation: (if it exists, indicate how active)

Other organizational memberships: (there are usually one or two key affiliations)

General status in community: (how perceived in the eyes of others—leader or follower, asset or liability, etc.)

III. LEISURE-TIME ACTIVITIES: (pin down the way the character spends his or her spare time)

Internal World

Intelligence: (some measure for comparison and how it manifests itself)

Personality type: (extrovert or introvert, optimistic or pessimistic, hot-tempered or cool, etc.)

General sense of self: (degree of self-confidence, self-esteem, etc.)

Sexuality: (how powerful a force, degree of comfort with, etc.)

Spiritual life: (nature and strength of—does God fit in somewhere and, if so, how and to what extent?)

Sense of morality: (how strong is it, and how does it manifest itself?)

Major secrets: (that he or she hasn't told anyone; prioritize if more than one)

Personal goals: (if more than one, prioritize)

Major disappointments: (if more than one, prioritize)

Special qualities and talents: (unique physical, intellectual, artistic, or spiritual traits)

As we take a closer look at the various elements making up the short-form, keep in mind that this early character work is just a starting point. As you explore your people more fully and get to know them intimately, these initial sketches will most likely need to be adjusted to fit the fuller personalities you uncover. As your idea is developed and refined, your people may very well have to change to fit into what your play is becoming. For now, however, the important thing is to get the exploration started.

What's in a Name?

Take another look at the character names you put down on your worksheet in Chapter 4. Do you really feel comfortable with these? That is, do they accurately give the feel for the characters that you want? Take a little time to think about this now.

Names have a way of giving a slant to a person and can seriously influence how someone is perceived by others. Everyone has certain names which for them conjure up types of personalities. A name can hint at a degree of formality or sexiness or athleticism or whatever. So make an effort to assign names that work for you, that fit what *you* feel about your characters' personalities.

Symbolism, on the other hand, or having a name carry some sort of special message, can become a nuisance and is for most plays too artificial. Just choose something you think you'll be comfortable working with and that feels right. Also, give each character a first and last name. You may not ever use the last name in your play, but you need to know what it is because it's imperative that you think of your characters as real people.

This is an important choice. You'll be writing these names hundreds of times. The mere act of writing them over and over will subconsciously send messages to you about the personalities they represent. They'll become as synonymous with your characters as your own name is to you. If a name isn't working, you can always change it. Even Henrik Ibsen's drafts show interesting renamings as he worked through his plays. However, be aware that after a certain point this isn't so easy. Characters, like real people, have a way of fusing with the initial names they're given.

Your Character's Physical Characteristics

It's important to get down some sense of who your people are physically. If these characters are ever to become real, breathing human beings for you, it's critical that you have a sense of what they look like, how they move, how they sound, how they appear when seen from a distance or from across a table, how other characters react to their actual physical presence.

I'm not talking here about what the actors who will be playing your characters should look like, although there's no harm in visualizing your ideal cast if this helps bring your people into sharper focus. **Terrence McNally**, for instance, says he always writes with specific actors in mind even if they don't end up doing the play: "This helps clarify for me; I can imagine what characters might look like, what they might possibly sound like. It just helps me to be specific."

Even if you do write with specific actors or people that you know in mind, don't feel at this point that you must write character descriptions as they'll appear in your finished script or try to convey how characters should be played in performance. That's another issue which shouldn't be confused with how you visualize your characters as you prepare to write. Rather, focus now on actual physical characteristics and start making some key choices about their "look" and "feel." Sharpen and clarify them visually and aurally for *you,* the writer.

Age and Date of Birth

In almost every case, the most important trait to determine is a character's age. Don't be vague about this. A twenty-eight-year-old sees him- or herself in a different way from a thirty-year-old. A woman who is fifty-six usually is not happy being described as "in her late-fifties." And exactly when the character was born—the precise day, month, and year—is important to think about. What kind of world did this person land in? What major national and international events had an influence on his or her growing-up years, on shaping the attitudes and outlooks of the character? Does the Great Depression or World War II mean anything personally to any of them? The Berlin Wall? The assassination of President Kennedy, or the war in Vietnam? The Beatles? The birth of the Internet? A date of birth gives a character a context and an automatic social history that will be woven into his or her personality.

One of the most frustrating things I come up against when I read a script is that the writer has not given the characters' ages. Odd as this may seem, it happens often. I'm forced to start reading the play with absolutely no idea of how old the people are. It's almost impossible to make any sense of the dynamics of the characters' relationships until I've managed to figure at least approximate ages for everyone. Then, if the play seems promising, I often find it necessary to go back and reread from the beginning. Withholding age information doesn't make me read more closely or pay more attention to the dialogue. It does the opposite. First it irritates me, and then, if the writing is good, it frustrates me because I can't get an accurate bearing on the characters as quickly as I should be able to. The writer has not allowed me to enter fully into the play, as would be possible at a performance where the physical presence of the actors establishes age immediately.

Remember, these are *people* you're creating here. They have lived a certain number of years, and every one of those years has shaped who they are. Assigning age, therefore, is a major decision—a critical piece of information to determine for each of your characters. However, if you're not sure at this point how old your people are, just put down something to start with. The wonderful thing about this process of writing plays is that you can go back and make adjustments. You can take away years or add them on as the evolving story dictates. Playwrights sometimes wipe out characters altogether. What's important is that you assign an age now so you'll have something to work with, something to respond to as you proceed.

Putting Them in Front of You

Like Terrence McNally, I find that the more complete a visual picture I can create of my characters, the more they come to life for me. Although I don't usually write for specific actors, I do try to see, in my mind's eye, the physical appearance of real people—their height, weight, hair and eye color, skin tone, posture, grooming, attractiveness, sex appeal, degree of ruggedness or refinement, clothes choice, and so on.

As an exercise, close your eyes and try to visualize your central character right in front of you. Put him or her in clothes appropriate for the play and carefully create your own visual picture. Start from the head down. Work at this until you can actually see the *person* standing there staring back at you, until you've created a real, living and breathing human being. Then study your creation. Spot the details. The button missing, the impeccably white running shoes, the stain on the sleeve— the grooming or lack of grooming.

Don't get impatient here. Take the time to try this visualization exercise. Developing a keen sense of your characters in all their human glory is critical, and the only way to do it is to focus in on the details. A visual picture of your central character obviously isn't the only thing you're going to need, but it sure helps as you proceed. The objective in character exploration is to gain an intimate knowledge and "feel" for your people. They have to become so close to you and you to them that their humanity and yours merge. You can't create real characters without true intimacy.

Now, get down on paper the initial physical description you've come up with. Keep everything concise. The idea here, as in previous exercises, is to tack down the essential details. If you're drawing a blank and nothing appears before you, force yourself to make up a preliminary description anyway, just to get started. When you put something down that doesn't seem right, you'll know it. And don't worry about it—no one else is ever going to see it.

My students sometimes balk at coming up with this kind of physical detail so early on in the process and feel uncomfortable trying to fill out an actual form. My response is that playwrights, particularly beginners, need to take advantage of every possible trick they can to get close to their characters, especially at the outset. And creating a detailed visual picture is one of the proven ways to activate in your writer's head a whole set of responses that will bring you into closer contact with these people you're inventing.

If you find yourself resisting, all I can say is: Push through it, plunge in, and start making initial choices in a trial-and-error effort. You have nothing to lose and a potentially much more fruitful character exploration to gain. Your task is to create characters that will come to life on the page and—let's hope—walk right off the page and onto a stage. Having a detailed visual picture as you move through your character explorations will only help you achieve that goal.

Your Character's External World

Placing your characters into their unique social contexts—the external circumstances your people have lived through and are currently involved in—

is essential. By doing so, you'll start seriously to dig into their lives and begin asking some critical questions about the forces that have shaped them and that continue to influence how they think and act. Every person has a definite set of social circumstances which has helped define who he or she is. You have to know what these are for each of your characters.

The Family Situation

First, make some choices about each character's blood-relatives—his or her family circumstances. There are a whole set of crucial questions you need to think about: Who are the parents? Are they still living? Are they still married to each other? Were they ever married? What kind of relationship do (or did) they have? What does (or did) each of the parents do for a living?

What kind of relationship did your character have with his (or her) father when he was growing up? With his mother? What kind of relationship does he have with each of them now?

Does your character have brothers and sisters? Where does he fall chronologically among his siblings? What kind of relationship did he have with each of them while growing up? What kind of relationship does he have with each of them now?

Are there any close relatives that have had an important influence on your character? Was it a happy family during your character's growing-up years? Was it dysfunctional? If so, how and to what extent? What emotional scars does the character carry from past family experiences?

If your character is a functioning adult in the real world, you also have to take a look at the family he has created for himself. Is he married or committed to someone? If so, is this his first such relationship? What kind of relationship is it? Does he have children? How many? What kind of relationship does he have with each of them?

If your character isn't married, has he been? If divorced, how has that experience affected him? Does he have a romantic or intimate relationship with someone now? How serious is it? If not, has he had one or more in the past? Does he have close, intimate friends? How important a role do these friend-relationships play in his life?

Notice that the questions center on the *relationships* your character has had or is currently involved in. This is a major key to understanding who your people are and why they do the things they do. People spend their lives interacting with other people and being influenced by them, especially those close to them. This is most true with a person's relationship with his or her parents, because without question it's here that the most shaping is done, both good and bad. It's important also to consider the other family and close-friend relationships as well. They've all made their mark.

Place in the Community

Outside the family, people have a multitude of ways in which they individually relate to their external world. Traditionally, in America, a person's standing in the community is largely determined by what he or she does for a living. Although this is slowly changing, a brain surgeon is still placed higher on the social ladder than a plumber, although both professions are crucial to society's ability to function. Certain professions simply carry with them a special status and respect while others have a negative stigma attached to them.

Deciding what your characters do for a living will automatically give you clues to a whole series of other important social factors, such as economic class, annual income, level of education, and status in the community. And then you should think about your characters' political and religious affiliations and any significant organizational memberships. Ask of each character: Is he (or she) a leader or a follower? Is he active politically? Do people in the community look up to him and ask advice? Do they consider him a nuisance and liability? What is your character's role in the community and is he or she comfortable with it?

Your character's occupation may seem to lack significance, but don't be fooled by this when it comes to placing him or her in a social context. Everyone has a role to play, a function to perform. A freshman college student has to maneuver through a social mechanism just as elaborate as (and perhaps more bewildering than) the President of the United States does. Placing your characters in their unique community settings will force you to begin asking important questions about how they relate to themselves and their world.

Leisure Time

Another angle from which to view characters' relationship to their external world is to look at how and with whom they spend their leisure time. Although occupation will often influence leisure activity, this is the one area where a person, at least to some extent, has the freedom to choose what he or she wants to do. As a result, you have the opportunity here to make choices that will truly individualize your characters. How people amuse themselves in their off-hours reveals a great deal about them. And whom they choose to spend this time with reveals even more. Does your character jump at the chance to run off with the guys to play basketball, or does he go off by himself and build model airplanes? What is her dream vacation? Would she travel alone, or with someone, and whom would she take with her?

Thinking about how your characters choose to spend their free time may seem at first like a minor consideration, one of those incidentals that can be picked up along the way—more than likely much further down the line. But think for a minute about when you're first introduced to someone. If, after an initial exchange, you determine that this is someone you'd like to get to know better, you start asking questions. And it's usually when you learn about what someone does with his or her free time that you either start to like that person or back off. It's this information that usually keys you into the kind of lasting connections, if any, there might be between you.

With your characters, it's no different. Making choices about their hobbies and free-time activities—even if adjustments have to be made later—will give you a sharper focus on these personalities you're bringing into existence and how they will relate to each other.

And because inner drives and secret passions are often revealed in what people do when given the choice of how to spend their time, you'll already be uncovering clues about what really makes them tick under the surface.

Your Character's Internal World

In the third part of the short-form biography you should sketch in how your characters think and feel.With this initial probe into their psychological and spiritual make-up—into what's going on in their heads and hearts—you begin to view them from the inside out. When it comes to writing good, truthful dialogue for these people, you'll need to feel comfortable living inside them. You'll need to be able, ultimately, to formulate and verbalize their *every* thought, presenting in words and actions their unique intellectual and emotional worlds.

Intelligence

In making some determination of each character's intelligence and its manifestation in thinking and behavior, it doesn't really matter what measurement you use, but it should be something that will allow you to compare relative degrees of intelligence between characters. As good as any method to get you started are I.Q. numbers—80 being below average, 100 average, 130 above average, and 150 and higher in the "genius" range.

Admittedly, assigning I.Q.s will give you only a general sense of intelligence for each character and a beginning point for comparison. The numbers say nothing about the *kinds* of intelligence or how a character uses his or her brain power. You have to make that determination and consider how this affects how a person talks and acts as well as how it influences the relationships that develop. For example, one person may have an edge in terms of quickness of response or glibness of tongue, and another may compensate with the ability to intimidate or wield authority or power. Consider *Who's Afraid of Virginia Woolf?*: Although both George and Martha have remarkable verbal adeptness, George has the edge in rational, analytical thinking, while Martha holds her own by consistently knowing what emotional strings to pull.

Personality Type

It's also useful to determine a general indication of personality type. Is your character an extrovert, outgoing, and naturally friendly, or just the opposite? If he or she is somewhere in between, where in between?

Think about the character's basic attitude toward life. Is it upbeat, generally positive, and optimistic or, conversely, a tendency to wallow in gloominess, negativity, and depression? Does he or she see the bright side of things and look at problems as opportunities, or just the reverse? Does your character tend to see only the good side of people and to give others the benefit of the doubt or, rather, to be judgmental and critical? Does he get angry easily or generally keep his cool? Is she fun to have around or, more often than not, a pain to spend time with?

Most people fall somewhere in between these extremes. In plays, however, effective characters push the personality limits in at least some areas, and this is generally true for central characters. That's what makes them interesting and alive onstage. It's what helps to propel them through the play and create the dramatic sparks that ignite scenes. So in this initial pinning-down process, make a conscious effort to give your characters personalities that make a definite statement one way or another.

General Sense of Self

Another critical early choice is to determine the degree to which your characters generally like themselves. There are a number of important self-esteem related questions you need to ask, such as: Are your characters comfortable with who they are? Are they at peace with themselves? Do they enjoy being alone? How self-confident are they? Where do they fall on the self-esteem curve? Do they feel superior or inferior to others? Are they riddled with self-doubts, or do they have an inflated opinion of themselves? Are they burdened with feelings of guilt? Do they like how they look in the mirror?

All interesting characters are struggling in some way with their own sense of self. In fact, most great plays are, in some way, dealing with this struggle. In *Death of a Salesman,* Willy Loman pushes himself to despair as he progressively loses his self-confidence and self-respect. We watch a man who increasingly is unable to live with himself. In *The Crucible,* John Proctor is ultimately driven to accepting death in order to restore his self-respect. In *Who's Afraid of Virginia Woolf?* Martha finally admits that she's afraid and that she needs to embrace herself honestly for the first time in her adult life. You don't have a potential play if your central character isn't at war with him- or herself in some way.

Sexuality

How characters relate to themselves as sexual beings is another "room" that must be explored. Often this inner, personal connection is a critical determining factor in how a person sees the world and responds to it.

Keep in mind that people connect to their own sexuality differently. Some are virtually controlled by the powerful sexual force in them and at the same time are totally at ease with it. Such people feel their sexuality in every move they make, and it colors how they operate in the world, how they relate to others of both sexes. At the other end of the scale are those whose sexuality is deeply submerged, locked away in an inner deep-freeze somewhere. It scares them to death. Their orientation to the world is or appears to be neutered. They have no idea what it means to ever feel sexy, and they have great difficulty connecting with themselves physically. Most people, obviously, fall somewhere in between these extremes.

In your short-form biography, reflect on how your characters' sexuality affects how they move physically and even how they sound when they talk. These and other sexual issues will help you unlock aspects of their private, secret worlds that in some way have to be laid bare for your use.

Spiritual Life

Surprisingly, this crucial area of a character's inner make-up is often overlooked in character exploration. In fact, a person's spiritual life (or lack of it) is often the most powerful, if hidden, influence on behavior. It's very private and deeply personal, but more often than not if you can get a person to open up about his or her relationship with God, or the Divine, or whatever label feels comfortable to that person, you'll be given a deep and powerful emotional response. Sometimes it's angry, bitter, and filled with denial. Sometimes it's tearful, sad, and full of longing. Sometimes it's an apparent indifferent response. Sometimes it's joyous and energetic. Even the adamant atheist can get emotional about God or, rather, God's assumed nonexistence.

The point here is that there's a place inside everyone that's the exclusive domain of the spiritual. To deny that is simply to deny a part of being human. Obviously, the spiritual side of a person can manifest itself in innumerable ways, within a Judeo-Christian perspective, an Islamic fundamentalism, a Buddhist asceticism, or one or more of the New Age orientations—and even agnosticism and atheism.

Your task is to acknowledge that *something* occupies each character's spiritual "room" and to make some choices as to what kind of connection each has to it. How strongly tapped into the spiritual is each one of your characters? To ignore this question will only diminish your chances of creating honest, real people. Explore it and you will open one of the most important doors into your characters' lives.

Sense of Morality

Although "morality" can be a loaded word and mean different things to different people, it's important to pin down a sense of a character's moral fiber. Every person operates under some moral system or way of thinking whether he has a belief in God or not. For example, one character living in Nazi Germany may feel it's his or her moral duty to betray a family of Jews; another might risk life and limb to hide the family.

What about more common things, like shoplifting? Or claiming deductions on income taxes? Or lying to a friend? Or sexual promiscuity? The list of everyday moral issues is endless. What standard does the character apply when questions of right or wrong present themselves? How does the character relate to the moral dictates of his or her religion, or of society, or of peer group? Clearly, answers to these kinds of questions will tell you a great deal about how your characters relate to themselves, each other, and the world around them.

Try inventing a number of situations drawn loosely from your play idea (but preferably outside the events to be dealt with in the play itself) in which your characters have to make clear moral choices about what action to take. Then force them to make it. This will allow you to at least begin testing their sense of morality.

Major Secrets

Every living person harbors at least one major secret, something they do or have done that they don't want anyone *ever* to find out about. Determining what this is can often shed a strong light on why a character thinks the way he does or behaves a certain way. **Marsha Norman** explains it well:

> Every one of us has something like a shameful secret. And we think that if everybody knew about this thing they wouldn't like us, they wouldn't want to be around us. Shame—whether it's something you did or not—we all have something that causes us to feel that we're different from everybody else and not finally understandable by anybody.

It's not too early in the process to make an initial choice here. Invent at least one dark secret that now seems right for each of your major characters. Try something on for size. If nothing else, it will stimulate your creative thinking about your people and help open doors to each character's true inner life.

Personal Goals

Everyone has ambitions or dreams. Some are modest and attainable. Others are way out there, beyond reach. Whatever they may be, the little choices people make day by day are at least partially influenced by the bigger goals they've set for themselves. It's precisely because of this that the more successful corporations and institutions come up with five-year plans. They know that if they have a set of goals they're shooting for—even if these change every year—it will help them make the hundreds of daily decisions they're faced with in the weeks and months ahead. Without such a plan, the organization has no guidance system and no vision for the future, and this can eventually lead to serious trouble.

People automatically do this for themselves. It's a sort of built-in mechanism. And if a person believes passionately in a personal dream, it can motivate everything he or she does. Nothing is allowed to get in the way of achieving the goal, making that dream come true. What about your characters? What goals, dreams, or ambitions have they set for themselves? Are they realistic, or totally unattainable? Are they positive and life-affirming, or negative and self-destructive? Are they self-serving or selfless in nature? How strongly do your characters believe in them? How important are these goals over the course of their lives?

Actors' agents are often quoted as saying they're looking for one part talent to three parts drive. Talent is important, they say, but what really gets them interested in signing someone is how hungry the actor is to succeed. They want motivation and push—people who won't take no for an answer. The agents need a full list of such driven actors if they hope to stay in business and put food on their own tables.

Audiences are like agents. They demand characters like that. They want to engage with people who are driven, who *want* something badly. Instinctively they know that's the only way they're going to be delivered "the goods," emotionally and intellectually, by the end of the play.

Likewise, to create that sense of inner life and direction in your characters you not only have to determine their personal goals but also make the attaining of those goals their top priority. It doesn't necessarily matter at this point if the long-term goals you come up with for your central character are part of the dominant need you put down on your idea worksheet in Chapter 4, although more than likely they will be connected with it in some way. Instead, what you're doing now is meant to go beyond the specific circumstances of the play itself and to simply embrace your central figure and all other characters as living, breathing human beings.

Of course, you can't ignore the play you're planning to write. That's the reason you're creating these people in the first place. However, it's important not to tie yourself too tightly to how you projected the dramatic shape of your play on the idea worksheet. Now's the time to stay loose and to experiment. Don't limit the range of your exploration by insisting on any preconceived plan of attack.

Major Disappointments

We all have at least one area in our lives we consider a failure or disappointment and for which we feel a substantial degree of remorse, regret, or frustration. Something important has not turned out the way we'd hoped it would, and this has left a mark. It's a universal human experience.

The disappointment can center on a special relationship, a career plan, an unrealized goal or dream. People push on with their lives, but as they do they carry a major failure with them, at least for a period of time. It affects their behavior, their choices, what they allow themselves to hope for in the future, what kinds of risks they're willing to take.

In your short-form biography, give each of your characters at least one of these humanizing frustrations. It's remarkable how this can often be the key to having a character come to life for you.

Special Qualities and Talents

As with frustrations, everyone has at least one thing to offer that is unique, a quality that makes him or her special. It can be physical, intellectual, emotional, or spiritual in nature: Extraordinary athletic ability, unusual beauty and poise, a highly developed sense of humor, uncanny business skill, great wisdom and judgment, a capacity for compassionate caring of the sick and dying, a powerful connection with God, and so on. These are positive traits that are thrown into the mix, things that indicate that a person has at least a potential for good, even if it's not being realized. In *The Crucible,* John Proctor is a successful, talented farmer and an honest man. In *Death of a Salesman,* Willy Loman loves his sons with a passion. In *Who's Afraid of Virginia Woolf?* Martha has a highly refined and brilliant sense of irony. These special traits season characters, giving them "color" and boosting their potential for surprise.

Using the Short Form

I suggest that you draw up a form to fill out for your short-form biographies and photocopy a stack of them. Keep them handy whenever you start new character explorations or go back to make changes. Try to get it all on two pages. This will limit the blank space you have and remind you to keep your initial answers short and to the point. Too much detail at this stage, when you're simply trying to sketch in your characters, will just bog you down. Fill out a short form on each of your characters.

It's also important to fill out a short-form on people who—at least at this point—you don't think are going to appear in your play but who have an important connection to one or more of your onstage characters, especially your central character. These so-called offstage figures—such as spouses, lovers, parents, or children—are often as important as some characters who appear and say lines.

Take the time now to determine which of these influential offstage people need to be explored fully and fill out a short-form on them. Doing this will undoubtedly open new doors into the emotional and behavioral life of your onstage characters. *They* know these offstage characters well—so should you. Getting to know them will bring you closer to that sensitive, intimate understanding that's so critical if you ever hope to bring your people fully to life on the page.

Giving Time to the Process

If you're at all like me, you need to keep telling yourself: Don't be impatient. One of the biggest stumbling blocks in writing a play is being too anxious to start on that first draft. Keep reminding yourself that you already are writing your play. Taking the time now to explore all facets of your characters' lives as thoroughly as you can—including those key relationships with people who won't ever appear in the play—will pay generous dividends later on.

Just remember: This is just the starting point. Your goal with the short form is to "try things out." So don't limit yourself. As you move more deeply into character exploration—and we'll go further in Chapter 6— you'll see where adjustments, if any, have to be made. You'll know soon enough when some initial hunch isn't right.

Indeed, nothing can develop and grow unless you simply begin the *process*, putting something down that will stimulate your creativity and move you deeper into the fabric of your characters' lives. That's what process means, and that's how your short-form biographies contribute to it.

There's something mysterious about actually getting your ideas down on paper instead of letting this multitude of details just float around in your brain. The physical act of writing somehow activates your creative and critical mind. As a result, your characters will begin to emerge and you'll have actual personalities to work with, to respond to. And even if all early attempts at getting down these "facts" about your characters have to be reconsidered, beginning this work—actually starting to *make choices*—will ease you into the process of creating real, truthful people.

DEVELOPING THE BACKSTORY

Most true playwrights instinctively know the answers to almost all subtextual questions that you ask.

—EDWARD ALBEE

Completing short-form biographies on all your characters is a crucial first step in the process of character exploration. But don't be fooled here. In the short-form you have made only a pencil drawing. To bring your characters fully to life, your exploration needs to go further toward inventing detailed, "real" pasts with rich emotional content. Short-forms in hand, you're now able to move deeper into the lives of your people and develop a thorough backstory for each of them.

The Long-Form Biography

If you're familiar with the milestone exercise presented in Chapter 3, you'll see that this next step, the long-form biography, basically involves completing a similar exercise on each of your major characters. It's the only approach I've found that uncovers a character's past in such a way that the writer is brought into meaningful contact with what has shaped this personality. It allows you to get to know your characters as if they were real people with whom you've established close, intimate relationships—the only kind of connection with characters that will, in the end, allow you to write an exciting play.

Here are the steps in the milestone exercise adjusted for the long-form biography. (You might want to review the discussion in Chapter 3 before tackling this for each of your major characters.)

- Write the character's name and date of birth at the top of a sheet of paper.

- Carefully reread your play idea worksheet and the character's short-form biography. Then make a conscious effort to imagine this character as a real, living person.

- Take a few minutes to create a list of milestones for the character. There's no real need to time yourself, but try not to take more than ten minutes or so. The point is to push yourself to come up with as many items as you can—at least thirty—as quickly as you can. Work fast and put down anything that comes to mind. Be brief and concise. Think in terms of those personality-shaping experiences and episodes in the character's life, those events—both deeply private and shared with others—that have left a definite mark emotionally or spiritually. Scan back and forth through the years. Put down everything that comes into your mind, even if it's a bit off the wall. Don't be afraid to try things.

- Specifically focusing on your play idea for just a moment, look over your list and see if there are any other milestones that might contribute, even indirectly, to the major conflict/dilemma of your play. Remember, conflict rises out of character, and since you're exploring and creating your personalities, you want to add to the list anything you think has even the slightest chance of heightening the play's dramatic impact.

  A warning: Take care not to manipulate your emerging personalities to fit too nicely into what you now think your play is going to be. Although it's important to keep your play idea actively in your thinking, don't let it control the character exploration. There's a danger of becoming too analytical and forced in this early invention. Now is the time to be open for surprises and be a bit freewheeling. Play ideas usually have a way of adjusting to fit the personalities that emerge from your character work.

- Now look over your completed list carefully and make a second list of the eight most significant milestones. It's making such choices that creates a personality. The eight you choose may not have any apparent direct relationship to your play idea—it doesn't matter. You're creating a *person* here. What's important is to identify the eight most personality-shaping events of the character's life.

• Make up a final list with the character's name and date of birth followed by the eight most significant milestones in chronological order.

Let's look at a possible set of milestones for Dave Marshall, our gas station attendant from Chapter 4:

DAVE MARSHALL

Date of birth: July 14, 1980

1. Breaking my arm when I was five.

2. The Canadian fishing trip with Dad at eight.

3. My fight with Dwight Khrone when I was twelve.

4. Getting caught shoplifting at thirteen.

5. Chosen captain of the junior high soccer team at fourteen.

6. The night Dad left Mom for good at fifteen.

7. The heavy date with Linda at sixteen.

8. Telling off Dad last month.

This list obviously doesn't paint a complete picture, but you can see how each item could be extremely significant in shaping the personality of the boy we see at the start of the play. Notice that the items run the gamut of feelings, from totally negative to very positive, and that they seem to be begging for a fuller exploration.

Now go through this exercise with each of your major characters. The final lists of eight milestones you end up with is the first step of the long-form biography. It forms the basis for the much deeper exploration to follow.

Getting the Characters Talking

The next step is to write an exploratory first-person monologue in which each character talks personally about his or her date of birth (that is, the circumstances surrounding it) and each of the eight milestones. (Playwrights, as we'll see shortly, tend to think of such monologues as stories their characters tell them.) In every case, the characters speaking should be as you now envision them when they first make their entrance in the play. In other words, each character is looking back at the milestones and talking about them from the current "present" of the play itself. Each monologue should be thorough enough to engage your characters in really talking about themselves and the significant events that have shaped them.

As you write, focus on the emotional subcurrents inherent in the milestones. Have your characters concentrate on their feelings about these moments of crisis and change. Let them get emotional. A straightforward, objective description of an event, even when told in the first person, won't go very far in exploring those hidden places in your characters. So coax them to open up. Persuade them to be honest and to look at the sometimes murky but always powerful emotional components of these life-shaping events. This will help you uncover that inner "stuff" that makes characters unique and endearingly human.

One of the benefits of getting your characters talking is that, in addition to allowing you to dig deeper into these personalities, you're able to start tuning into the voice of each character. It's a sort of warm-up for the writing of the play in dialogue. Each character's diction and thought patterns, word choices, and command of the language are essential things to start getting an ear for.

Marsha Norman says this kind of preliminary "voicing" of the play is critical before starting her first draft. "Monologues help you 'happen in' to the person. That really helps. You sort of speak in their language for a while. . . . You hear how they talk, hear what's funny to them, you hear the kinds of metaphors they use, whether they talk about cooking or fishing."

Arthur Miller explains: "I don't think I write a play unless I can hear it. I have always felt that playwriting is an auditory art. . . . It's really basically what you hear. If I can hear characters speaking, it's a big leg up, it's a big event."

Athol Fugard expresses it this way: "I need to have, metaphorically speaking, a kind of a tuning fork. I need to know that I've got the pitch of each voice, and in what key they are going to be played before I start writing."

I suggest you start with the date of birth because it demands that you deal, from the character's point of view, with revealing and potentially valuable information. A person's feelings and attitudes surrounding the specific circumstances of his or her birth can shed considerable light on what makes this person tick. The nature of the parents' relationship at the time, their attitude toward the new arrival, the family economic situation, any special stresses on the family, and so on, are useful things to discover, especially when the character is talking about it in his or her own words. These circumstances affect, however subtly, the way a person relates to himself, his family, and the world. Sometimes surprising facts, clearly of major significance in a person's life, present themselves. You never know until you get them talking.

Let's look at a couple of milestones as our own Dave Marshall could have related them:

Date of birth: July 14, 1980

No big deal. Except for Mom, who always tries to make this huge thing out of birthdays. It's okay, I guess. I mean, to have a special day and all. I kind of like it, really. It means money in my pocket, which is definitely a plus.

I was the third and last kid. The first boy. Uncle Steve told me Dad was relieved when I appeared on the scene, because he wanted to keep going until he had a son. There's always been a special thing between us. Especially since the break-up. Mom once told me that my coming along when I did helped him get through the transfer from Minnesota to New Jersey, which he hated. That's cool. I've never found out the details of that . . . probably never will now.

Wow. He was thirty years old then. If he hadn't been transferred, I'd be this kid in some burg in Minneapolis. Forget that. Mom also said they almost decided to quit at two girls. When she's pissed off at me she says she wishes they had. Sometimes I wish that, too. Anyway, I really don't have any special feelings about my birth. Never thought much about it. Most of the time I'm glad it happened.

My fight with Dwight Khrone when I was twelve

This oversized kid, Dwight Khrone, lived a block and a half from my house, over between 5th and 6th Street. He was always a little strange. So were his parents. I remember feeling sorry for him because he didn't have any friends. But he was big, and when he wanted to hurt somebody he didn't have any qualms about that.

The summer I turned twelve, my best friend Pete and I built this cool, three-room treehouse perched high up in a huge cedar tree between our houses. We weren't sharing it with anybody, and when Dwight asked us if he could join our club, we said, "No way." He didn't like that at all. So one afternoon when we were out swimming, he marched over to the cedar with a crowbar in his hand, climbed up the branches to the trap door, and started prying off the floorboards.

Pete and I got back and caught him still up there. I lost it. Started screaming and cursing, throwing stones and sticks up at him. Pete tried to calm me down, but I was locked in. As Dwight started climbing down the tree, trying to dodge my missiles, Pete panicked and ran home. I was left facing this angry kid almost twice my weight, who was bleeding from one arm where a branch scratched him on the way down.

It was a weird feeling. I had an incredible energy and clear focus: I wanted to fight this guy. Nothing else mattered. Everything sort of disappeared around us. I jumped on him and started pounding as hard as I could. We were on the ground. All I remember is screaming "You asshole, you bastard!" and punching him over and over. I didn't feel any pain. I don't remember him hitting me back. Then suddenly he pulled himself free, got up, and ran off. I stood there watching him go, breathing so hard I thought my lungs were going to burst.

After a minute I realized my nose was bleeding. There was blood all over my T-shirt. I'd never been in a fight before. And then I felt this amazing rush. I'd just beaten up Dwight Khrone and sent him running home. I felt powerful. My body felt different. I seemed bigger all of a sudden. This was new for me. And at the time, it felt real good.

This gives you some idea of how getting your characters talking can start to unlock details and a distinct voice. It's also a lot of fun. Usually when you start these forays into milestones, the writing seems to take on a life of its own. Let your characters go, and if they keep on talking, let them talk. Don't rush through this, for what you'll learn is invaluable, though perhaps very little of it will be directly applicable to your play.

Shared Milestones

If your characters are from the same family or are close friends, they will often share one or more of the milestones. When this happens, it's interesting to see how each person relates to the same past experience, emotionally responding in his or her unique way. You'll discover the differences in the characters' perceptions of events, in their emotional makeups, and in their defense mechanisms. Comparing the two monologue responses will help you figure out how these two people might relate to each other and what's operating under the surface in terms of their interaction. Whenever the opportunity arises, you should explore these shared milestones.

Drawing from the Unconscious

You may be surprised by what your people "tell" you. That's one of the mysteries and joys in this process. When you get them talking about themselves and specific key events in their lives, these fictional personalities start merging with your own past, your own emotional makeup. But, at the same time, the characters who start coming to life are entirely new and different. As pointed out earlier, they seemingly emerge as people who begin thinking and feeling for themselves and telling you things in their own voice—things you didn't know or hadn't thought of. Writing the long-form biography you will tap into a creative engagement with your characters.

It's a mystery how the writer's mind activates when you actually start putting words on the page. Something is triggered in the creative side of the brain which allows you to dip into riches below the surface, beyond conscious, deliberate thought. **Edward Albee** remarks:

> One of the wonderful things I find about writing is the way we
> can surprise ourselves: "I didn't know I thought that. Goodness,
> is that why I want my characters to do that? I didn't know that."
> So you inform yourself of what you've been thinking about.

Such "informing" certainly can take place in this pre-draft exploratory work. You can sit and muse about your characters for hours and little occurs in terms of the nitty-gritty details of your play. But start working through the long-form biographical exercise and things start happening. Real people start speaking about real experiences and feelings. Personalities with all their shadings and intricacies begin to be uncovered.

When I wrote the date of birth milestone for Dave Marshall, for example, I had no idea he'd say that sometimes he wishes he'd never been born. And he hints at it twice. That's interesting information. It suggests that there's a dark side to this character that's worth looking into further. If I were working on this play, I would definitely explore when and why he felt this way and determine how serious these feelings really are. This might lead me to a major discovery about him. Then again, it might not. In terms of the process, the milestone monologue first opened the door to this potentially significant piece of Dave's emotional makeup.

Another thing you may discover as you work through this exercise is that a character is totally in denial about some traumatic event or fearful of facing some monster from the past. Your job is to get the character to confront the experience, describe it honestly, and relate the personal feelings involved with it. Don't let characters off the hook because you've convinced yourself that their personalities wouldn't permit them to discuss a certain topic. Again, **Edward Albee** remarks on this aspect of character work: "We play that trick on ourselves, don't we? We pretend that the characters are real and that we can't have them say anything they don't want to. Well, this is foolishness."

I agree. Simply remember that this is a private exercise, with the characters talking to themselves about themselves. Insist that they open up and start dealing with these dark areas, even if what they have to say is incomplete, halting, and relatively incoherent. Afterward, you can always add additional notes in the third person at the end. Be careful here, however. Don't ever talk about a character if it's at all possible for a character to talk about himself. Keep your third-person comments in the milestone exercise to a minimum. Don't slip into writing lengthy descriptions of your characters and how they feel about things. It's always more useful to have your characters describe themselves.

The Rewards of Patience

Impatience to get into the actual writing of your play before thoroughly embracing your characters is a common stumbling block for playwrights. A little voice keeps telling you that you don't need all this prep work, that you can explore your people once you get them talking and interacting in the draft itself.

In one sense, that voice isn't wrong. Some writers work this way. Their first drafts are nothing but explorations, trying things out, testing ideas, getting people talking to each other and seeing what happens. **Terrence McNally**, for example, says:

> I think a lot starts happening when I begin writing the dialogue—that's when they start becoming specific, and I have to really zero in. You start out with types and conflict, what the relationships are, who's involved with whom romantically, who's mad at whom. But it all starts happening really when I start writing it. . . . I guess I'd say my work is more improvising at the typewriter than anything.

And **Tina Howe** says: "I can only find the truth of the moment through the words themselves. It's always the words that lead me there."

Be careful here, however. These two writers and others who work this way *have* done a lot of prep work before sitting down to write. It may not be all in the form of long-form biographies, but they've started to answer the basic questions about their characters and how they think, feel, and express themselves.

My experience tells me that usually when that little voice of impatience wins out—especially for beginning playwrights—the writing suffers. Things will work pretty well for several pages and be perking along, and then you start running out of gas. The dialogue starts sounding wooden and false. The characters lose their energy and spunk. You can't "hear" them anymore. An awful numbness sets in, and everything grinds to a halt.

In almost every case, the reason for this is that you don't know your characters well enough. They haven't become a part of you. It's like trying to leave on a long car trip and forgetting to fill the tank. You don't get very far because an essential step has been ignored. **Lanford Wilson**, for example, admits that this has happened to him. His remedy is character biographies:

> I've written pages of biography—what they think and what they feel . . . but this is because they've stopped talking to me and I don't know where I am. And so I just try to get to know them better, so that maybe they'll start talking again. If they were still talking, I'd be writing dialogue. And they're not, so I'm writing their history and trying to discover who they are.

Taking the time to introduce yourself to your characters and giving them the opportunity to introduce themselves to you through exploratory work like the long-form biography will give you a much keener awareness of what really makes your characters tick. As a result, when you do start your first draft, the play can feel like it's writing itself, or, rather, that you're just sitting there writing down what the characters do and say.

When this kind of "automatic writing" starts to happen, you'll know you're on to something, that the process is working as it should. Your characters are so real to you that the actual writing of the play is an adventure in observing and listening to distinctive people. It's an amazing feeling when this happens, when the proverbial Muse lays her hand on your head and your people come fully to life. What triggers these good days, of course, is that you've taken the time to prepare yourself for the task. **Arthur Miller** puts it well:

> If one of the characters starts freewheeling and spinning out
> his surprising observations or reactions to something, so that
> he or she becomes autonomous, life takes place. You work and
> work hoping that will happen, and when it does happen, those
> puppets get out of your hand and they begin to breathe. And
> that's when you know something happened. But, as I say, to
> arrive at that point is a lot of work.

It is not often understood that the word "writing" really refers to a creative process that begins with formulating and developing an idea
through *pre-writing*. And for playwrights, character exploration is at the
heart of pre-writing. In doing long-form biographies, then, you're
already actively in the midst of creating your play. When you've brought
your characters vibrantly to life for yourself, you're halfway home. Now
your people will go to work for you and bring you the rest of the way.

Exploring with Dialogue

As you're working on your long-form bios, you may get the urge to try
a bit of dialogue between two of your characters, just to get them talking to each other. Or you may feel like getting a character into a dialogue with someone who features prominently in his or her life but who
won't appear in your play. Often a character's milestones will suggest a
variety of situations for such dialogue exploration. Don't ignore this
urge: It's an inner voice telling you it's time to do some more exploring, to see how your people behave with others verbally, how they
respond and maneuver, how they interact. As we've seen, some writers
do an extensive amount of this kind of improvisational and exploratory
writing.

One cautionary note here: This business of writing plays is so delicate
and fragile, it's usually best to steer away from scenes that you think are
going to be in the play itself. Once you start writing a version of a scene
or two from the play, it's hard to stop. It's very easy to plunge into your
first draft before you're really ready. And once you've written a scene
from the play, however exploratory you think it may be, it's sometimes
difficult—when you're actually writing your first draft—to approach that
part of the play again with freshness and excitement. You might discover
that something's been defused because your characters have already
talked their way through a version of that scene.

Of course, every writer has a different response to exploratory writing. **Edward Albee** says he can't do any at all, because "writing it down for me is getting it out of my mind." Instead, he creates a situation *not* in the play and, in his mind, does a form of actor's improvisation with his characters. Other playwrights have no difficulty with extensive dialogue exploration from the play itself. In fact—as we'll see in Chapter 10—this is how they write their plays.

As a general rule, however, it is usually safest to hold off tackling the material of your actual play until you've made an honest attempt to do thorough character explorations—to make as many discoveries as you can before you put your people into your play. To state this another way: The more you know about your characters before you start your first draft, the more they will be able to engage with your play on their own terms. Getting them into the actual play prematurely can short-circuit this process.

The Character Timeline

After completing your first-person milestones, try going back to your original expanded list and create a timeline for each of your characters' lives. Start with the date of birth and work through everything, placing each event or experience on the timeline with a word or phrase. Put down anything you think might be of some significance, including important historical events that your characters had no direct part in. When you're done it should resemble one of those timelines used in history courses, only here you've charted the important events in the life of your character up to the start of the action of the play.

If you make sure the spacing between years on the timelines is the same for each of your characters, you'll even be able to set them all out in front of you and compare when various events occured. If the characters share a long backstory, this can be especially useful; undoubtedly some of the events listed will be the same. You can keep track, then, of different characters' ages when things happened to them and of where they were in their development when confronted with shared experiences. At a glance, you can have an overview of your characters' lives and relations to each other in the past. These simple summaries help make sense of all the material you've been accumulating, putting it into a workable perspective.

Those Unturned Stones

With completed milestones and timelines in hand, now is the time to look for any other events or experiences that warrant further exploration. If some aspect is still a little cloudy or unclear, even slightly, look carefully at it. Consider doing another milestone monologue. Look over your short-form bios and write down questions about the specific circumstances your characters will face in the play and how they might react to them. After musing over these questions, sleep on them.

As **Marsha Norman** suggests:

> Turn them over to the guys in the back room, as I call them
> . . . the unconscious, or subconscious, part of your mind that
> works better than the other part in terms of thinking about
> people and their dilemmas.

The important thing at this point is not to leave any potentially significant elements unexplored. Don't limit yourself to the eight milestones. Other factors will certainly present themselves. Because character exploration is a process of peeling off layers, you never know what or when new secrets might come into focus. When they do appear, explore them.

Taking Stock, Making Adjustments

When you've utilized *all* the techniques for the exploration of your major characters, conduct a careful review of your preliminary idea. Ask yourself the obvious question: Does your play idea worksheet still appear to represent the play you want to write, given what you now know about your characters?

Sometimes, depending on the discoveries you've made, your initial idea will have to undergo a major shift. You may realize that you really want to write your play about one of the secondary characters. Or the dominant need of your central character may not be what you thought it was after digging into his or her life-shaping experiences. You may discover that what you really want to communicate with the play is quite different from what you thought before you explored your characters fully.

Now's the time to ask some hard questions. Look at your most current worksheet. Do the discoveries you've made about your people meld with your play idea and support it, both in terms of the story you want to tell and the emotional "mix" under the surface? Is there something you know now about one or more of these personalities that no longer allows them to function in the play the way you thought they would? If adjustments need to be made, make them. Fill out another worksheet. Sleep on it and then look at it again. Shape your idea into the play you now want to write. Keep working with the worksheet until it clearly reflects what you're excited about developing further.

It's always possible to go back into your character work and make adjustments if you can't bring yourself to alter your initial idea or if you can't find a way to change it successfully. Usually, however, it's best to trust the characters who are beginning to reveal themselves and to respect what they're telling you about where your play is to be found. It's hard for characters to lie. The long-form biographies are so personal and revealing (if they've been done properly) that to ignore the messages they're giving is like short-circuiting electric current. Characters *are* your play. How they feel and think and act, what motivates and drives them— it's these things that supply the energy that will bring your writing to life.

You may discover that your original idea still works beautifully. It's always a blessing when your initial hunches have proved correct. Now you have this rich "support system" undergirding your characters and the situations you're going to be placing them in. Whether you have to make adjustments or not in your idea, what's important here is that the character work you've done must align with the idea you've outlined. To continue developing an idea that is *not* supported, enriched, and intensified by in-depth character explorations is begging for frustration.

Again, writing a play is a cycle of discovery and adjustment—and then *more* discovery and adjustment. It's a messy business, but it's an adventure. When you get to the writing of your first draft you'll make a whole new set of discoveries, and more rethinking will be demanded. In describing how she writes, **Wendy Wasserstein** explains why she keeps going back over her material again and again as she works:

> Maybe I'm afraid of moving on with it, and maybe I'm insecure about it, but maybe I'm still finding the play, and reviewing it again and again, and thinking I want to get in touch with this again, so I'll know where I can go.

She's describing process, of course, and in writing plays, that's the operative word.

CREATING THE WORKING DRAWINGS

Because my basic instinct is one that is undisciplined, I apply a lot of form to my writing. I want it to take a shape on some level. . . . It's extremely structured; I sort of insist on that.

—WENDY WASSERSTEIN

The development of your idea is now at the point where you need to create some "working drawings" of how the actual script is going to be put together. It's time to become the structural engineer and plan how to shape your play-in-the-making, so it contains a growing and deepening tension, ever-intensifying in focus, and a steady sense of forward movement to ensure that the play will work as an effective theater piece. For as **Arthur Miller** says: "The plays that resonate, I think, and that stick with us, are *made.*"

Designing a Structural Framework

It's at this point in working on a play that many people make a critical mistake. They've done a lot of preliminary thinking and writing about their idea and characters; they know where the play's going to be set; they have a general idea of the major conflict and how it will be resolved. Naturally, they're eager to begin, to get their people up there and talking to each other, to start producing some actual pages of script. "Enough!" they say, "It's time to start writing the first draft."

You could do that now, and it might prove to be a good exploration. Just be aware that you'd be skipping over a crucial pre-draft step, and at some point you'd more than likely have to backtrack to do it. It would be like leaving on a long hike through a wilderness having assembled your equipment, food, and water, but without having procured a map and settled on a reasonable route. You may have a good idea where you hope to end up, but if you plunge into the woods now, odds are you'll get hopelessly lost within hours. And as you push on, stumbling through the bush with rising panic, you'll probably end up somewhere close to where you started from, staggering out of the woods exhausted and discouraged. You will have made a big circle—which is what usually happens when people get lost in the woods—and although you thought you were going in a straight line toward your destination, in truth you've made no real progress.

I suggest—especially if this is your first play or one of your early efforts—that you spend the additional time to put together an initial structural framework for your play, rough as it may be. No doubt it will change as you proceed and things will have to be reworked. By now, I hope, you're used to that state of affairs as simply part of the process. What's important here is that you plan an initial route to follow as you push through that first draft.

Occasionally, successful playwrights state emphatically that this is precisely what you should *not* do. They observe that they start writing with no idea where their plays are leading them. They plunge off the cliff, and award-winning plays "happen." With no intention to mislead, they'll say—and some have insisted to me—that they don't consciously follow any rules or principles of dramatic construction and that somehow their innate artistic instincts pull them through.

In truth, if the plays are successful, these playwrights have applied the rules and have followed an arduous process in spite of themselves because their dramaturgical instincts have become so finely tuned. They've simply learned the territory and can guide themselves through the writing of a play much as an experienced Indian guide can traverse the Canadian wilderness without referring to a map. **John Patrick Shanley**, for example, says he doesn't consciously apply any craft elements when he sits down to write the first draft of a new play. However, he explains how he spent many early years in preparation:

I read, oh, fifty great American plays. I read *Playwrights on Playwriting* and *Directors on Directing,*—very good books. I read *Famous American Plays of the Thirties, Forties, Fifties, Sixties.* I took acting classes, I took directing classes, I took playwriting classes. I studied art history, the history of theater, and theatrical craft—I did all that stuff. And I wrote play after play after play. . . . And then at a certain point I could take the craft that I had been working on all those years and put it to a purpose that had some personal meaning for me.

Shanley then goes on to say:

I've written I don't know how many plays—at least thirty full-length plays—in my life, and at least ten films. So I've done a lot of writing. And I studied structure a lot, and I worried about it, and I asked strangers "What is a plot?" I tell you, I tried to figure out what a plot was for two or three years before I finally got the idea. And you forget that you ever struggled with those things because you're so busy now with "Do I have anything to write *about*?" I don't belittle things like plot—it's just that that part of it has become sort of second nature. But there was a great deal of preparation before.

Romulus Linney puts it this way:

There are certain things that you learn as a playwright that you'd learn as basketball player. . . . You just start running up and down the court and the things that you've spent your whole life drilling yourself in just suddenly take over. It's very much the same sort of thing. As a writer you want that automatic process to be going on.

It's clear that every successful playwright has his or her own way of working. But in each case, it's also clear that they've developed a process that ultimately gives solid structural shape to their finished plays.

The same can be said for what is generally referred to as *new writing for the theater,* which claims to throw out all the rules of character development, conflict, and plot and instead champions plotless circular, collage-like, nonlinear writing. Indeed, this kind of writing for the theater does exist and does find its way to production. In fact, it's been with us since the appearance of the Dada and Surrealist movements early in the twentieth century and numerous examples that stretch back further. However, every successful work in this vein that I've ever seen or read still has structure. With mastery of the basic, ageless laws of dramatic construction, the creators of plays that on the surface appear to fly in the face of the rules were in fact just applying most of them in a new way.

Also be warned not to accept at face value a popular theme in dramatic literary criticism which insists that the "well-made play" is passé. In this strain of criticism, a disapproval once reserved for artificial and contrived plotting has been heaped upon all kinds of stage works that adhere to basic rules of dramatic structure, as if good form were as hopelessly out of date as the creakiest nineteenth-century melodramas. At times the critical writing in this area takes on a passion that is difficult to explain rationally. Moreover, there seems to be deep-seated aversion to any discussion of craftsmanship when it comes to how good plays are constructed. According to some pundits, there can be no "rules" or "laws" applied to writing for the theater.

This line of thinking can be misleading for playwrights because, in one way or another, all good plays have a basic structural framework; they are all *well made*. The structure may manifest itself in a predominantly emotional rather than physical-action journey for the central character (and for those taking the journey with him or her) but that structure is always there. The play couldn't work on the stage otherwise.

Athol Fugard says:

> An aspect to the business of playwriting that I'm very passionate about is craft. The word is play*wright*, W-R-I-G-H-T . . . *maker of.* I know that in the vocabulary of the arts are terms like "inspiration" and "the Muse," but I am very nervous about all that. I mean, a play is a *made* thing, and the crafting aspect of it is something that gives me infinite joy.

Romulus Linney explains:

> There comes a time when you have to cut into the work, when you have to decide—the way a surgeon decides where to cut into the patient—that you've got to cut into the dramatic construction and shape it structurally.

The point is simple: Don't be persuaded that it's possible to throw out all the traditional principles of dramatic structure as they have functioned for two and a half millennia and expect to create a piece that works in the theater. Plays that ignore the rules are written everyday. The problem is that the vast majority of them spend their lives on shelf boards rather than stage boards.

Emily Mann sums it up: "You have to follow those rules, I think. Every time you try to get away from them you sink, you die. I don't think you can get away from it."

Those Hidden I-Beams

I can think of no better way to get a grasp of the importance of this next step than to look at the process involved in constructing a large building.

Imagine you're walking along a big-city street and come across a construction site for an office tower. There's a viewing window in the ten-foot-high fence, so you take a look. You discover that the builders have only recently begun the process of putting up the building. The enormous hole is dug, the footings have been poured, and from them steel girders rise several stories. A huge crane is lifting more of the I-beams onto the structure. The construction site is strewn with piles of building materials—reinforcing rods, plastic plumbing pipes, electrical conduit, and so on. Cement trucks rumble in and out. Workers in hardhats are riveting, pounding, operating equipment, looking at plans.

Whenever I look over a scene like this, I'm fascinated by how something this big, this complicated, can be constructed with such precision, one bolt at a time. To me it seems overwhelming, an impossible task. But the buildings get built, and when they're finished we look at polished stone and tinted glass gracefully rising above us. All the inner workings and support structures are hidden from view; out of sight, out of mind. We're presented with an impressive facade that we may either like or despise, but it doesn't occur to us to ask what's holding this enormous edifice up or keeping it from collapsing. We walk inside without a thought to our safety. It's expected that the recessed lighting will stay on and the toilets will flush, not to mention that the ceilings will stay put and the floors will not give way.

What allows buildings to be constructed successfully, of course, is that they're first painstakingly designed and planned. People labor for weeks, months, and sometimes years over the drawings as they evolve. Engineers figure out the loads and the stress limits on materials. Architects incorporate structural requirements into their designs and draw up specifications. Eventually a finished set of plans emerges and bids are sought.

The prevailing contractor charts the building process in every detail, locating all materials and signing on subcontractors. Only then does shovel hit soil.

A play must go through an analogous process. It's too complicated and multilayered a project to attempt without careful planning and the drawing up of a structural blueprint. In fact, I would venture to say that plays, of all the forms of fiction, are the most dependent on structural design for their ultimate success. Writing good dialogue and creating wonderful characters are essential, but a playwright without a sound working grasp of dramatic structure is destined to fail. As **Lanford Wilson** reminds us: "You're always trying to build something with integrity. It has a reason to be shaped the way it's shaped."

You've already located and purchased the building site (your idea and premise) and investigated, researched, and collected your building materials (your characters and their dilemmas, conflicts, and histories). Now you have to come up with the most effective way to put these materials together on your site. You need a plan, a design of how your play should be constructed.

Finding Your Play in Your Story

The first step is to determine where the action of your play should begin. I say "action of your play" because your *story* involves much more than will ever appear in the play itself. As discussed in Chapter 3, plays are about big events in people's lives and almost always focus on the last chapter of a much longer tale. Everything else is backstory. Your first task, then, is to find where this final chapter starts. Once you've made that determination you'll know what materials you have to work with as you begin sketching out the play's structural shape.

Edward Albee observes: "The only important thing about writing plays is to know when to start and when to stop." The play itself, he says, is like "a set of parentheses around the life of the characters." Your job is to determine where those parentheses should be placed.

The simple timeline suggested in Chapter 3 to aid in searching and testing potential ideas for plays should now be looked at again. Review all the exploratory work you've done. By now you know a great deal about the history of the central character's dilemma and of the other characters who play a part in it. In fact, if you've gone through your character explorations successfully, you should have much more material than you could ever portray onstage.

To make sense of it all, to get it in perspective, a useful exercise now is to chart out a detailed backstory timeline of the central character's problem from the moment it first appeared until it explodes in his or her face. Such a timeline will help you locate where the action of your play begins. Use at least three or four connected pieces of computer paper and, setting the paper out the long way and starting at the left, chart every important event in the central character's dilemma. Put down every occurrence you think has contributed to the problem, even indirectly. Refer to your play idea worksheet, the short- and long-form bios, and any other notes you've made. You may have to go back many years as you trace the chain of events that leads to the action your play will deal with. Think about the roots of the dilemma, what the original triggers were, and then identify each step in the development of the problem up to where you now think the action of the play will begin.

In most cases, events of the more recent past which have contributed to the central character's dilemma will take on the most weight (obviously, this will vary with each story). If your play is about a middle-aged woman who can't relate to her father because he was an alcoholic when she was a teenager, then it's important to go all the way back to her teens and chart the key events surrounding the first appearance of the problem. Most often, however, it's the more immediate past that produces the most significant backstory events.

As you come up with items, lay them out visually on the timeline with a concise written description. Put down just enough to make it identifiable to you. It works best to mark off sections on the timeline into years or months, depending on how concentrated the series of events becomes during any one period. Allow yourself enough pages so the timeline doesn't get cramped.

Locating the Starting Point

By the time you've finished this exercise, you should have a fairly good sense of where your play should begin. This is almost always just before the final crisis, the day or week before, the afternoon of. Everything that's gone on earlier is important and potent, but it's also still backstory. Attempting to dramatize every step of the evolving dilemma is a mistake. The play has to focus on the big event, the final blowout.

Everything that's led up to the crisis feeds into it, but should remain in the past, out of sight, between the lines, and under the surface. The backstory should fuel the play, never flood it. Remember the iceberg? Good plays are supported by rich, deep backstories that are felt intensely, but rarely make an actual appearance onstage.

One danger here is falling in love with an episode in the backstory that you want desperately to write about. I've had running battles with students who insist their plays have to include large portions of backstory material. Even when I point out that these are basically undramatic—at least in terms of the idea being focused on—they go ahead and incorporate the material anyway. Of course, that's ultimately the writer's option, and maybe it's important to include some of this material in a first draft, if for no other reason than to see the material "out there" on the page. Keep in mind, however, that as a general rule prolonged direct references to backstory or actual scenes dramatizing backstory episodes almost always rob plays of forward movement, causing them to stagnate. These references and episodes are usually the first to get axed in the second draft.

Rarely does a play work that focuses on more than the culminating events of a dilemma. Every page has to contain an underlying and building tension that, in most cases, can only be achieved if the problem is nearing its *crisis,* or breaking point. That tension has to be felt in the opening scene. The play has to hook the audience early on and reel them in as each moment ticks by in performance.

Imagine the backstories of *Death of a Salesman, Who's Afraid of Virginia Woolf?,* and *The Crucible.* They're all incredibly rich and textured. However, the plays themselves deal with Willy Loman in the last few agonizing days of his life, Martha on the final brutal night of a twenty-year struggle, and John Proctor on the eve of the hysteria that will sweep him up and force him to take responsibility for his actions.

To add another example, Tennessee Williams's *A Streetcar Named Desire,* presents us with Blanche DuBois making her last desperate cry for help after years of tumbling downhill.

Both *Salesman* and *Streetcar* have moments which fleetingly dramatize backstory episodes, but these are in the context of the present dilemma Willy and Blanche are facing, and they take place in (or break into) the middle of scenes in the present. These inclusions of backstory segments work because they intensify the specific and immediate dilemmas and directly contribute to the present-tense tragedies unfolding before us. Both Miller and Williams allow us inside their central characters' heads as they agonize over past events. As a result, we feel the impact of these experiences on their dilemmas in the here and now. In *The Crucible,* on the other hand, we don't actually see Proctor's initial encounters with Abigail, but we can still feel the heat from them.

Another excellent example is Marsha Norman's 'night, Mother. In the play's first scene Jesse tells her mother that she's going to kill herself that evening. Try to imagine the backstory timeline for this dilemma. It obviously stretches back many years and involves many characters, intense experiences, and a growing sense of despair. A good number of these are made clear either directly or indirectly in the play itself. The point is that the playwright chose to begin the action of her play on the final night of the story. As a result, from that first scene on, we're caught up in the play. The choice of where to start the play was the most critical structural decision she made. As **Marsha Norman** told me:

> It's very important to choose correctly the two hours from the character's life that you're going to watch. The choice of time is, to me, critical. You must pick two hours in that life from which the whole life is visible. If you choose two hours that are too soon, then the problem hasn't quite developed yet; the person doesn't have the strength really to grapple with it yet. If you choose two hours that are too late, it's kind of all over, and they're bitter already.

All successful playwrights know that plays have to deal with what's happening before our eyes. Most importantly, very early on they have to give the audience the awareness that they're going to witness the final event in a long struggle.

As you look over your completed timeline, carefully consider how much of the story you actually need to dramatize. Keep in mind the old adage "less is more" as you consider your possibilities. Remember that what you want is for the audience to "lean into" your play, to be summoned to listen carefully, to engage in filling in the blanks, to figure out the backstory for themselves as the characters interact with each other and the central dilemma becomes clear.

Is There More Than One Play Here?

Now's the time to consider if some important event in your backstory may actually be the basis for another play entirely. It's not unusual for playwrights to draw on the same backstory for more than one play. Two of Eugene O'Neill's later plays, *Long Day's Journey into Night* and *A Moon for the Misbegotten,* grow out of the same general backstory material.

In a much broader sense, August Wilson's major plays, including *Ma Rainey's Black Bottom, Fences, Joe Turner's Come and Gone, The Piano Lesson* and *Seven Guitars* are part of a cycle drawn from one sweeping and loosely-knit backstory about the struggle of African-Americans in each decade of the twentieth century. Granted, such a cycle reaches far beyond the backstory material of any one character or set of characters, but Wilson is drawing from the specific history of a people, a history that definitely informs each play. For O'Neill and Wilson, each of their plays is complete as an independent work, and they weren't written in any chronological order. There is, however, a shared history that undergirds each play.

Perhaps a more direct example of this is Lanford Wilson's family trilogy consisting of *Talley's Folly, Fifth of July*, and *Talley and Son.* All three plays take place in or around the same house, and although *Fifth of July* takes place years later, the other two are set on the very same evening. At least for *Talley's Folly* and *Talley and Son*, the backstory timeline is the same. Wilson simply realized he had two plays to write from the same specific backstory material.

What's important here is that you don't make the mistake of trying to fold two or more plays into one. As you scan over your backstory timeline be tough on yourself. Remember that plays deal with concentrated, explosive events supported by a wealth of backstory material. Reread your idea worksheet and make an informed choice as to what you're going to dramatize in this play, and start an idea file for the other potential plays that may be suggesting themselves.

A specific exercise at this point is to select several successful plays that have held up over time and study the wider story each play relates. Analyze why each starts where it does. How does the starting point heighten the dramatic tension? Why are you interested in what's going on? How complete a backstory could you outline on each play? To what extent does each deal with the culminating event of a long struggle?

The Three-Act Structure

With your starting point set (at least for now), the next task is to invent how the play should be put together in terms of action or plot—what actually happens between the time the lights first come up and their final fade at the end. It's time to take the initial plunge into creating the structure of your play. You've already made a start on this work, of course, with your idea worksheet. You know who your central character is, what his or her dilemma is, how this dilemma manifests itself in action, and how it's resolved.

This journey is often referred to as the central character's *arc*. **John Guare** explains:

> You're in trouble if the character doesn't have an arc apparent in the main disagreement or argument of the play. . . . That seems to be the message from Aeschylus on down. So you have to have an arc built into it, or that character will be still-born. There will be nowhere for them to go.

John Patrick Shanley describes it in terms of his play *Four Dogs and a Bone*:

> The play has a character, a writer, who goes from a very emotional, diffuse, tortured place to a very focused and cynical one by the end. That's the arc he has to go through. From "I am an *artiste*" to "I am a deal-maker, and I'm going to grab all the power I can"—that's the journey he has to go through.

In other words, the arc of a play is the dramatization of the change that takes place in the central character from beginning to end. Think of it as the trajectory path of a missile being launched and rising high, speeding across the sky, and then eventually falling to the ground far from where it began. Your character has to follow a similar path or arc.

Your job now is to take a close look at this trajectory and expand upon it. It needs to be embellished and opened up and then crafted to fit into a structural framework.

All workable dramatic material—be it play, screenplay, television sitcom—can basically be divided into three structural or dramaturgical parts: the setup, the struggle, and the solution. In the theater, these three parts are usually referred to as Act I, Act II, and Act III. It's important to be clear that this reference to "acts" does not refer to what happens before and after the intermission in a standard "two-act" play. Rather, we're talking about the hidden structure of a play, whether it's a ten-minute one-act or a long four-act drama like O'Neill's *Long Day's Journey into Night*.

Length has nothing to do with the number of structural acts in a successfully constructed piece of dramatic material. All plays have the three basic structural parts—the three S's—setup, struggle, and solution. **Emily Mann** explains: "For me, even if it's a two-act play, even if it's a one-act play, there are always three movements. . . . And that's consistent in every single piece, absolutely consistent."

It's rare in today's theater for plays to break for intermissions at the structural act breaks. A notable exception is *Who's Afraid of Virginia Woolf?*, which is indeed divided into three acts. In our contemporary theater, however, if there is an intermission, it almost always falls somewhere in the middle of structural Act II, just after an important peak in the action has been reached. The program and even the script itself labels everything before the intermission as Act I and everything after as Act II, but, again, these "acts" have nothing to do with the structural acts of the play. The three acts we're talking about are structural elements that are never exposed to view.

The Sonata Form

Many of the playwrights I interviewed likened the structure of their plays to the sonata form in classical music, which—not surprisingly—also has three basic structural parts. These are called exposition, development, and recapitulation. Writing *'night, Mother,* for example, **Marsha Norman** recalls:

> I just felt that it had a kind of sonata form for me from the beginning. There really had to be a structure that the audience could *feel*. There had to be this rising and *mmm—* and stop, and quiet, and up and *mmm—* and stop, and quiet, and *mmm—* and the end.

Terrence McNally says:

> Whatever I know about play structure probably comes from listening to a lot of music. And most of the music I listen to is classical. There's the sonata form, for example. I can't read music, but I think I have a sense of how long things should be, and how you set up the theme here, and how you develop it, just like music.

Athol Fugard puts it this way:

> Music has been and remains one of the sustaining support systems in my life as a writer. When I listen to music, it sort of leads me on an emotional journey by the way it organizes emotional energy. The sonata form, for example: The way you

play one theme against another theme, the way you can have both themes running at the same time, the way music organizes the emotional responses—that has been very, very instructive to me as a writer.

Tina Howe also has a musical perspective: "I really get into theme and variation, so that, as important as the journey of my characters is, I am just as interested in the music of the piece."

And **Lanford Wilson** explains:

I believe I build a play musically. I think I always have. There are leitmotifs and themes. I studied music, not an instrument but the voice, for years and years in a chorus in school and in church. And I believe that's where I learned about structure.

Edward Albee, Michael Weller, and others also acknowledge the structural similarities between plays and classical music, especially the sonata form.

The point here should not be missed: These playwrights all independently acknowledge a debt to a classical musical form for their sense of dramatic structure. And they admit that while creating their plays they're fully aware that that structure consists of three basic components.

Let's take a look at each of these three parts. Keep in mind that the intention here is not to present a magic formula for structuring plays, but rather to help you understand how the different structural units function in a typical successful straight play.

Act I: The Setup

The function of Act I is to lay out the terms of the evening. Within ten to fifteen minutes into any average full-length play an audience will expect to discover who the play is about and what his or her conflict/dilemma is. Your task here is to launch your story, and win the rapt attention of your audience so that they stay with you. You have to tell them how to listen to your play and what to listen for. The important point is to realize that, from a structural standpoint, all plays have an Act I, whose critical function is to pull the audience in by setting up the basic elements of the story you're telling. Usually, Act I comprises a fourth or less of a play's running time, although there's no formula or set rule as to its length.

Act II: The Struggle

Once the play is launched in Act I, the main part of the voyage can commence. Act II comprises the heart of the play and structurally consists of the central character struggling with his or her dilemma by encountering mounting barriers and roadblocks. The attitudes and actions of the other characters are put in confrontation with the needs and desires of the central figure. The central character's own actions and choices contribute to the struggle. The resulting conflict takes on dimension and coloration as the audience witnesses the central character struggling in different ways and with increasing intensity to overcome whatever problem is being dealt with. The struggle unfolds in such a way that by the end of the Act II, the central character has become deeply embedded in the dilemma, and it's harder than ever to foretell how the tense conflict will be resolved. On average, Act II comprises from half to three-quarters of a play's running time.

Act III: The Solution

You already have a clear idea of how you're going to resolve your central character's dilemma. Act III deals with how this is accomplished. The dividing line between where Act II ends and Act III begins is that point when the central character is faced with a barrier of such magnitude that he or she will *inevitably* be forced to do something extraordinary to get rid of the dilemma. **Emily Mann** reveals how she knows she's in Act III: "You get to a point where you absolutely have to have a kind of explosion."

This explosion—when the central character is forced to take a final action that in one way or another deals with his or her struggle in a defining and irrevocable way—is called the *climax* of the play.

Act III dramatizes this last defining action—the climax—and the resolution it leads to. What happens may not always be happy or pretty, but the dilemma is finally put to rest. Act III is usually as short or shorter than Act I, a fourth or less of a play's total running time.

Usually plays have a moment or short scene at the very end which functions much like the coda in a musical composition. This is traditionally referred to as the *denouement,* from the French word for "untying." The final, brief part of Act III, it serves to ease the audience out of the play as the lights go dark for the last time. You always know when a play or movie is "over." The story's been told, the tale's been spun, the climax of the action has passed, the resolution's been presented. All that's left is to spin out as gracefully as possible, leaving the audience with just the right feeling.

This moment usually writes itself as your story comes to an end. You'll feel the momentum of the entire play behind you and the very definite rhythm and mood it has created. The denouement always rises out of this "place" where the play has finally arrived, and its shape and content presents itself when you get there. At this point you should just be aware that ultimately it's part of the structural shape of your play.

Analyzing the Masters

The dictionary defines *analyze* as follows: "to separate or break up (any whole) into its parts so as to find out their nature, proportion, function, relationship, etc."

I urge you to begin doing this with successful plays on a regular basis. Go see them and read them and study how they're put together, how the structural parts function. **Terrence McNally** confirms: "It's so important to know a writer like Chekhov or Ibsen or Shakespeare really, really well. You can't read *The Cherry Orchard, The Wild Duck, Hamlet,* or *King Lear* too many times, or see them too many times."

John Guare says essentially the same thing: "I love to read plays. I'm reading all the time. I think it's critical. You constantly have to keep reading and rereading plays to study the technical problems that they solve."

In other words, make a habit of studying the masters. It's the best way to learn how to write good plays and especially how to gain a working grasp of dramatic structure. What you'll discover—and this should not come as a surprise—is that virtually all good plays, from the Greeks through Shakespeare to the twentieth-century plays we examine in this book, share the three-act structure regardless of how many scenes or acts the playwright (or an editor) has divided the script into or where the intermission falls.

So think structurally. Find those I-beams. Locate where the structural components start and stop. It isn't easy to think this way at first as you stare at pages of script or experience a play in performance, but after consciously looking through this structural lens at a few plays, the commonality of the components will begin popping out at you.

Familiarizing yourself with how structure functions in the best plays ever written will pay great dividends as you go through the process of building your own plays. Without always being aware, as if by a sort of osmosis, you'll automatically start applying the same standards and common principles. The simple truth is that if you want to be good at this or any other art form, you have to study unendingly how the proven masters do it.

Inventing Plot

When I asked **Tina Howe** if she worked with plot outlines before attempting to write her first drafts, she said:

> Oh, outlines, outlines, outlines! Months of hopeless, detailed, endless, horrible outlines. I paste them on my windows. It's a process of starting with a few ideas and then just building them up. When the windows are covered, I start doing the room. Eventually my husband comes in and says, "When are you going to take the play off the walls and put it down on paper?" I do an enormous amount of plotting, which is basically a way of convincing myself there's something there. My outlines are maps to help me on my journey.

Athol Fugard told me:

> I need to know very clearly for myself what I'm taking on. I've never been surprised, for example, when I sit down to write a play. I know the beginning, I know the middle, and I know the end. I've heard wonderful stories from other writers who have said, "You know this one character suddenly ran away from me, and I found myself going off in a direction I never intended." I've envied them because I think I'm a bit of a fascist when it comes to my own writing. I don't allow any deviation from what I have decided is going to be the shape of the "new republic."

Whether you end up outlining as freewheelingly as Tina Howe or being as strict and methodical as Athol Fugard, the next step in coming up with a structural design is to determine what scenes, beats, or pieces of action absolutely have to be in the play in order to tell the story you want to tell. And this includes "emotional plotting," as Terrence McNally calls it— what's going on between characters on a feeling level, beneath the surface.

You have your play idea worksheet, your character bios, the backstory timeline, and the knowledge that somehow your play should have a three-act structure. Now you have to start inventing the *plot*—the action, both physical and emotional, that will transform your idea into a play.

At this point it's important to stress that what's presented here is not the only approach to the playwriting process. Many playwrights do not spend a lot of time working out details of plotting before they start writing their plays. Others, like Howe and Fugard, do. The purpose here is simply to guide you through a thorough and logical sequence so that you can discover for yourself the degree to which this kind of careful preliminary planning may be helpful in your own process. I urge you to test it out, to follow the procedures presented here. If later you determine you're one of those writers who likes to make these discoveries exclusively as you go along, you still have a useful "fallback" procedure if and when you get stuck.

Also keep in mind that as you gain experience at writing plays, the need for charting out your course may diminish. For example, when asked if he did outlines, **Athol Fugard** said:

> I used to get involved in that for my own benefit, just putting it on the wall above my table, as a sort of diagrammatic realization. . . . I find that I need that less and less. My facility, if I can call it that, for being able to hold the structure in my head without having to put it down on paper has improved. And so now I don't do that any more, but I was very dependent on it.

Here's an exercise in plot invention that will get you started. Put a stack of 3 x 5" index cards in front of you, and on the top card write a brief description of the most important, most intense moment in the play for your central character as you conceive of it now. This should be the climactic moment, the one that *must* be in the play based on your most current play idea worksheet.

It's what used to be generally referred to as the *obligatory scene,* so called because it's the moment or the specific encounter that the playwright is obligated by the terms of his or her story to give the audience. Without it, the story would not have been told in a satisfying way. It is the big "moment of truth" for your central character, the major turning point in his or her struggle.

When you're finished, set the card aside, and on the next several cards write brief descriptions—one per card—of the other obviously important moments or specific pieces of the action, the ones that have to be in the play in order for the story to be told and for the climactic scene to make sense. Concentrate on your central character and his or her struggle and keep going until you've captured every significant physical or emotional action of the play, each on a separate card. Nail down the *essence* of each specific moment—the revealing of a critical piece of information, a confession, a moment of violence, a loss of temper, a tender exchange, and so on. Let your mind go here, allowing one moment to suggest another, and then another. Put down any possible scene or moment that comes to mind, even if you're not sure where or how you'll eventually use it.

Don't worry about the order in which these moments come to you now, or what act they'll fall into. What usually happens in this exercise is that you find yourself working backward. In order for the climactic scene to happen, you need another scene or moment before it, and that moment has to be preceded by another. Keep in mind that as part of a process your cards represent the preliminary rough sketches of the possible components of your play. Don't question how plausible they are or how logically any one of them might fit in. As you write these additional cards the relative importance or emotional size or weight of the moments should be of little concern.

Also, as you work through this exercise don't be stymied if you've conceived of your play as one long conversation between two people. Think structurally of that conversation; see it as a series of components that you will eventually put in the most effective order. This conversation has emotional movements and shifts, as well as physical action such as a kiss, a slap in the face, or the throwing of a martini glass against a wall. And it's the putting together of these pieces of both physical and emotional action that creates a preliminary structure for the play.

Keep going with the exercise until you can't think of any more possible moments, scenes, events, or exchanges. For a one-act play you should end up with at least fifteen to twenty cards and for a full-length play two to three times as many. At this point, the more the better. Later on, it will become obvious which ones don't belong in the play.

Next, write on three separate cards *Act I*, *Act II*, and *Act III* and set them out to mark separate areas on the table. Go through your stack of cards and try to determine which act each card belongs in. Place each card in its appropriate act. If you're not sure, take a guess.

When you've separated all the cards into acts, try arranging them in a preliminary order within each act. You'll most likely realize when you do this that the cards don't always logically fall into a natural order. Experiment with shifting them around until you've come up with what feels most right to you now. Add cards as you think of connecting scenes and actions. Insert them where you need them.

When you're finished with this, you'll have an initial structural outline—the beginnings of one—for your play spread out in front of you. Of course, it's rough and unsteady; you're just starting to invent the pieces of your puzzle. But it's a start.

You'll begin to perceive how the makings of your play may fit together. Certain things will pop out at you. If you have twice the number of cards in Act I than you have in Act II, for example, you have an indication that your second act needs to be developed further or that, possibly, what you've considered Act I material is really Act II material. The nice thing about working on cards, as opposed to writing out outlines on legal pads, is that you can add and subtract pieces as you refine and easily move them around to see how they fit other places. It's a system that allows for molding and shaping, much as a potter works with a piece of clay. Most significantly, you are—from the very beginning—conceiving of your play both as a *whole* and in *structural* terms.

The discoveries made in this exercise often prove to be amazingly accurate. Many times the play you end up with is still clearly reflected in your index-card outline. Of course, changes are usually necessary, and sometimes finished plays end up in an entirely different orbit, but this exercise is still worth doing. Coaxing you into connecting actions and moments, it nudges you into that first draft with the initial road map you need.

David Ives explains this aspect of his process: "Before I start writing, I generally know the events that are going to happen. I present myself with a structural idea that is then free to change."

The Dramatic Intensity Curve

Another useful tool to help you get a visual sense of the overall shape of your play is to attempt to chart the play's rising and falling action through the three acts. This *dramatic intensity curve* helps you visualize how your play should function in terms of audience involvement with your central character's unfolding story. It gives you a feel for how all the pieces might fit together dramatically into a unified whole.

"Whoa!" you might say. "I thought this was a book on how to write plays, not an introduction to price theory economics. How can I possibly chart out on a graph the rising and falling action of a play I haven't even written yet?"

My answer: Relax. Applying this seemingly nonartistic exercise to something as mysterious as writing a play will give you more of a sense of control and mastery. All great art has a carefully worked out compositional design which ultimately blends form and content in a seemingly effortless finished work. If that is your goal, give this a try.

The illustration below presents a dramatic intensity curve for a typical one-act play. On the horizontal plane the estimated running time of the script is charted out. In this case I've used thirty minutes, the average length of a one-act, but any time span could be substituted. On the vertical plane is calibrated the dramatic intensity—that is, the degree of developing audience involvement in the story being presented, both emotionally and intellectually. Or, to put this more figuratively, the *weight* of audience identification with the central character is mapped, the *depth* of their empathy with him or her, the emotional stakes the audience finds in the play. Granted, this is an arbitrary "calibration" and not a real measurement. The purpose here is to get a feel for the increases and decreases in dramatic intensity for the audience as the play is performed.

Notice in the illustration the proportioning of the three acts over the running time. Act I is seven minutes long, Act II is eighteen, and Act III is five. (Again, I'm not suggesting a formula here.)

Of course, the audience is unaware of these structural acts as a play is performed. And this is as it should be. Only the playwright need concern him- or herself with such hidden elements of the craft.

The dramatic intensity curve rises and falls numerous times throughout the play, forming many peaks and troughs of various extremes. Each

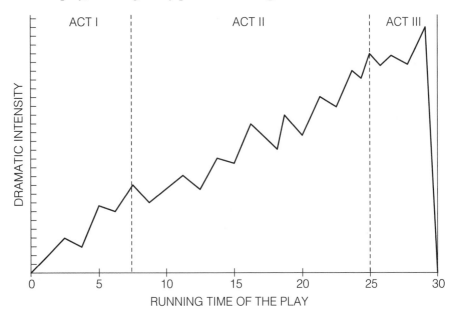

build to a peak is a unit of action with increasing intensity and each fall to a trough is a unit of action representing a retreat, reflection, transition, or regrouping of some sort. All plays have such recurring peaks and troughs throughout, from the opening moments to the final blackout. It happens automatically, as it does in real life. There are heightened, charged moments and then quieter, slower moments. The constant ebb and flow is much like waves at the seashore. Some are small and gentle and then others arrive that are much larger and more powerful. In intensity, a play in performance is just like the surf, always in flux.

Note as well that the peaks as they progress through the running time of the play are charted ever higher on the curve, much like stock prices over a good bull market year. As the audience gets caught up in the ebb and flow, it's critical that their involvement increases and intensifies as the play runs its course. You want them to come out ahead and to gain dramatic riches at the end of their "investment."

A series of peaks with decreasing intensity will put people to sleep very quickly, as will a series of peaks with equal intensity. A peak of lesser intensity may follow one of higher intensity, but this has to be the exception, not the rule. Without exception, the dramatic intensity curve for any successful play works its way progressively upward to the final big moment in Act III, with the audience becoming increasingly gripped by and committed to the story unfolding before them.

As **Emily Mann** puts it: "There's one energizing force that must go from the beginning and has to *peak*, and go to the end." As discussed earlier, the denouement after the climactic scene is a falling action and is usually necessary for the play to reach an effective final fade-out.

Using your cards, try charting your own dramatic intensity curve. Use the illustration as a model, but don't force your developing structural design to fit this curve; let your material dictate its own. Take a guess at your approximate running time and calibrate this out in minutes along the horizontal axis. Obviously, the actual length of your play is something you can't really know at this point, but make an educated guess. If you have absolutely no clue, use thirty minutes if you're working on a one-act and ninety minutes for a full-length. Starting "as the lights come up," chart each moment or scene as noted on your cards. Try to give a fair assessment of the dramatic intensity of each and locate its peak on the graph. Finally, label with a word or short phrase on the chart each of these pieces of action so you can easily identify the parts making up the whole of the curve.

Granted, there is no concrete way to measure the varying degrees of dramatic intensity. The purpose of the exercise is not to chart out a definitive or precise configuration of your story as it plays out in time which you then have to follow to the letter. Instead, what you will discover (being honest with yourself) is whether or not you're anywhere close to the structural shape you need to write a play that will ultimately work in the theater. For example, if your peaks "plateau" or start heading downward throughout Act II, you know you'll have to rethink how you've put your story together.

Emily Mann goes on to explain:

> The stage is about *time,* and you have to know how to manage
> and sculpt and make alive time. If you don't understand that, if
> you take 45 minutes for your first movement and then you
> have 15 minutes free for the second and an hour and ten for
> your third, you are dead. It won't work. I don't know whether
> it's the human pulse, or how we listen, or how we feel, or how
> we react, but it simply won't work. There are things that we
> have to do when writing for the stage.

Whatever the dramatic intensity curve of your play looks like, the important thing at this point is that you'll have a heightened awareness of what has to occur for your play to work structurally. And that will put you ahead of at least ninety-five percent of the people attempting to write plays today.

The Plot Treatment

Your final bridge to the first draft is an expansion upon what you've already put down on your index cards in a *treatment.* Writing out in paragraph form a narrative of the play as you now see it unfolding is similar to what film and television writers do when they prepare an idea for a film or television show. Usually two or three pages long, this renders the material with a visual feel or treatment that producers can respond to. They then give their input about the idea before giving a "green light" for the creation of a first draft.

Borrowing this technique for playwriting can be extremely useful. It activates your creative juices and gets you thinking more specifically than ever before about how your story will unfold in theatrical terms. You're forced to make your first connections between the scenes you've already invented and to find ways to tie everything together and keep the action flowing.

It's not easy to do this. It involves considerable invention and the willingness to plunge in and try things. And, as in all these preliminary explorations, nothing you do here has to necessarily end up in your finished play. The plot treatment is simply meant to help you think through a possible version of your story from start to finish before you tackle a full-blown dialogue version. It gives you the opportunity to work through the entire play in terms of what happens from moment to moment. You may not entirely like how it sounds when you're finished, but you will have found a way through to the end in terms of action. Maybe not *the* way, but at least a route.

The best way to write the plot treatment is to imagine you're sitting in the ideal theater and are about to see a performance of your finished play. Try to visualize the other audience members, the stage, everything. Then have the house lights go out, the stage lights come up, and as the play begins, start writing down in order everything you see happening before you. Describe people as they enter and how they act and interact. Try not to write down much, if any, actual dialogue, but rather describe what is said. If you do include dialogue, use only snippets of exchanges or lines that capture the flavor of specific moments.

Work through the entire play this way. Refer to your timeline, index cards, dramatic intensity curve—anything that might be useful. The end result should be a narrative of two, three, or more pages that is a detailed description of what might happen in your play from beginning to end.

Don't expect or even try to make this treatment sound flashy or have it read like a work of literature. Resist slipping into writing extended dialogue segments or actually getting into writing your first draft. That's coming soon enough.

The Spontaneity Factor

The biggest objection I get from students about writing the plot treatment (and other pre-draft structural analyses) is that it will take all the fun and adventure out of actually writing the first draft. They argue that you've already made all the major discoveries and that the writing of the draft will be a paint-by-numbers drudgery, boring and uninspiring; that all creative excitement will have been sucked out of the experience because your characters have not been allowed to speak for themselves and tell you where they want the play to go.

My experience is that the opposite proves to be the case. Writing the plot treatment actually frees you up when you start the first draft because you've worked through a version of the action of the play from a structural standpoint and you know there's at least one way to get from "as the lights come up . . ." to the final blackout. You have that road map in hand. And once you start out on your trip you can throw it aside whenever you want, you can get off the freeway and take the coastal route for a while, or wander up an inviting country lane to look at stone walls for a few hours, or, on impulse, head over to a neighboring town to visit a distant cousin for an evening.

There's no law that says you have to adhere to the route you've charted out. If and when your characters prompt a change in your course, let them have their way. Welcome the unexpected and explore every impulse.

As **Tina Howe** remarks: "The process is all about allowing yourself to take those detours. You must explore the full range of your characters." And this from a playwright who papers her room with outlines.

John Guare, who also works with preliminary outlines, says:

> Oh, you want to get lost. A play is a journey. The idea of a great trip isn't to say, "Gee, you know, we got there, piece of cake. I had my Triple-A maps, got right on the turnpike, and got off at the right exit—no problems." A great trip is when there's this detour, then another and another, and then: "Wait, I'm lost." But that's what should happen.

The important point here is that the road map is still there on the seat beside you when and if you do get lost. It's still available when your people agree with you that it's time to push on toward your final destination. It'll help show you how to get your party back to the main road or figure out an alternate route that will still get the group where it eventually needs to go.

Writing a solid first draft of a play is not easy. You find yourself staring at pages of dialogue, some good and some not so good, with your characters often talking—and carrying on at length—about things that you hadn't planned for them to talk about. Things will happen that are total surprises. People may do things that will shock you. But, as Guare affirms, that's what should happen. Always be encouraged when your characters seemingly start to take over, leading the play in a new direction. This shows they have life and vitality in the world you've placed them in.

The difficulty arises when your characters lead the play so far off in a new direction that you can't recognize the terrain and you don't know how to proceed. Suddenly they turn back to you and drop the reins in your hands again. And they almost always will do this. Then you're staring at possibly dozens of pages of script. The words are there on the pages, but they aren't telling you what to do next. The dialogue is all detailed and focussed on the immediate subject at hand, as it should be, but you've lost your sense of forward movement. You find yourself lost in a veritable sea of lines, most or all of which you might like, but which don't point in a definite direction.

John Patrick Shanley describes this state of bewilderment as the play "jumping the tracks":

> If I start a play, and it's really interesting and exciting, and the sense of the emotional, moment-to-moment truth is there, and the things that people have to say to each other are clean and big and theirs, and I sense it's going somewhere, then that's great. However, if the place that I start from is bigger than the place I finish in, then I know that I've jumped the tracks somewhere and taken a wrong turn. I've gone onto a little side road off the main highway and want to go around the main highway to the end. So I have to wait to figure out how to get back onto that highway again.

When this happens—and it often does with beginning playwrights—writing your first draft can become an exercise in frustration. You force yourself to keep writing, trying any idea that comes to you and hoping to work your way out of the quagmire. More often than not, however, you find yourself more confused, staring at even more pages. Finally you decide either to quit or go back to the drawing board and rethink. You discover that, indeed, some preliminary plans would probably help guide you from one leg of your journey to the next and to your final destination. You realize you need some kind of road map to respond and react to, which can stimulate your thinking and help you make the kinds of choices that keep you moving forward. You're willing to concede that it's difficult to figure out as you go because you can't see the forest for the trees.

Writing a play, then, is a constant balancing act between the rational and irrational, between the planned and unplanned. As **John Guare** says:

> That's part of the schizophenic nature of being a playwright. We have to work without putting restrictions on ourselves, just to get it out alive. And then we have to begin functioning as our own dramaturg, the rational part of ourselves that has to look at the clay that we have and shape it consciously. That's

where the craft of play*wrighting* comes into play, why it's spelled w-r-i-g-h-t. We are wheelwrights, shipwrights. We are shapers. And we have to shape the material we've created subconsciously.

And again, to quote **Tina Howe**:

> I think the cruelty of the form is that to write a good play the architecture has to be impeccable. A play is only as good as the ideas within it. The form demands rigor and a sense of structure. It demands intelligence, rational thought, figuring things out, and laying the groundwork. But then the cruel part is that to let the play *live* you have to surrender control and let your characters go. You have to let them stumble, fall into walls, and be mute, let them drift and be lost. If you hold the reins too tight, they won't spring to life. So it's a constant balancing act. The structure has to be tight, but you have to leave room for spontaneity, mystery and silence.

Michael Weller sums it up:

> I like to have it planned out in a certain way so that when the writing starts I can just relax and know that I'm vaguely going there. I think I would just be way too worried if I had no idea where I was going.

The structural work discussed in this chapter, then, is intended to liberate you as you write your first draft. All your working drawings lead you into a deeper familiarity with the material you're working with and give you both a sense of confidence with and a structural control over your developing story. When you get into the first draft you can "let your characters go" while you remain in charge. And if things get derailed, you'll be well equipped to get the play back on track.

As **Romulus Linney** says: "In the first draft, the arc and the shape and the basic bones of the play have to be there in some form or I'm going to get lost. I can then shape around that, but that basic *thing* has to be there."

In other words, coming up with a structural plan activates your thinking, gives you focus, and primes you for the next creative task ahead.

8

WORKING IN THE STANDARD FORMAT

A playwright notates his play very much as a composer notates

his score.

—EDWARD ALBEE

This chapter and the next look closely at the craft of actually putting words down on a page. Chapter 8 covers the standard professional format for plays and lays out how to work with its various components— tools you can use to great advantage if you understand how and why they function the way they do. Chapter 9 then presents the basic techniques involved in the writing of dialogue and stage directions.

If you already have a working grasp of the professional format for plays and are completely confident in your ability to write lively, exciting dialogue, you can skip these next two chapters. The process of creating your play picks up again in Chapter 10, with the writing of your first draft. However, I urge anyone who is the least bit uncertain about how to use the tools of format or could benefit from a review of the techniques of good dialogue writing to take a close look at Chapters 8 and 9 *before* proceeding. They cover in great detail aspects of the craft that are useful and, in some cases, essential as you continue with the making of your play.

Even if you are most comfortable working longhand when first getting your words out on the page, what's presented in Chapter 8 is still important to digest. It provides a *grammar* for how plays are presented in manuscript, and knowing the rules of this grammar—understanding the way they can help "lift" your writing—gives you a definite advantage as you produce your pages. If you're just starting out as a playwright, you have nothing to lose and much to gain by learning how to work in the proper format from the beginning.

Obviously, no matter how you work, the point of gaining an early working knowledge of format is not to freeze you up creatively, but rather to facilitate your ability to get down what you see and hear in the most dynamic fashion. Work as loosely, roughly, and freely as you want in your early drafts. Don't worry about a "finished product" look when the words are first spilling out of you. Get them down any way you can. Just know that very soon you'll need to see your work typed or printed out before you. And that's when knowing how to work in the proper format will pay off.

The Importance of Presentation

Writing for the theater has a built-in frustration. Simply put, plays are written not to be read but performed onstage before an audience. The ultimate goal of any playwright is to get that play up there on its feet while, backstage, the manuscript gathers dust on the dressing room floor. The problem is that in order to get a play on the stage, it first has to be read on the page by someone in a position to decide whether or not it should or could or will be brought to life. The script itself is only a means to an end.

The playwright, unlike the poet or novelist, is faced with a special challenge: How do you write a play so that the intermediate step of putting it down on the page works to your advantage? How can the manuscript actually help to suggest performance? What can be done to coax the reader of a play into seeing and hearing it as it would unfold in an actual production?

How a play looks on the page is more important than most people realize. I often hear scripts described as "dense" or "heavy," only to discover when I finally have the opportunity to look at them myself that it's the way the words have actually been put down on paper that's elicited this kiss-of-death label. The script has been formatted so it's visually difficult to read. By not following a few simple, field-tested procedures, the writer has limited the play's chances to ignite for the reader.

Anyone who reads large numbers of scripts can't help but acknowledge the importance of presentation. Ask any literary manager or professional person hired to read and evaluate plays for a theater or some sort of script competition. It's simply easier and more fun to read a script that is put down on the page in the proper way. It reads better. It comes to life more fully. It has the ring of fine crystal. Obviously, a poorly written play nicely presented isn't going to get very far. But a good script poorly presented is its own worst enemy.

Ultimately, of course, how your work looks on the page says something about you, the playwright—namely, how much you know about the business of writing plays, and whether or not you're savvy enough to present your work in the most advantageous manner possible.

Contrary to what many books on playwriting suggest, there is a standard manuscript format for plays. This basic format, presented in Script Samples 1 through 4 (see pages 143–146), has evolved over the years and is generally accepted as the professional norm in United States. I recommend you become familiar with it and use it faithfully. You have to figure out some way to get your play down on the page, so it only makes sense to learn the right way.

The standard format has evolved the way it has because it is first and foremost a script for actors to work with in readings and rehearsals. And that's the way you should think of your script—as an intermediate step to production. You want to present your material in such a way that other theater artists who will be getting involved in it can use it effectively and with ease. That's why the standard format looks the way it does, with all the white space, clear visual differentiation between lines of dialogue and stage directions, and character names spelled in capital letters. It's a practical format, perfect for use in rehearsal.

The good thing about this is that it's not only easy to read, but even *looks* easy to read. There are relatively few words on each page—nothing cramped or crowded. The length of the script in the standard format may be a few pages longer than a script in another format, but the dividend is this ease of the read. Don't underestimate this. I've struggled through many poorly formatted plays—a few of which have turned out to be quite good. I'm so used to the standard format that when my eyes land on a strangely formatted play I know right away it's going to be a much tougher read, at least at first. And that's a terrible way to start off.

Here's what Samuel French, Inc., the largest publisher of plays in the world, has to say about the standard format in their "Guidelines" handout:

It is not only the most readable format, but also, in the minds of most producers and their readers, a play in this format might just possibly be worth careful consideration—whereas a manuscript in another, less readable format is probably the work of some beginner who doesn't know beans about the needs of the professional theater and, hence, is worth only a cursory reading.

That's rather blunt and to the point. It's also accurate.

The Various Formats

As we begin this discussion of format, it's important to know the difference between the many formats for dramatic material currently in use. Script Samples 3 and 4 present the typical first pages of a play in the *author's manuscript*. This is the standard format—the one you should learn and use.

Compare this to Script Sample 5, which presents three formats commonly in use for *published* plays (including hard- and softcover trade editions and the various acting editions); these formats obviously don't resemble the standard format at all.

When a play is published it will either appear as a trade or library edition—a book for the general readership—or as an acting edition used by theaters when producing the play. As Script Sample 5 makes clear, the typical formats—and they vary widely—are designed so the play can be printed on as few pages as possible. The publishers have not considered that the standard format increases the readability of a play. (They have no real reason to concern themselves with this issue since the plays they're publishing, with rare exceptions, are already known and successful; people will read them anyway.)

Also be aware that manuscript formats for screenplays and teleplays (or TV sitcoms) differ from each other and from stage-play format (See Script Samples 6 and 7). Notice how both present the dialogue indented and the visuals and/or stage directions at the left margin—just the reverse of the play format. It's interesting that as the various formats have evolved in the different mediums, the one most distinguishing feature is how the dialogue is placed on the page. In plays it has the primary position at the left margin, and in films and TV it takes a secondary position. This is as it should be, of course, for the theater is basically a verbal medium, and film and TV are visual mediums.

THIS QUESTION OF FORMAT

a scene

by Buzz McLaughlin

[Put date of draft here]

Copyright © 1997 by Buzz McLaughlin
[Put contact address and phone number here]

Script Sample 1
Play Format
Title Page

```
CHARACTERS

CAROL, 28

RICHARD, 23


TIME

The present, late afternoon


PLACE

Carol's cramped and cluttered Literary Manager's office at an
established theater on Theater Row, New York City.

Scripts are stacked on the desk and floor.  File cabinets and
bookshelves line the walls along with theater posters and
memorabilia.  There's one small window.  The room has the feel of
a no-nonsense, active place where a lot of work gets done on a
daily basis.
```

Script Sample 2
Play Format
Character/Time/Place Page

(As the lights come up, CAROL sits behind the
desk holding a script. RICHARD sits opposite
her, clearly upset)

                    RICHARD
Come on, you can't be serious. The format is wrong? I
mean...this is...How anal can you get?

                    CAROL
Call it what you like, it's the truth.
          (referring to the script)
This screams "amateur."
              (She sets it down in front of him)

                    RICHARD
          (getting up)
I can't believe this. Did you even read it?
          (pacing)
I mean, did my format problems make it impossible for your
normally receptive mind to handle the <u>words</u>? It's the words, you
know, the words that count here. Or am I missing something?

                    CAROL
I think you are. And yes, I did read your words, Richard. Calm
down.

                    RICHARD
Why should I? People like you drive me nuts. What difference
does it make how I put it down on the page? It's what I have to
<u>say</u> that I need a response to. Man, I can't--
          (He faces CAROL)
Oh, well, why bother? I should be used to this by now.
          (grabbing his script)
Format problems. Thanks for the tip.
          (starting out)
See ya around.

                    CAROL
Sit down.

Script Sample 3
Play Format
First Script Page

                    RICHARD
That's okay, Carol. I've got other places to take this. Don't
feel the--

                    CAROL
          (firmly)
--Will you please shut up and listen?

          (He stops in the doorway)

                    CAROL (Cont'd)
I like your play. I think it has great promise. I think you're a
talented writer. The theater needs writers like you. I've told
you that before. But you've got to get over this attitude that
somehow you're entitled to early and great success. That you've
got all the answers. That everything you put down on paper--even
the way you put it on the page--is brilliant and above comment or
criticism. Nobody wants to work with someone like that.
Correction: nobody can work with someone like that. At least not
for long.

          (She gets up and crosses to him. RICHARD stares
          at her defiantly)

                    CAROL (Cont'd)
I've wanted to work with you. To help you.
          (taking the script from him, flipping through it)
But this is the third play you've brought me looking like this. I
tell you how to format it correctly and you ignore my advice.
You've decided it doesn't matter. Well, I know it matters. To me
and to most people who spend their days and nights reading endless
submissions like the ones stacked in this office. I keep bringing
up this format thing--silly as you think it is--because I want you
to be the best you can be. To represent yourself as the
professional you have the potential of becoming. But until you
get that ego of yours under control, I'm no longer interested in
working with you.
          (She holds out the script to him)
Goodbye, Richard.
          (He glares at her, then grabs the script, and
          exits in a huff.

          Blackout)

Script Sample 4
Play Format
All Pages After the First Page

As the lights come up, CAROL *sits behind the desk holding a script.* RICHARD *sits opposite her, clearly upset.*

RICHARD   Come on, you can't be serious. The format is wrong? I mean . . . this is . . . How anal can you get?

CAROL   Call it what you like, it's the truth. *(Referring to the script)* This screams "amateur." *(She sets it down in front of him.)*

RICHARD   *(Getting up)* I can't believe this. Did you even read it? *(Pacing)* I mean, did my format problems make it impossible for your normally receptive mind to handle the words?

As the LIGHTS come up, CAROL sits behind the desk holding a script. RICHARD sits opposite her, clearly upset.

RICHARD. Come on, you can't be serious. The format is wrong? I mean . . . this is . . . How anal can you get?

CAROL. Call it what you like, it's the truth. *(referring to the script)* This screams "amateur." *(She sets it down in front of him.)*

RICHARD. *(getting up)* I can't believe this. Did you even read it? *(pacing)* I mean, did my format problems make it impossible for your normally receptive mind to handle the words?

As the lights come up, CAROL *sits behind the desk holding a script.* RICHARD *sits opposite her, clearly upset.*

RICHARD: Come on, you can't be serious. The format is wrong? I mean . . . this is . . . How anal can you get?

CAROL: Call it what you like, it's the truth. *(referring to the script)* This screams "amateur."

She sets it down in front of him.

RICHARD: *(getting up)* I can't believe this. Did you even read it? (pacing) I mean, did my format problems make it impossible for your normally receptive mind to handle the words?

Script Sample 5
Typical Formats for Published Plays

```
FADE IN:

INT.  CAROL'S OFFICE - DAY

CAROL sits behind the desk holding a script.  RICHARD
sits opposite her, clearly upset.

                    RICHARD
          Come on, you can't be serious.  The
          format is wrong?  I mean...this is...
          How anal can you get?

                    CAROL
          Call it what you like, it's the truth.
               (referring to the script)
          This screams "amateur."

She sets it down in front of him.

                    RICHARD
               (getting up)
          I can't believe this.  Did you even
          read it?
               (pacing)
          I mean, did my format problems make
          it impossible for your normally receptive
          mind to handle the words?  It's the words,
          you know, the words that count here.  Or
          am I missing something?

                    CAROL
          I think you are.  And yes, I did read
          your words, Richard.  Calm down.

                    RICHARD
          Why should I?  People like you drive me
          nuts.  What difference does it make how I
          put it down on the page?  It's what I
          have to say that I need a response to.
          Man, I can't--

               (He faces Carol)
          Oh, well, why bother?  I should be used
```

Script Sample 6
Screenplay Format

```
INT.  CAROL'S OFFICE - DAY

(CAROL SITS BEHIND THE DESK HOLDING A SCRIPT.  RICHARD
SITS OPPOSITE HER, CLEARLY UPSET)

                    RICHARD
          Come on, you can't be serious.
          The format is wrong?  I mean...
          This is...How anal can you get?
                    CAROL
          Call it what you like, it's the truth.
          (REFERRING TO THE SCRIPT)  This
          screams "amateur."
(SHE SETS IT DOWN IN FRONT OF HIM)
                    RICHARD
          (GETTING UP)  I can't believe this.
          Did you even read it?  (PACING)  I
          mean, did my format problems make it
          impossible for your normally receptive
          mind to handle the words?  It's the
          words, you know, the words that count
          here.  Or am I missing something?
                    CAROL
          I think you are.  And yes, I did read
          your words, Richard.  Calm down.
                    RICHARD
          Why should I?  People like you drive
                    (MORE)
```

Script Sample 7
Teleplay Format

I emphatically urge you to stay away from any of these other formats or some combination of them as you start working on your play. You're writing a new work for the theater that needs every break it can get. The standard format used in the new play business puts a good number of them at your disposal.

Elements of the Standard Format

Script Samples 1 through 4 illustrate how you can give the manuscript of your play its most readily accepted visual presentation. We'll review the elements of this standard format one by one.

Title Page

Starting at the top, the first page of your manuscript should, obviously, be the title page. Script Sample 1 shows what it should look like. It normally includes six pieces of information:

1. The title of the play, usually in capital letters. Put it in bold type and a slightly larger font if you have such features. Another option is underlining. Within reason, do what you can to make the reader's eye immediately go to the title.

2. A phrase describing what kind of play it is—a play in one act, a comedy in two acts, a play in six scenes, and so on. Keep this short and simple. *Use 12-point type for this and everything to follow in the script.*

3. Your name, preceded by the word "by."

4. Identification of what draft it is by listing the completion date. I suggest you avoid the wording "first draft," "second draft," and so on. The date is enough. You'll know what draft it is. There will perhaps be times when you won't want to include this identifying date on a submission, but usually it's helpful to know which version of your play is between the covers. This becomes especially useful when you've printed up and circulated more than one draft of the play. Not identifying your revised drafts can lead to potential problems, such as when different people give you responses and you don't know what version they're referring to. So it's important to identify every draft, from the first one on.

5. The notice of copyright. If you do this precisely the way it's shown in Script Sample 1, including the small "c" with a circle around it, you

are legally protected without actually having to register your script with the Copyright Office in the Library of Congress in Washington, D.C. It gives notice to all readers that it is your work and that all rights are reserved. Formal registry of copyright is necessary only when a professional production is in the works or the play is about to be published.

6. Your permanent address and phone number. Writers with agents representing their work almost always list the agent's name, address, and phone instead of, or in addition to, their own. If you have an agent, I suggest you list your own address and phone anyway, until that point in your career when your name is so famous that it's prudent to keep yourself one step removed. (Agents are discussed in Chapter 12.) If you're a student, list both your school and your home addresses and numbers. Sometimes a script will lie around for years before a potential producer or director connects with it, so be sure there's a way you can always be contacted.

Characters/Time/Place Page

Script Sample 2 presents a typical character/time/place page. It immediately follows the title page, unless there's a page of dedication or a special author's note to the reader which would be placed between the title page and this page. There are several details to highlight:

1. *Character Names.* These are listed "all cap"—that is, entirely in capital letters—both here and throughout the script.

2. *Character Ages.* With rare exceptions, I suggest you always give the ages of the characters here. As discussed in Chapter 5, one of the most irritating things for a reader is knowing neither how old a character is nor the age spread between characters. I once got more than thirty pages into a script that listed no ages up front before discovering that a character I'd judged to be roughly the same age as another was, in fact, a generation older than the other character. I was forced to go back to page 1 and reread the play with this critical new information—something that would have been visually obvious in performance but which, given the way the characters were relating, I had no way of discerning on my own.

When reading a play it's often necessary to use this page as a reference as more characters are introduced and it becomes more difficult to keep track of ages and other information. For this reason, it's best to list all ages here and get it over with, not bury this information in the script itself as characters are introduced.

3. *Character Relationships.* It's often helpful to list the relationships characters have to each other, especially if they're familial—siblings, husband and wife, parent and child, and so on. Again, these elements usually become clear in performance but aren't always conveyed as quickly as you'd like on the printed page. Including this information here allows the reader to focus in on the dynamics of a relationship as when seeing the play performed.

4. *Character Traits.* Other than ages and familial interconnectedness, it's usually best to let the play reveal your characters. Personality traits or the physical appearance of your people might be critical information for an intelligent understanding of your play, but more often than not the unfolding of your story in dialogue and action will make these clear soon enough. Sometimes even a few details of character description can actually give away major surprises or tell readers things they want to discover on their own. So the general rule is: Don't put anything in your character descriptions that can be inferred in a reading of the script. If you do present a detailed description here, you risk not only being redundant but also short-circuiting the reader's creative engagement with the material.

If you think it's imperative to give some brief description up front, only include elements that the audience would see when the character *first* appears onstage. In other words, avoid going into what the character is thinking or feeling. Don't divulge what the character has just been doing, that he has a terrible temper once it's unleashed, that she's too intelligent for her own good, and so on and so forth. Again, readers want to figure these things out for themselves and, besides, you're writing a play, not a novel.

5. *Time.* Always list the general time in which the play is set, such as "The present" or "Summer, 1951," or "A fall weekend in 1968," and so on. If the play is one scene of continuous action, it's usually useful to include here also the time of day in which the action takes place, such as "Late evening," "Early morning," "3:30 a.m.," and so on.

If the play has several scenes, you can either list each scene with a brief indication of time (such as "Scene 1: 7:30 on Friday evening;

Scene 2: Very early the next morning; Scene 3: Late that afternoon). Or you can simply list only the general time for the entire play here and indicate specific times in each scene's opening stage directions. The latter is more commonly used, for readers are then given the information when they need it as the play unfolds. Whichever way you end up indicating time, keep in mind that this page's only function is to orient the reader to the play about to be read. So just use common sense and keep it simple and clear.

6. *Place.* It's important to offer the reader a frame of reference as to the general world the play is set in, such as the region of the country, the city, or the specific locale, and so on. As in Script Sample 2, this is usually listed first as a separate paragraph and, simple as it is, it can supply important hints as to overall tempo and pace, accents, and even how characters physically relate to one another. It gives readers a general take on what's to follow and keys them into how to enlist their imaginations as they read it.

Then, in a second paragraph, describe the specific setting for the play. If the play takes place in more than one locale, it's often best to conceive a "unit set" in which all locales are included in one overall design. And although you, the playwright, are not expected to be a set or lighting designer, when there are many scenes in different places, it's appropriate to suggest how you envision the play moving from scene to scene on the stage through the use of lighting and/or specific actions by the characters. This is especially true when your stylistic conception of the play is highly theatrical. Generally describe how you envision this scheme working for the play as a whole, and then be more specific in the stage directions within the scenes themselves.

In describing your setting, whether a single room or a unit set involving several locales, always be as brief as possible and avoid dictating the precise locations of furniture, doors, windows, and so on, unless a precise location is absolutely essential to the understanding of the play. There's nothing more tedious before you've started reading the play than to be forced to wade through an unneeded, overdrawn description that locates the couch downstage left, the door to the kitchen upstage right, a large portrait of a child on the upstage center right wall, and so on. Include only the essential and the unusual items with perhaps a suggestion of their locations, but wherever possible allow the reader to create his or her own precise visualization of the setting. Instead, "invite" the reader by establishing the "feel" of the place.

Moving to the first page of actual script, let's look at the various format elements.

That Friendly White Space

Although not a hard and fast format rule, the first page of the actual script should have a top margin a few lines deeper than other pages. This sets off the start of the actual play and visually helps ease the reader into this as-yet foreign world. Likewise, at the end of a scene, leave the rest of the page blank and start the next scene at the top of a fresh page. As strange as it sounds, this kind of white space helps a script breathe and makes it more reader-friendly.

Margins

Your standard left margin should be fifteen spaces or an inch and a half from the edge of the paper, no more, no less. Be precise, because there's a practical reason for it: You need this much space to punch holes and bind your pages together and still have an adequate left margin. If it's less than an inch and a half, you run the risk that the binding will obscure the words. If it's more than an inch and a half, you're leaving too much white space and your playscript starts looking like a TV script.

The left margin is reserved exclusively for the actual lines of dialogue. Nothing else *ever* starts here.

The only caution about the right margin concerns word processors or computer software that allow you to justify the text. Some programs lengthen spaces between words on each line so that a right margin can be justified. As a result, the spacing is uneven and the line looks jumpy. There really is no advantage to justifying your text, but if you prefer it, do it *only* if your program is sophisticated enough to avoid this annoying effect.

Tab Settings

There are two tab settings, as seen in Script Samples 3 and 4:

1. The first tab is ten spaces (or one inch) in from the left margin. This is where *all* stage directions begin and the only place you should put them. And it's only stage directions you should ever put at this tab.

Never put a stage direction on the same line with dialogue; rather, it should always start on a new line indented to the first tab setting. The reason for this is, again, readability. An actor always knows this is where action is described. There's never a chance for confusion between a line and a stage direction because each has its own position on the page.

For stage directions longer than one line, you should also indent on the *right* ten spaces or an inch in from the margin. Visually, this tends to set all stage directions off even more from the dialogue. This is a subtle thing, but it's another one of those tricks worth employing. All word processing software includes a right/left indent feature that accomplishes this automatically.

2. The second tab is in twenty spaces (or two inches) from the left margin. This is where you put the all-caps character name that identifies the speaker of the lines under it. There's no need to center the name above the speech, although this is easily accomplished, especially with computers. Nothing else should ever be put at this tab except, when necessary, the words "Cont'd" or "offstage," which are discussed below.

Character Names

Again, character names should always be typed in capital letters at the second tab setting and whenever a character is referred to by name in any stage direction. The reason for this is simply to help alert the actor that his or her character is being referred to; the capitals draw attention to the name. The only time you don't capitalize the name of a character is when it's spoken in the dialogue—unless, of course, you intend the actor to shout the name very loudly.

I find it interesting that in film and TV format the character names are in all caps only the first time they appear in a script and thereafter lowercased. Again, this reflects the predominantly visual nature of storytelling in screenplays and teleplays, where the camera reigns over the writing.

Splitting a Speech Between Two Pages

When at least one line of a character's speech appears under the character name at the bottom of a page, it is not necessary to re-identify whose line it is at the top of the next page. The exception to this is when a stage direction at the bottom of the preceding page makes it unclear that the continuing line belongs to the same character. It's also not necessary to add the word "More" at the bottom of a page when a speech continues, as is the case with film and TV scripts.

Between the bottom of one page and the top of the next, avoid at all costs separating the character name from the speech to follow. Word processing systems are very fond of doing this when you've gone back into the script to add or subtract material to a page. Get in the habit of going back over your manuscript just before you're ready to print out a copy to be sure these splits are eliminated. They're a real nuisance at readings, for actors can easily lose track of who's speaking as a page is turned. It's also sloppy and unprofessional.

There is software on the market for playwriting (as well as for film and TV) that automatically formats as you write, and they eliminate this problem when you make additions and edits. Be careful when considering using any of these, however; some of them have actually been programmed with serious errors in format! They're also quite expensive. I suggest that you carefully inspect how the format is programmed before investing in such software.

External and Internal Stage Directions

There are two kinds of stage directions: external and internal. (These are discussed in Chapter 9.) In Script Samples 3 and 4, external stage directions are those which describe an action or actions that take place *between* two lines of dialogue. They're literally outside the lines being spoken and are in addition to them. They always appear on the page as units of action separated from what immediately precedes and follows.

Internal stage directions are, as it were, interior to a speech, indicating how it should be spoken or describing an action that takes place while a line is spoken. That is, they describe only *concurrent* action, inflection, or tone of voice. These directions are always very short—a word or phrase. Do not describe an action involving another character or an action that is, in fact, completed before or after the line the stage direction is a part of. Internal stage directions can be placed either at the beginning of a spoken line (between the character name and the start of the line) or anywhere within a line.

Line Spacing

As is shown in Script Samples 3 and 4, you should *double-space* between the last line of a speech or stage direction and the character name that appears before the next speech. You single-space nearly everything else— all lines of dialogue and all stage directions. After any character name, *single-space* to the first line of dialogue or to any internal stage direction that you might want to insert between the name and the speech. Also single-space within a character's speech when you insert an internal stage direction.

Use of "Cont'd"

If, after a portion of a character's speech, you insert a stage direction that actively shifts the attention of the audience *away from* the character speaking, the format requires two things:

1. You should *double-space* before and after this stage direction, which will remove it from "inside" the character's line.

2. You should identify the continuing speech after the stage direction as belonging to the same character who was speaking before the stage direction. Insert the character name again, followed by the abbreviation "Cont'd" in parentheses *on the same line*. There are two examples of this in Script Sample 4. The reason for this specific abbreviation of "continued" is simply tradition.

If you don't follow this procedure, it's sometimes difficult, if not impossible, to tell whose line it is after the stage direction. In some cases, a scene could seem to make sense if the line following the stage direction were assigned to a character other than the one you wrote it for. Sometimes the context does not make it obvious whom a speech belongs to. Obviously, you want to avoid confusing your readers and actors. The example in the middle of Script Sample 4 shows how this might happen. If the continuation of Carol's line beginning with "I've wanted to work with you" were not identified as hers, for a moment an actor could conceivably construe it as Richard's, since it follows a stage direction describing his action. That's why this format rule should always be applied.

Do not use "Cont'd" after internal stage directions. Again, look at Script Sample 4. Notice how the focus of attention of the audience doesn't always leave Carol during her long speech, even though there are internal stage directions within it. We stay with that character through these stage directions. There's no confusion and so no need for re-identifying whose speech it is.

Characters Speaking from Offstage

The only other time you should put a stage direction on the same line as the character name is when the character speaks from offstage. Simply put "offstage" in parentheses directly after the character name. The reason for this placement is that you may want to include a normal internal stage direction for the offstage line, and this allows you to do so with no possible confusion.

The Period in Stage Directions

A generally accepted rule in working with the standard format is to eliminate the period at the end of an external stage direction immediately preceding a line and never to use a period after an internal stage direction. The reason for this is that as readers we automatically process the period as a stop, like the "stop" in a telegram, and a period at the end of a stage direction just before a speech halts the flow of action just when you want action and dialogue to fuse. Think of stage directions and the speech immediately following as part of the "theatrical sentence" you're composing. Admittedly, this is a subtle point, but it does make a difference in the way our eyes scan a script and translate what is seen into micromessages sent to the brain. This little, seemingly harmless dot sometimes damages the flow, and when that happens the rule is simple: Don't use it.

The Paragraph in Stage Directions

It's often to your advantage to break up long stage directions into paragraphs when a complicated action or series of actions is being described. Usually, breaks are made when there's a definite shift in focus for the audience, such as the entrance of another character or a new and significant piece of action. On the other hand, if the focus of attention remains on the same character throughout a stage direction, it might be best to leave it all as one long paragraph for reasons of flow. Whatever the situation dictates, don't overuse this tool. When you do use it, start each paragraph at the first tab setting, where all stage directions start—that is, do not indent the first line of a new paragraph the customary five spaces, as is standard in narrative writing.

Parentheses Around Stage Directions

The rule is simple: All stage directions—including external stage directions several paragraphs in length—should be bracketed with *one* set of parentheses.

Interruptions

The way to indicate that one character is interrupting another character is to put a dash (commonly rendered as two hyphens right next to each other) immediately after the word where you want the interruption to happen *and* to put a dash immediately before the start of the speech of the character doing the interrupting. For example, look at Carol's interruption of Richard in Script Sample 4. Using dashes in this way, it's never necessary to include the internal stage direction "interrupting" before the line of the interrupting character. Instead, you're doing it visually with punctuation, which is preferable because it speeds the flow of the read.

Characters Cutting Themselves Off

When a character abruptly stops talking in the middle of a sentence, use a dash at the point he or she stops speaking. See how this works in Richard's line in Script Sample 3. This is the same as the interruption, except there's no dash placed at the start of the next line. You should assume that well-trained actors and directors should know the difference.

The Ellipsis

This tool comes in handy in several situations. If you want to indicate a character's verbalized thought trailing off and disintegrating before our ears, put the dot-dot-dot after the last word you want spoken. This prompts from the actor a very different quality than the dash—a trailing off as opposed to an abrupt cutting off. If a character is having difficulty putting something into words, stammering or groping for the way to say something, ellipses should be used. Finally, if a character is on the phone and we hear only his or her side of the conversation, ellipses are used to indicate the character's pauses as the person at the other end speaks. For example, a portion of a phone call in one of my plays goes as follows:

> Hi . . . Sorry, I got my hands full out here . . . No, I'm alone . . . Not so good. I've already started talking to myself. Actually to my father . . . Forget it . . . It was a joke, okay? So what'd you find out? . . . Yeah . . . Those sons of bitches . . . I can't . . . I know, I know, but you'll have to— . . . I just got here . . . I've got to . . .

I can't imagine how this could have been written without this tool.

Indicating Special Emphasis

At times it's necessary to indicate which word or words in a line are to be stressed to make sure it will be read and played the way you intend. This is called *pointing* a line and is almost always done by underlining a specific word or words. For example, a line like "She wouldn't say she was sorry" might be pointed "<u>She</u> wouldn't say she was sorry," or "She wouldn't <u>say</u> she was sorry," or "She wouldn't say she was <u>sorry</u>." Depending on which word gets the emphasis, the real meaning of the line is totally changed. See Script Samples 3 and 4.

Be careful with this, however. Only point words when the desired emphasis is not obvious in the context of the moment. There's nothing more irritating to actors and directors than a script in which a good share of the lines are already frozen in place by the writer. It's the job of these artists to interpret the script and find the best possible way to bring it to life. Overusing this tool, therefore, can be at best redundant and at worse insulting.

You can indicate that a character is shouting a line in one of three ways: by an internal stage direction; by underlining the line; or by putting it all in capital letters. It's all a matter of the moment and of degree, of course. The general rule is to use discretion. Save these weapons for when you really need them.

I suggest you stay away from italics and bold type for indicating emphasis. Even if you have a state-of-the-art laser printer and copier, both these features often have a tendency to reproduce poorly. Keep in mind that theaters often make extra copies of scripts over which you'll have no quality control when they are photocopied.

Simultaneous Speaking

There are different ways to indicate characters speaking at the same time. If you want your characters to begin talking unintentionally at the same time, deal with it as you would an interruption. Have the first character start a line, followed by the other interrupting, followed by the first trying to continue, only to be interrupted again. You can't continue this for very long, of course, but you do accomplish the effect you want.

It's best to avoid indicating in a stage direction, "The following three lines are spoken on top of each other," or some such phrase, because it's clumsy and brings you, the playwright, into the moment—something you generally want to avoid.

If you want a sustained overlap that goes on for several lines where characters are intentionally talking over each other, then you have two options. One is to break each character's speech into fragments and then, using ellipses (not dashes) before and after each line fragment, alternate them on the page. The fragments spoken by each, if put together, should fit into one continuous thought or series of connected thoughts. A good example of this can be found in the famous opening scene of Albee's *Who's Afraid of Virginia Woolf?* as George and Martha are about to open the door for their guests. Albee "orchestrates" the overlapping with the use of ellipses so that the audience hears everything that is said, but the effect achieved is that the characters are speaking over each other.

The other option is to temporarily rearrange the format and set up two columns of dialogue on the page, one for each character. This works well with extended overlapping because it allows you to indicate precisely on what lines (and even what words) the overlaps occur.

Use this two-column method only for extended parallel dialogue, however. It looks a little silly to go through the trouble of setting up the two running columns for, say, four or five overlapping lines.

Finally, a general caution: You can't have characters speaking simultaneously for very long or it all becomes unintelligible; you run the risk of having the overlapping section draw attention to itself for its own sake. Because of this, it's usually better to create the illusion of simultaneity by having characters continually interrupt each other through a section of dialogue, as in the example above from *Who's Afraid of Virginia Woolf?* This way, everything is heard and the play continues its forward movement.

Page Numbering

Put page numbers in the upper-right corner. All scripts should be numbered consecutively from the first page of dialogue to the last page regardless of how many acts or scenes are contained in it. The title page and character/time/place page are never given page numbers, and the page number does not appear on page 1. For plays with more than one scene or act, put the act and/or scene preceding the page number, representing the act number with a capital roman numeral and the scene with a lower-case roman numeral. Here are some examples:

I, i, 17   II, iii, 94   ii, 27   I, 29

Assembling the Script

When you're ready to prepare your script for photocopying, be sure that you use the 12-point type option, as mentioned earlier. This will approximate the "pica" size—the larger of the two traditional type sizes. Adhere to this religiously—it is the standard in the profession. Select a font that seems the cleanest and most readable. Make sure that your master copy has been printed with the utmost clarity so the script will photocopy well. Laser printers are by far the best for this, and if you don't own one it's worth the extra effort and expense to locate one to use for this purpose.

The best script cover is the simplest—the title page itself. Ask your copy center to use a heavier stock of paper for the title page and pick up some blank pages of the same stock to serve as back covers. Have the script photocopied on three-hole punched paper and bind the copies using roundhead brass fasteners of the proper length (a half-inch to an inch longer than the thickness of your assembled script) and with heads considerably larger than the punched holes. Using pliers, clamp the fasteners down securely so they hold the script snugly and won't twist or turn. Almost all professional scripts are put together in this way.

The general rule is not to get carried away when you finally prepare your script for presentation. Just keep it clean, neat, and humble. What you want to avoid is making it look like it's already been published. The script you finally send out and around to potential producers, agents, and other theater people should be thoroughly developed, fully revised, and as polished as you can make it, but always tell yourself that you're offering up a draft of a work-in-progress. Therefore, it should look professional, but its presentation shouldn't send an unspoken message that the play is absolutely set, or frozen, in its current form, not to be touched by anyone. I always get suspicious when a submission is "over-prepared" for the printed page. That should only happen *after* it's won the Pulitzer Prize.

At the same time, however, given the rapid pace of current advances in computer and printer technology, it's worth your while to periodically investigate what's available on the market concerning script preparation. We are in a time of vast change in how all information is transmitted from one person to another, and playwrights are not being left unaffected. Anyone who ignores these developments will run the risk of being judged outmoded or not keeping up with the times. Old habits die hard, but I urge you to familiarize yourself with the new tools as they appear. You never know what might work for you until you try it.

Getting Familiar with the Format

Reading through the features of the standard format is a start, but you also have to get comfortable working with it. I offer this exercise which has proven extremely valuable for students. You'll need a tape recorder and a blank tape. Arrange for one or two people you know well to meet with you for a fifteen- to twenty-minute visit. Explain that you're going to record your conversation with them and use a portion of it as a playwriting exercise. Then turn on the recorder, set it aside, and start talking with them about anything at all. At first your friend(s) will be very aware of the recorder, but within a few minutes they'll forget about it entirely. Record at least fifteen minutes of this conversation.

Later, when you're alone, play back the tape and select the two- to three-minute section of the conversation you think is the most lively and interesting. Then, using the standard format, transcribe at least three pages' worth of what's on the tape. Get down everything accurately, including inflections, tone of voice, and physical actions. Capture the dialogue exactly the way it comes off the tape. Don't change anything.

This isn't an easy exercise, and it takes some time, but it's guaranteed to get you familiar with the format. Most of the problems playwrights confront in getting dialogue down on the page will be faced and wrestled with. I urge you to take the time now to do this, so that when you start on the first draft of your play you can concentrate exclusively on what your characters are saying to each other instead of on how to put it down on the page.

Another benefit of this exercise, of course, is that in addition to seeing how all this translates to the page, you can examine how real-life people actually use words and physical actions while communicating. The next chapter takes a detailed look at this.

BRINGING IT TO LIFE

As a writer what you have to search for is that sense of life, however mysterious it is and wherever it comes from.

—HORTON FOOTE

As you sit down to write a play there's one overriding goal before you: To craft the work in such a way that the audience will be drawn in immediately and remain fully engaged throughout. What I'm talking about is no less than a grand seduction. One way or another your script has to have a power, an appeal, an alluring quality that pulls people in. It has to establish for the audience a sense of trust; that they know they're in good hands; that you, the writer, know how to give a script forward movement, shape, voice, and that special "feel" of truth.

When I read a good play, I'm always struck by its similarity to other good plays I've read, in terms of how it accomplishes these things—how instantly it commands my attention, draws me in, and keeps me interested. I say to myself, "Ah, here's a pro. Here's somebody who knows how to do it. Here's a voice I feel compelled to listen to."

This chapter takes a look at the common principles and techniques shared by all good writers in creating dialogue and stage directions, the two means by which plays get onto the page. If you're relatively new at this business of writing plays, I urge you, as I did in Chapter 8, to take the time to gain some mastery of the tools presented here. They'll help arm you for the task ahead and ultimately give you a better chance at creating something that will have the breath of life in it.

Just as a beginning cabinetmaker would not make his first chest of drawers using the most select wood in the shop, I strongly urge you not to use your developed play idea when you first practice applying what's presented here. Eager as I know you are to get started writing your play, take the time to engage in writing some scenes purely for exercise, for muscle flexing, before plunging into your first draft. The thirty suggestions for practice scenes presented at the end of the chapter are for this purpose.

The Art of Carrot Dangling

Your job in writing a play can be compared to that of a driver of a horse-drawn wagon full of vegetables who's expertly manipulating a carrot tied to a long pole in front of the horse's nose—the purpose of which is to keep the wagon moving to a stable down the road so the horse can be fed the whole wagonload of vegetables. You're the driver, the horse is the audience, the carrot is your script in performance, and the wagon contains the "goods" of the play—its ideas or content, what you want to communicate.

As the driver, you control the forward motion of the wagon. Because he's hungry, the horse keeps moving, trying to eat the carrot that's constantly being dangled before his face. If the carrot gets close enough for the horse to snatch it, the wagon will stop as he eats it, never arrive at the stable, and never deliver the full feast to the horse. Likewise, if the carrot gets too far from the horse, he'll stop in his tracks because he'll give up hope of ever getting his teeth into it. Keeping the wagon steadily moving forward toward the stable depends on how well the driver keeps the horse tantalized by the carrot.

And that's precisely what you have to do. Your onstage action—delineated by the single instances of dialogue and stage directions in your script—has to keep the audience constantly leaning into your play, making them work to keep up with it, yet not making it so difficult or obscure that they tune out. Ideally, every line you put down will teeter on the edge of falling off into obscurity or falling back into the predictable and obvious; it will hover on that invisible boundary between saying too much and too little. You have to find a way to balance yourself on this precarious edge. It's the only place from which good dialogue can flow.

Let's look at the numerous components of successful carrot dangling.

The Question of Style

Any discussion of the technique of writing good dialogue (and stage directions) has to begin with clarifying the two fundamental styles of theater available to you: *representational* and *presentational.* It's difficult to proceed with the writing of a play unless you have a fairly good sense of which style you're going to be working in.

The vast majority of plays are, to one degree or another, representational in style, meaning that they aim, fully or in large part, to represent, or be a reflection of, reality. The characters are to be seen as real people living in a real world which has no direct contact with the audience. Indeed, there's an invisible "fourth wall" between the characters and us, the spectators. We get drawn in and become involved emotionally with what's happening, but basically we remain observers, removed from the world onstage. In this sense, our experience is nearly the same as when watching a dramatic film.

Presentational plays, on the other hand, acknowledge throughout that they're presenting a piece of theater to a live audience. Characters never hide behind a fourth wall, and the audience is constantly reminded that they're in a theater watching actors performing a play. Such works are always highly theatrical in the sense that they expose and make use of the various artistic elements of a theater performance. Actors talk directly to the audience, sometimes even walking up and down the aisles and speaking to individual audience members. The set often reveals the backstage activity taking place during the performance. The audience is always reminded of the theater event that they're a part of. It would be as if, in the middle of a dramatic film, the camera suddenly panned to the cameraman and director and we saw on the screen all the lighting and sound equipment. An aspect of the circus is often captured in such plays, where everything is acknowledged as artifice and the story is told in front of the audience as a "show."

Although representational plays are always predominantly realistic in style, there can be presentational elements woven into the telling of the story. For example, a character in the play may sometimes function as a narrator and address the audience, as does Tom Wingfield in Tennessee Williams's *The Glass Menagerie.* Even when such a device is utilized, however, the story itself is almost always told representationally, with the characters living out their drama behind a fourth wall. Another example is the highly theatrical *Equus,* by Peter Shaffer, in which Martin Dysart, the psychiatrist, addresses the audience throughout, and the boy's sad story is dramatized with actors called upon to play highly stylized horses. Even here, however, the story is still basically told representationally, in that the audience is invited to witness the characters functioning in a separate reality representing real life. We watch these people live out their tale in a world distanced from our own. Thus, although representational plays can have a high degree of theatricality and use presentational elements, they basically remain works removed from the audience's immediate and present reality in the theater.

The techniques discussed in this chapter are primarily geared for use with writing representational, realistic plays because, as I've said throughout, I believe that first gaining a mastery of this style is the best way to learn the basics of the craft. You're faced head-on with the challenge of creating pages that bring characters truthfully to life. You aren't allowed to hedge your bets or possibly fool yourself into thinking you're writing something wonderful and theatrically alive when in fact you're only dressing up wooden puppets and putting them through their stylized paces. The bottom line is that writing for the theater succeeds only when you're able to create living, breathing people who speak and act truthfully in the world of the play. Without question, the representational style is the best arena in which to learn how to do this well.

Once you've mastered this style, it's much easier to begin opening up your plays stylistically while infusing them with the power of truth. This same progression has been the norm for centuries in the training of visual artists. Pablo Picasso started by executing brilliant representational drawings before moving into abstract work. Playwrights who hope to one day make a significant contribution would be wise to follow a similar path.

Becoming an Eavesdropper

In writing the first draft of a representational play, you might think of yourself as eavesdropping on real people in a real place having real exchanges with each other. You secretly watch what they're doing, listen to their conversations, and then put down on the page exactly what you see and hear.

Michael Weller describes the way this works for him:

> I only hear people talking, and then I put down what they say. . . . In a way, it's like listening to the radio. It's always on, and you just listen to the people chatting away. It's a little more complicated, but it's something like that.

Working this way requires that you never dwell on how your audience might react to what is said and done by these people or force words into your characters' mouths for the audience's benefit. Of course, this doesn't apply if you incorporate moments in which characters step out of the story and talk directly to the audience; these stylistic breaks have to be approached differently. What I'm referring to here is the telling of the tale from inside the characters' world, which undoubtedly will take up most of your pages.

The Megaphone Effect

The moment you either (1) consciously start dwelling on whether or not the audience will understand what your characters are saying or (2) begin pondering if the audience has enough information to make sense of the situation in the play, you run the risk of what I call the "megaphone effect." This is the kiss of death in dialogue writing. It rears its ugly head whenever characters suddenly start telling each other things they already know about themselves, other characters, or the circumstances they're involved in for the benefit of the audience's understanding. There's nothing more false, wooden, and tedious than characters talking at each other about things they should be taking for granted.

Never allow yourself to intrude on the characters' reality in this way. Be very tough on yourself with this.

Write for the Smart

It helps to think of the audience you're writing for as a collection of the most intelligent people you know. Imagine them as the friends who generally understand what you're trying to communicate before you've finished verbalizing it, as the people you've met who impress you as having quick, active minds and seem to be always a step or two ahead of everybody else. Don't worry about all the rest, the ones who take a little longer to understand ideas, who need things explained two or three times. These people will simply have to work harder to keep up with your play. Perhaps, in the worst case scenario, there will be those among them who "drop out." Under no circumstances should you let those few put your carrot in danger of being eaten by the brightest members of the audience while the wagon is still en route to the stable.

The general principle, then, is to let your audience figure out what the characters are talking about. In other words, make them work at it. They *want* to make the connections and fill in the blanks. This is why the cliché "less is more" rings so true when applied to playwriting. The power of your work increases the more the audience is allowed to engage creatively with the material, and you accomplish this by leaving things unsaid. As **Edward Albee** puts it: "You get paid for what you don't write."

Exposing the Subtext

Remember that the script is only the tip of the iceberg—the surface layer of a deeply submerged whole. Your job is to write your pages in such a way that there are constant glimpses into that submerged part of the story, or *subtext*—that rich stew of intellectual and emotional "stuff" always just under the surface—that you've explored in your character work . You tap into this deeper level and make it felt and understood by what you leave unsaid. Forced to engage actively with the play to get the whole story, the audience makes their own connections between the surface and what lies underneath.

Always write with this dynamic in mind. It's this quality more than any other that separates good plays from bad.

Terrence McNally describes this another way by saying it's essential to keep the focus on what the characters are doing, rather than on what they're saying:

> Whenever I get stuck, it's because I'm asking, "What should he say to that?" Then I know something is dead in the scene. See, in real life when people ask us something, we don't usually stop to think a lot. So if you're writing a scene and you start asking yourself, "He said this, now what is she going to say back?" then I'd say there's something dead in the situation, because in real life that is not a big issue, being at a loss for words. And if as a playwright you keep getting stuck, it's because you haven't put your finger on the life of the scene, what's really going on. That's what I mean about knowing what the characters are doing. Because words are very much the tip of the iceberg. There's a whole other thing going on.

Getting Inside the Play

To write good pages you must be able to transport yourself totally into the reality of the play. You have to *be there,* inside that world with your characters. You know you're having a good day when somehow you've managed mysteriously to leave your own present-tense reality—the writer sitting there at a desk—and to travel to and exist in that other time and place for a sustained period. It doesn't happen every time you sit down to write. But when it does, the hours flash by like minutes, and you're shocked that you've actually been sitting there unaware of the morning turning to afternoon or that it's grown dark outside.

As **Marsha Norman** says, "One of the best things about writing is to get lost that way—it's great. It's exactly that feeling of being *in* the play."

When you have a day like this, you become sensitive to every detail of the characters' world—the quality of the sunlight, the smells, the temperature, and so on. The people are absolutely real in every particular. And when they speak, you can hear their breathing and watch the expression in their eyes. You can feel precisely the degree of comfort or awkwardness they feel with each other. You can read their minds, know their thoughts, and see every subtle movement and physical response in their faces and bodies. In short, on a good day, you become the play and all its parts.

Terrence McNally, for example, is able to say in all honesty that on the good days his characters write his plays. He explains:

> Now, I don't mean to sound naive, but when I'm really writing well, I feel as if I'm channeling. . . . Probably if you went to a séance, and you really believed in the whole process and what the medium was saying, and you actually heard the medium speaking in your father's voice or your good friend's voice— that's what I'd say it must feel like. Because I don't feel I'm writing the play at these moments. Their words are coming through me.

Putting it another way, **Edward Albee**, in speaking of the trick playwrights must play on themselves in order to get characters talking, says:

> They don't exist in a rational sense . . . we are creating them, we are inventing them. And they can't say anything that we don't want them to say, but we have to play that trick on ourselves. We have to pretend that they have the dimension and that they are doing it, or else we can't give over to our creativity fully. We have to explore that.

Thus you have to commit yourself completely to the task you've put before you. And this means sensitizing every pore and brain cell. It means really believing in make-believe. It means willfully jumping off the cliff of your own reality and guiding yourself into the world where your characters live. For this is the only way you'll ever capture on the page anything vital and exciting, something that has the feel of life in it.

Minutia Is Gold

When you get yourself inside the play completely as you write, one of the first things that jumps out at you is the amazing specificity of information and facts that your characters are immersed in and throw back and forth at each other. This, of course, is exactly what you want. By way of the minutia of the characters' lives you get at the truth of any moment and allow your audience to grab on and pull themselves into the world of the play. It's how you give them access to your work.

What's operating here, of course, is the writer's paradox discussed in Chapter 3: Making your play universal in its appeal will depend on its being specific, detailed, and personal. Always concentrate on the seemingly little things, the character-specific details of thought and action that, without fail, reveal so much. It's not just about someone brushing his teeth; it's knowing the brand of toothpaste and whether he uses waxed or unwaxed dental floss. These are the things we relate to. Your dialogue and the subtext beneath it has to be a tapestry of such details and minutia.

Terrence McNally confirms this when he says:

> It's a question of being specific. How hot it is, what day of the week it is, what time of day it is—I have to know these things before I can write a scene. . . . When you're specific, the world becomes so large.

The Architecture of Conversation

The exercise at the end of Chapter 8 is a great way to start looking technically at what goes into writing good dialogue. Here you put down on paper how people really talk to one another. No matter what was discussed in that recorded conversation, the lines ring true on paper because they *are* true. Real life is what you captured on the page. When you write dialogue, you want to create this same sense of truth. Your characters have to be real people in real conversation. Your transcription scene, therefore, holds many clues as to what goes into authentic-sounding dialogue.

Here's a partial list, in no order of importance, of elements found in typical dialogue drawn from real life. See how many you can find in your own transcription scene:

- People are often more interested in saying what they have to say than in listening to what another person is saying.

- People often interrupt the person speaking.

- People often interrupt themselves in the middle of verbalizing a thought and rephrase their thought or completely change the subject.

- When people get excited, they often talk over each other.

- People often repeat themselves, restating ideas and using the same words and phrases over and over.

- A person can often be identified by the use of certain slang or pet words such as "like," "awesome," "incredible," "you know," "man," "dude," and so on.

- People often speak in incomplete sentences.

- People often have a difficult time getting out exactly what they're trying to say.

- Some people swear a lot.

- People almost always use contractions.

- People rarely say the name of the person they're speaking to.

- Pauses are part of a conversation.

- Usually there's some kind of physical gesture or action connected with verbal communication.

- What people are doing physically during a conversation often works its way into the dialogue.

- One person will often give verbal encouragement while another person is speaking, such as "right on," "uh-huh," "you tell it, man," "yeah," and so on.

- One person will unintentionally pick up the diction of another person in the same conversation.

This list could go on.

Start examining what's happening when people talk to each other. Listen closely to conversations. Train your ears to hear in a new, analytical way the shape and coloration of ordinary speech in a variety of settings. Study the changing pace and tempo—how one person manages to dominate, how arguments build and dissipate, how word choices and use of language create distinct individual voices, how physical gesture and action influence and contribute to the verbal give and take.

Emily Mann, who uses a similiar exercise with her students at Princeton, declares:

> It's critical that you start to hear how people really talk. My
> students go off and interview each other, and then sit and write
> what they remember was said. Then, the next exercise is to
> transcribe what they *really* said. And they find out they hadn't
> listened at all. They had put all their own stuff onto the other
> person. They had no idea about how people really speak.

Every possible characteristic of real-life conversation should be at your disposal when you write dialogue. But you can only make use of these if you know specifically what they are.

The Sentence in Dialogue

As you begin putting down on paper how people communicate orally, you quickly realize the extent to which the rules of grammar are broken in casual conversation. There isn't always a verb in every sentence, and often a response will only consist of a word or two. When people talk to each other their only goal is to communicate thoughts and ideas. They never stop to think how it might look written out on a page.

Your job, of course, is to lend accuracy to your characters' utterances, no matter how many rules are broken. For example, if a character is shocked by someone's request for something, he or she might respond:

> "Never. Do you hear me? No way. Ridiculous. Impossible. Out
> of the question."

I count one complete sentence out of six. The periods serve an important function here of separating this series of short but distinct thoughts, each meant to hit the other character like a dart. The whole line becomes the "sentence."

It's imperative that you put down on the page exactly what your people really would say, articulately or not. That's your only concern, so use or break whatever rules of grammar and punctuation necessary to accomplish this.

Creating Distinct Voices

A common trap beginning playwrights fall into, usually without realizing it, is writing lines for different characters that all sound the same. The voice of each character is indistinguishable from the others. This almost always creates a flatness in the writing; it eventually becomes monotonous. Don't make the mistake of leaving it up to the actors to supply the needed contrasts between voices. Actors, of course, will help. However, the writing must offer up characters who have their own distinct diction and way of speaking. All good playwrights provide this. It's a given.

People start forming their thoughts into words a millisecond after their brains have conceived them and usually start sentences before they know how they're going to finish them. One person might consistently speak in beautifully shaped, articulate sentences. Another, though eager to communicate something, has difficulty putting thoughts into words and is constantly interrupting him- or herself in a struggle to latch onto a precise image or expressive phrase. As a result, the former may convey a strong sense of confidence and an intimidating presence, while the latter may come across as timid, less intelligent, and unsure. The point here is that people deal differently with this process of birthing ideas into words; brains are connected to tongues in different ways. Keeping this in mind will help you create distinct, individualized voices in dialogue, giving each of your characters a diction of his or her own.

As discussed in Chapter 6, writing exploratory monologues helps immeasurably in discovering how your characters talk and what makes each voice unique. Look these over and attune yourself to the subtle differences in word choices and the ease or unease with which each character forms thoughts into words. Look for repetition of certain favorite words, the use of sophisticated or pretentious words, frequent or rare use of vulgarity, and so on. If you discover that the characters sound similar, try making adjustments. Experiment with ways of making the voices distinct, even in subtle ways.

Using Vulgar Language

There are four general truths to keep in mind concerning the use of vulgar language in plays.

First, its impact diminishes the more it's used. This is a simple fact. Accordingly, if swearing is used sparingly, it will have more power when a character finally makes the choice to use it. There are logical moments to let loose with a few expletives, such as when a character is in a fit of anger, and these almost always have more punch if you've held back beforehand. If a character is prone to use bad language when speaking normally, so be it. Just be warned that repeated use will most likely *reduce* the impact you might want in big emotional outbursts.

Second, an excess of vulgarity can have an unintended comic effect. I once was at the preview of a serious off-Broadway play about soldiers in Vietnam. The production was beautifully mounted and acted. From the first moments of the performance, however, the audience started snickering. They eventually laughed outright at what was obviously intended as serious material. The problem was that the dialogue was very true to the speech of young grunts in a combat unit, and the word "fuck" and its numerous variations peppered every line. As accurate as this was, in the play it sounded funny, and people couldn't help hearing it that way. It was clear that the writer needed to cut back drastically on the use of obscenities. Doing so would have easily eliminated the unwanted laughter without reducing the feel of the foxhole world. If you have characters who speak vulgarly, try not to overdo it. In the theater, a little filthy language goes a long way.

Of course, David Mamet immediately comes to mind as an exception to this. He uses a great deal of profanity in a number of his successful plays. But Mamet's genius for writing dialogue for vulgar male characters, as in *Glengarry Glen Ross,* is so stylistically refined that he manages to pull most of us (but not all) along in spite of the language. He sometimes intentionally provokes laughter as his characters, debasing the English language totally, descend into gibberish. Accordingly, I suggest you study closely how he accomplishes this and then proceed with caution when you find yourself creating foul-mouthed characters. Just be sure you know what you're doing when you use it.

Third, the audience you're writing for often affects how you use vulgarity. While one group would be revolted by any cursing, another would be able to comfortably absorb extremely offensive language of all kinds. And different audiences will be offended and upset by different kinds of cursing. I've discovered in teaching playwriting to young African-American "street" kids, for example, that they would very rarely have a character curse using variations on the names Jesus Christ or God. For cultural reasons, most people in their world (who comprise the audience they write for) just don't use this form of cursing, and they know it would be extremely offensive. The "f" word and a wide range of other colorful expletives, on the other hand, are used constantly. Of course, with almost any audience, if you use words or phrases such as "Jesus Christ" in cursing, you should be aware that you're likely to alienate people in the audience who are believing Christians or members of the clergy or who believe on principle that the things held sacred by any faith should not be profaned for the sake of a touch more "realism" in a play.

The same point can be made about the more extreme ethnic slurs that pepper our language. If alienating people is your intention, or if you don't care, so be it. However, it's always worth taking the time to consider your target audience and what will be tolerated and what won't. A good basic discipline is to be tough on yourself whenever you have a character curse. Ask yourself: "Is it absolutely necessary, given the character's personality, to convey the sense of the moment and the character's emotional state?" If so, keep it in. If not, try finding another way of conveying what you want without the potentially offensive language.

Fourth, it's often possible to remove profanity from a script or replace it with less offensive language and not miss it at all. This may at first seem like a preposterous statement, but it's true in most cases. I'm not suggesting that you sanitize your plays. Rather, I'm saying that even in the most angry, emotionally charged moments, it's rarely the cursing that makes it work, but the deeper underlying dramatic support supplied in the writing, coupled with the actor's ability to tap into the inner emotional state of the character at that moment. In some of the best plays ever written these heightened moments of anger have little or no profanity at all.

Plausible "Mechanics"

Before writing dialogue around the performance of some specific physical task, such as making a pot of coffee, having someone run down to the corner store for something, or mixing drinks, be aware of how long it takes to execute the task. A common pitfall among beginning playwrights is incorporating an activity into a scene without carefully considering the "mechanics" of time and effort involved in actually doing it. If you have a character put a pot of water on to boil in a scene, the pot can't begin whistling thirty seconds later. Likewise, someone drinking a can of beer normally isn't asking for another a page or two later, unless the point is that he or she is chugging it down. When this kind of reality distortion occurs, the red light of a lie detector flashes in the mind of every audience member. When the mechanics of the task are being presented dishonestly, the scene plays false, no matter how good your dialogue is.

Work out the mechanics of an activity, then, before you attempt writing it. Preparing a meal, getting drunk, running off to change clothes, and so on, are the kinds of activities that tend to weave themselves into conversations in a very organic fashion. If you haven't considered carefully how these tasks are accomplished and the time it takes to accomplish them, you'll ultimately have no choice but to rework the scene. That often means having to rewrite it entirely.

Interestingly enough, you can cheat a bit on how long something takes in performance as opposed to real life. It just has to give the appearance of reality. Audiences are mercilessly demanding on this point. They insist on plausibility.

Incorporating Objects

One of the best ways to add life to dialogue is to incorporate the use of objects into the action. Often the dramatic point of a scene can be punched up by having characters refer to, hold, exchange, or otherwise use an item that literally or symbolically represents what's being talked about. This ties characters into their setting and situation in a specific, organic way. Often the use of an object in a scene can communicate more powerfully than words. The use of Richard's script in the Chapter 8 script formats, for example, functions this way. The physical use of the manuscript by the characters brings home the point much more effectively than if they just talked about Richard's play. As you read and study plays, note how often objects are used and the way they add life and focus to the writing.

The Finesse of Stage Directions

Working with stage directions is an art unto itself. Used properly, these are invaluable tools to enhance your writing, helping the script to lift off the page. Used incorrectly, they can bog your pages down and constantly short-circuit the forward flow. Don't be fooled because they seem merely to be suggestions of actions for actors to execute onstage, because in performance they're never read and often not adhered to, and because ultimately they are—as is everything in the script—only a means to an end. Your play must work on paper first. Therefore, how you use stage directions is as critical as the words you give your characters.

Emily Mann, a director as well as a playwright, says that as a writer she directs her plays on paper and that stage directions are a critical part of her work: "Directorial ideas are very vivid images for me, and I consider them part of the writing so that people can see it as they are reading it."

The most important rule concerning stage directions is that they should succinctly describe only the present-tense action the audience will see and hear. For the reader, they should function only as enhancers, suggesting the look and sound of the play in performance. A common beginner's mistake is to include descriptions that do more than that. You want to resist editorializing. If suddenly you become novelistic and begin describing the thoughts and feelings of your characters or their motives for doing this or that, you clog the script's ability to convey the feel of your play as it will be experienced by the audience.

It is not dialogue alone that pulls people into a creative engagement with the play, inviting them to fill in the blanks and make connections the script only hints at. Stage directions are an integral part of accomplishing this, but only when they explain just the essence of actions—the simple, straightforward, and unadorned physical things that are happening at specific moments onstage.

A Warning on Internal Stage Directions

A common pitfall is overusing internal stage directions as defined in Chapter 8. It's sometimes necessary to utilize them frequently in the first few pages of a play or whenever a new person is introduced, for they help you establish unique personality traits or attitudes. However, the temptation is often great to define the tone of voice, the accompanying look, or the detail of physical action. You may want to make sure that readers, directors, and actors get the point, but you need to rigidly discipline yourself to resist putting it in if there's a good chance they will get the idea without it. What you want to avoid at all costs is stating the obvious—that's the kiss of death. You also don't want to miss the opportunity for people to creatively figure out for themselves how a character is coming across.

The best way to avoid this pitfall is, again, to write for the most intelligent, perceptive people you know. Ask yourself: "Would this smart group need a stage direction here to get what I'm after in this line of dialogue at this moment?" Less perceptive readers will be forced to work harder to get the point of a moment, and certain subtleties may go over the heads of some actors and directors. But that's always better than including something they already know or are in the process of figuring out for themselves.

This is not to say that internal stage directions aren't a wonderful tool. Just be aware that established professional playwrights never overwork them. Take time to study the published version of a number of successful contemporary plays—those written in the last twenty years or so. But be careful: You should use for reference the so-called library or trade editions and not the acting editions of plays, for the latter are texts prepared with additional stage directions that describe the blocking and behavior of the actors in the professional premiere staging of the play; they usually include not only the author's original stage directions but the production stage manager's as well.

When the published script represents what the author actually wrote (which is almost always the case in trade editions of contemporary works), you'll find that internal stage directions are used skillfully and always sparingly.

Describing the Pause

Probably the most important nonverbal element in plays, at least in realistic or quasi-realistic plays, is the pause, or silence between lines of dialogue. Many writers insert the word "pause" or an equivalent to indicate such moments. Harold Pinter is the all-time master at this, and I urge you to look at his plays to see how artfully he orchestrates and weaves them into his work.

I caution you, however, on the overuse of the words "pause" or "silence" and the like when indicating a desired break in your dialogue, because you may be missing the opportunity to bring your script more fully to life by describing the action taking place during such moments. If two characters stare at each other with hostility, that's a significant action. So is one character walking to the window and looking out with his back to the other. You may still determine that the word "pause" best suits your needs at a particular moment, but be tough on yourself here too. Describing the action during the pause instead, if done carefully, can heighten the impact of a moment visually and guide readers to a deeper engagement with the play.

Also keep in mind that it's during pauses that the most profound glimpses into subtext can occur. Often the most important moment in a scene is during the silence that ensues after a poignant line, the moment when a profound decision or realization is made. The audience witnesses this happening during the silence.

These moments are part of the writing. You, the author, are creating a play that includes both verbal and nonverbal elements, and it's how the two interplay with each other that determines the shape and rhythm of each scene and the work as a whole. All nonverbal physical actions influence how your characters relate to each other and what they say and think. And this is especially true for the silences.

Finally, because both plays and music are performed "in time," it could be said that the playwright, like the composer, uses a form of notation when putting his or her work down on paper. **Edward Albee** points out: "A composer deals with whole notes, half notes, eighth notes, dotted eighth notes, all the rest. A playwright does exactly the same things—loud, soft, fast, slow."

This is especially true when capturing a sense of time duration either during a line or between lines. At times you need to be quite accurate in describing pauses and silences, regardless of length. It's one of the significant ways you control how your script moves from moment to moment through a scene.

As the Lights Come Up

Over the past forty years or so, lighting has just about replaced the use of stage curtains, except in the magnificent traditional theaters in the large cities. Today you're much more likely to be ushered into a theater that has the set for the play exposed on the stage with some sort of pre-performance (or, as it's generally referred to, pre-set) lighting washed over it. When the play starts, the house lights, followed by the lighting on the set, fade out. After a few seconds of pitch darkness, the lights come up for the start of the play. The "curtain" has gone up.

Many playscripts today begin with the words "As the lights come up . . ." or "Lights up to reveal . . ." or something similar. This is accepted practice. It's understood that there will probably be an exposed set lit in some way as the audience enters the theater. Most likely some carefully chosen pre-show music will be playing. It's understood that the house lights will fade out at some point. And it is here in the blackness, just before the lights come up, that you the playwright begin your job. Don't concern yourself with what happens earlier unless it's absolutely critical to the opening of your actual story.

This same use of a lighting "curtain" holds for the ending of scenes as well. There are generally two ways to state this, depending on the effect you want. One is to use "the lights fade out" or something similar. This suggests that you envision a relatively slow "pulling back" into darkness after the final line. The other is to use the word "blackout," which means an abrupt, clean stop to the action.

Don't become the lighting designer here. Be concise and to the point. Suggest lighting to help establish the mood and/or general effect you want, but don't get too precise or long-winded. Your job is to tell the story, not to describe on the page how to produce or design the play. This is true even for presentational plays where lighting and set design might feature prominently in how your piece is to work in performance. There's nothing worse for a reader than to be forced to wade through detailed descriptions of exactly how a playwright envisions each theatrical moment playing visually. And directors and designers do not value having the playwright impinge or "head off at the pass" the creative contributions they can make—and these people can serve your play in wonderful ways you could never have foreseen. The wise thing to do is lay out the basics and let your characters and your story sell the play. Leave the actual designing to the designers.

Stage Right, Stage Left, Upstage, Downstage

By the same token, you should avoid getting too specific or technical when describing characters moving around the stage. As is the case with the description of setting(s) discussed in Chapter 8, a good general rule is to describe crosses from one place to another and other physical action only in relation to the setting, not in terms of where it may occur on the traditional proscenium stage. In other words, don't move someone "stage right" or "stage left," or "upstage" or "downstage," or any variation of these (including "SR," "SL," "US," "DS," and so on).

What happens when you do use such technical directorial labels is that you pull your readers out of the world of the play you're trying to coax them into and remind them instead of the artifice of it all. Instead, describe crosses and physical action by referring to pieces of furniture or set pieces, such as: "He moves to the window and looks out" or "She crosses to the table, picks up the letter." This way you're able to keep the reader inside the world of the play, within the *characters'* reality.

In presentational plays, of course, this rule doesn't usually apply, because from the start you're acknowledging the theatricality of the event you're writing for. You want to be constantly reminding the readers and audience that they're in a theater witnessing actors playing at being characters on a stage, pretending to be this place or that place. You're presenting the reality of the theater experience itself and want to reinforce that throughout.

Regardless of style, all crosses and physical movement you describe should be only the essential actions necessary to the telling of your story, and no more. Just as you shouldn't become the lighting designer, likewise you shouldn't become the director. Overworking your stage-movement descriptions only impinges on a director's staging choices and, in most cases, produces more irritation than clarity in the reading of the script.

A Sense of Place

An important element common to all good plays in the representational style is a strong sense of place. This is the way the setting—the physical environment in which the play or scene unfolds—becomes part of the play and of the characters' lives, influencing their behavior, their moods, how they dress, how they look, even how they talk.

If, for example, a play takes place in the living room of a small cluttered house in southern Minnesota during a heat wave in July, the heat should be "felt" whether or not it's directly referred to in the dialogue and physical actions. It should simply be there as a part of the whole, a given that the reader can sense and experience. In the same way, the cramped and cluttered nature of the room should be felt and experienced.

Some writers find this sense of place essential to their process. **Terrence McNally**, for example, says:

> I have to have a very, very graphic idea of what the set looks like. . . . I write very few stage directions in either my

published texts or what the actors get to see. But in my mind I have to see. It's to keep me specific while I'm writing.

McNally's plays generally exude a strong sense of place as a result.

The ways in which setting or environment are made evident in the script have to be subtle, rising naturally out of the lines and actions of your characters. Most of this information is indirect and felt between the lines. However, it's important that from the start you think of establishing and sustaining a strong sense of place as part of your job; don't push off this responsibility to the set, lighting, and costume designers. These artists will obviously play an important role in producing the effects the play needs, but the buck starts and stops with you. If a sense of place is not built into the script, it will never fully materialize in production.

Crying, Tears, and Generally Losing It

A major danger area is the description of characters bursting into tears, crying, sobbing, or otherwise losing their composure. It happens often in plays, to be sure, but be careful how you actually put this down on paper. When a good actor incorporates these moments in performance they ring true. The difficulty lies in the way it looks and works on the page.

The simple fact is that descriptions of intense emotional moments usually read as overdone and even silly. The phrases "his eyes fill with tears," "tears stream down her cheeks," "he breaks into sobs," and the like, wind up being inappropriate because the images they conjure up rarely match the reader's mental picture of how the character is behaving at that moment. They call attention to themselves and distract the reader.

In highly charged moments, it's generally best simply to hint at the physical manifestation of the emotions being dealt with. If you've done your job in the writing, the reader will already know what's occurring or about to happen. Your actors will have even less difficulty knowing. Your subtle, carefully crafted hint, therefore, actually aids readers in visualizing the emotional breaking point and how it manifests itself. They automatically make the tears, sobs, displays of temper, and so on, fit what "plays" for them. And you'll pull them deeper into the experience of your play.

And yet, in your first draft, you shouldn't worry about how descriptions of highly charged emotional moments come out on the page. Subtlety is usually not achieved in the first sweep. Let those tempers be hopelessly lost, and let the tears flow exactly as you see these moments happening. Write it all out. It's only later that you should go back and work at making it all palatable for your readers and actors. We'll consider this more in Chapter 10.

Directors Who Ignore Stage Directions

Mercifully, history and tradition are on the side of the playwright when it comes to the sanctity of the written word—at least, the dialogue. It's generally considered off-limits to change a line of dialogue without the permission of the playwright. Professionally, the Dramatists Guild's minimum basic contract totally prohibits unauthorized changes. The writer, in fact, has the power to shut down a professional production if this occurs. This is where writing for the theater differs enormously from writing for television and film. In the latter fields the Writers Guild—the professional association of film and television writers—bargained away artistic control decades ago, in favor of up-front payments. Not so for playwrights in the Dramatists Guild, fortunately. (See Chapter 12 for more on the Guild.)

Concerning stage directions, however, things aren't quite so clear. Students often ask me: "At what point does the playwright's job stop, and when do the director and actors take over? Won't these other artists ignore my stage directions and do it their own way, even if I'm precise in how I use them? To what extent are they obligated to respect my suggestions about how a physical action should be executed or how a line should be read?"

The degree to which written stage directions should be adhered to or ignored when putting a play on its feet is an important issue for playwrights. (I rarely meet one who doesn't have justifiably strong feelings about it.) Stage directions are there because the writer has determined they're necessary to get across the full sense of a line or moment. They're part of the writing, part of the fabric of the work. The way a character's line is written is often determined by the physical action that has just taken place, is about to take place, or is taking place while he or she is speaking. Attitude, degree of assertiveness, the emotional color of the words uttered, and so on, are all affected by what a character is doing at the time. So when a director or actor decides to ignore the writer's stage direction or reinvent an action for a particular line, the result is usually something other than what was originally intended. Often the whole sense of the moment is changed.

This is a serious problem for playwrights working in the American theater. A current and prominent theory of directing insists that physical action is the director's exclusive domain, that this is how the director puts his or her artistic mark on the work. This approach to directing is fine with the classical authors such as Shakespeare or the Greeks; their works contain few, if any, stage directions to begin with, and even those have often been supplied by editors, not the playwrights themselves. Laying a heavy directorial hand on such plays in terms of concept, setting, and period is often interesting and at times successful. With new or contemporary plays, however, it's a different story.

Recently there have been a number of court cases as playwrights have sued producers for ignoring stage directions. The most famous case to date involved a production of Samuel Beckett's *Endgame* at American Repertory Theater at Harvard University. Beckett sought an injunction to stop the production because the director had decided to set the play in a subway station instead of the neutral wasteland carefully described in the script. Beckett insisted that this would radically change the overall effect he hoped to achieve with the work. Ultimately he lost the case, however, and had to settle for a notice in the program stating that the setting for the play was not that intended by the playwright. Still, the case certainly made an issue of the importance of stage directions and all nonverbal elements of a play as conceived by the playwright.

With new plays, this directorial heavy-handedness should never be allowed. The director's job should always be to work in close collaboration with the playwright, putting on the stage as near an approximation of what was originally intended as possible. In other words, in almost all circumstances stage directions in the script should be taken seriously. If changes are contemplated, the playwright should be consulted and agree to them before they're incorporated into the staging.

I can already hear directors howling disapproval of this position. But there's nothing worse for a playwright—the original creator of the material—than to see his or her play distorted and maligned in its staging, where carefully worked-out orchestrations of lines and physical action have been eliminated and something else inserted which communicates a different thought or feeling. If as a writer you care about your work, and

I'm assuming all writers do, then you have to insist that directors respect what you've written and discuss with you any contemplated "adjustments" before they're put into the production. If they will not agree, don't work with them. If you do, be forewarned: You're setting yourself up for frustration.

Obviously, this whole issue has to be approached with reason. The majority of directors and actors working with new plays do so because they like working with playwrights and want very much to put on the stage what the writer has envisioned. In fact, most are absolutely dedicated to this goal. And often better solutions are found for expressing something in words or action than those you've come up with. Again, it's wonderful when this happens—for the playwright, almost magical. You fall in love with these artists working with your material because they're bringing your vision more fully to life than you thought possible. They're making your play look very good. Yet this will not happen automatically. You always need to make clear the terms of your collaboration. You need to work closely with your director, being constantly watchful as to how your play is taking shape.

Above all, you have to make sure you've captured your complete vision in the script itself. In this business the bottom line is what's on the page.

Reality versus Illusion

As you begin writing, it's important to keep in mind that, at their best, dialogue and stage directions may possess the characteristics of real life, but still belong only to the world of illusion. On the surface, the script has to read so realistically that it sounds like a transcription scene itself. Under the surface and hidden from view, however, is the structural framework that really controls the shape, speed, and intensity of the play. Throughout the writing process you're constantly pulling structural strings and guiding the play in the direction you want it to go. It's often necessary to modify, distort, or condense how something would happen in real life to make it work theatrically. The reality is that the writing of a play is all artifice. Your job is to give it the sound, appearance, and feel of real life.

You might wonder why something this obvious needs to be included in a discussion of playwriting techniques. It's because I've worked with a number of playwrights who hold onto material that isn't working on the stage, insisting "that's the way it happened in real life" and, therefore, "that's the way it's going to stay" in the play. Of course, as the writers they are in control here. They can hold onto as many pages as they like regardless of the strength of evidence indicating they should make adjustments for the sake of the play. And, in most cases, their instincts will eventually lead them to make the necessary changes. However, when playwrights steadfastly refuse to change material because "that's the way it really happened," the result is often self-defeating. What ends up onstage may be accurate, but it can be lethal to the success of the play as a whole.

Practicing the Craft

One of the most difficult aspects of teaching playwriting is convincing students they need to practice the craft before attempting to write their masterpieces. The beginning music composition student would never consider sitting down and writing an entire piano sonata as an early project. Without training, the mind simply isn't up to the task of conceiving such a work when the skills to write it out on the page are only being mastered. The same could be said for a beginning visual artist who dreams of painting large oils that one day might hang in the Museum of Modern Art. It would be impossible to start producing those oils without having a mastery of painting techniques, composition, the interplay of form and content, and the means of translating all that onto the canvas.

Beginning playwrights, however, already have vast experience talking and interacting with people. They've spent a lifetime observing and listening to how people engage with each other. And they already know how to write words and sentences. Their fingers have had years of practice writing and/or typing them onto pieces of paper. The illogical conclusion, therefore, is that the writing of dialogue is something a person should be able to do well automatically. All one has to do is gather the necessary writing material and/or equipment, find the time and a nice place to work, and brilliant lines will just flow out naturally.

Needless to say, the writing of a good play is as much an art as composing a good piano sonata or creating a wonderful painting. And the skills needed to do this must no less be learned through practice and training. Don't be fooled because the materials or components of the art form are people's words and behavior. If anything, this makes the writing of plays that will work onstage an even more difficult task. It's a slippery business because, as discussed throughout this chapter, your job is to create the appearance of reality—to seduce the audience into the world of your play, to get them to believe in your characters and identify with them even though they are a complete fiction. In short, your task is to have your audience recognize and respond to truth in the midst of artifice.

Therefore, if you're just starting out as a playwright or think you might still have something to learn about the craft (which should safely include just about everybody), I strongly suggest you draw from your store of patience and take the time to write at least five practice scenes of the type suggested below before beginning the first draft of your play. The purpose, of course, is to help you gain at least a measure of mastery with the techniques we've been discussing.

Good as your developed idea and character bios may be, plays stubbornly refuse to come to life on the page if you can't write good dialogue and stage directions. If you haven't gained a working knowledge of the tools of the trade, in writing that first draft you will run a genuine risk of being quickly discouraged.

Exercises in Carrot Dangling

Think of a short conflict scene (four to five pages tops) between two characters not in the play you're working on. They know each other well. One person wants something very badly, and the other doesn't want the first to get under any circumstances what he or she wants. Have them argue heatedly over a very specific thing. Invent a thorough backstory for them and complete a short-form biography for each.

Next, write the scene so that the actual point of contention, the thing wanted by one of them, is *rarely or never directly mentioned in the scene.* Make your readers figure out what the two characters are arguing about; make them have to lean into the scene and use their intelligence; force them to engage creatively and get inside the material. Refer to the situations listed below for examples of the kinds of scenes that make for good practice material.

As you write, think of "the art of carrot dangling" and try to apply everything discussed in this chapter. Become the eavesdropper. Avoid megaphoning information. Write for a smart audience. Use details and specifics. Allow glimpses of the submerged iceberg. Put yourself inside the play. Create distinct character voices. Try to integrate the use of an appropriate object. Establish a strong sense of place.

When you finish a draft, go back through it and work on subtlety. Cut out anything you might not need in the dialogue or stage directions. As the saying goes, "If in doubt, cut it out."

When you think you've gotten it just right, give it to two or three of your target audience members—the intelligent ones you had in mind while writing the scene. After they've read it, and without telling them anything about the scene, ask them to describe in detail the characters' physical appearances and personalities as they saw and felt them. Have them explain what they saw and heard happening, and when, if ever, they figured out exactly what the argument was about. Have them describe the setting and how strongly they felt a sense of place.

Don't get into a conversation with them on any of these points, and never let them ask you what you were trying to accomplish in the scene. As soon as you do that, their reactions are no longer trustworthy, because, as friends, they'll only tell you what they think you want to hear. So aim for honest reactions out of them and, making no comment, listen closely to what they have to say.

This type of feedback is the only valuable kind for playwrights. It will tell you plainly where you succeeded and failed in staying ahead of your readers and the degree to which you managed to communicate what you intended.

With their responses fresh in your mind, go back to your writing table and see how you could make the scene work better. Don't hesitate to throw things out, to edit and trim, especially at the front end where first drafts tend to run long and express the obvious. Be honest with yourself and tough-minded. Rewrite where you have to. Then try testing it again with two or three different target readers. In this way you'll begin to get a feel, a "touch," for how to bring your pages to life, for what works and what doesn't.

You need to work your muscles as a playwright—and rarely can you overwork them. Most established playwrights I know "work out" writing these scenes in their notebooks or journals all the time, especially when they're between plays. So go through this procedure with several practice scenes, and try a variety of situations. Try the same scene in a different setting. Test things out, and stretch yourself with different types of personalities. Work on establishing different moods. Try writing some that are very funny, others that are very violent, still others that are very sad. Some with lots of action and some with very little.

The operative word here is *practice*. Accordingly, resist using characters or situations from the play you're working on. Think of these scenes as separate training exercises and approach them as such. Save the play for when you think you've developed some control of the craft. Once you start writing scenes from the play itself, the material automatically begins taking shape, whether you like what comes out onto the page or not. And it's impossible to go back and unwrite something completely. You've disturbed and tampered with precious virgin soil, so to speak. So experiment and practice with material that's an end in itself.

Suggested Practice Scenes

Although ranging widely in intensity and mood, these situations all involve some sort of battle between the characters. In some, the conflict is out in the open and immediately apparent; in others, it is submerged in the subtext of the situation. If one of them strikes a chord in you, work with it. Better yet, use these situations to help you spark ideas for scenes of your own.

1. A young man, a sophomore at an Ivy League college, pays a visit to his successful business-executive father and announces that he's quitting school in the middle of the year to join a rock band and go on tour. The father won't hear of it, but the boy has already made up his mind. The scene takes place at the father's large, well-appointed office.

2. A boy, 17, and a girl, 18, are in a hospital waiting room. Their heads and hands are bandaged and the boy has an arm in a sling. Less than an hour before, the car they were in went off a country road and hit a tree. The boy was driving. They're now awaiting word on the condition of another boy who is in the operating room, critically hurt. The girl and the boy in the operating room are going steady. All three were drinking in the car at the time of the accident. None of the parents has yet been reached.

3. Three women (of college age or older) have been spending the summer traveling through Europe together. As the scene opens, one of the women has just left their hotel room to return to the States because she wasn't having a good time. The other two have never gotten along with each other, but their hostility has grown acute during the four weeks they've been together. The woman who left was

fed up with their constant fighting. The other two are stunned by the sudden shift in plans, realizing that without their friend, they couldn't possibly stay together. They're forced to begin dealing with their animosity.

4. Two bachelors, good friends in their late twenties, are celebrating at a bar the night before one of them is getting married. The groom-to-be announces that he doesn't want to get married after all. His friend tries to convince him that he should.

5. At a restaurant, an unmarried high school teacher in her late fifties informs her younger brother that he'll have to help pay for the nursing home where their ailing mother is about to be admitted. For many years the mother has lived with the woman, and until recently she has managed to take care of her. The brother, married with four children living at home, owns a business that isn't doing well, but he's kept this a secret from his sister. Now he tells her he can't help out financially. The sister sees this as the latest in a series of attempts by her brother to weasel out of any responsibility regarding their mother.

6. A boy, 16, and his girlfriend, 15, have run away from home in New Jersey and are on a state highway somewhere in Nebraska heading for California. It's the middle of the night, and they've been hitchhiking for three days. Now they're out of money and have no place to stay. The girl is having serious second thoughts about what they're attempting and has decided she wants to go home. The boy won't consider returning.

7. In the kitchen of their apartment, a young woman, 18, confronts her single, divorced mother, 38, with her decision to leave home after graduating from high school. She's made arrangements to move into an apartment with two girlfriends. Having recently broken up with a man she thought she was going to marry, the mother desperately wants her daughter to stay with her. The daughter is just as desperate to get out from under her mother's problems and control.

8. Two single lawyers—a man and a woman, both 29—meet unexpectedly one evening in their firm's library. Both are ambitious, eager for advancement. Their friendship is professional; there's no romantic interest. That day the woman has been awarded a big case the man

expected he'd be getting. This is a big break for her and almost guarantees that she'll become a partner in the firm. The man is bitter. She's aware he wanted the case.

9. Two young men, both 20 and best friends, are taking a lunch break at a construction site during a severe July heat wave. Intelligent and athletic, they've both been stars on their high school sports teams, but neither has gone on to college. Both have steady girlfriends, and the couples spend a great deal of time together. The father of one of them owns the construction company they work for. As the two have lunch, one announces he's decided to start college full-time in the fall. This is a big shock to his friend, who has no desire to change his life-style or lose his friend.

10. A talented actress, 26, visits her father, a successful theater producer, at his New York apartment and asks him to help her get a part in a new play he's producing. He's never wanted her to go into the business and has consistently refused to open any doors for her. Having had zero luck in landing a job for over two years, she's desperate. The role she's interested in would be perfect for her.

11. Two college seniors, a man and a woman, meet by chance in the library stacks. Each is involved romantically with the best friend of the other, although the four don't spend much time together. As a result, though these two don't really know each other very well, they know a lot about each other. In the scene, they realize for the first time that they're attracted to each other.

12. A brother, 16, and a sister, 19, are alone in the kitchen of their home, having just been told their parents are separating. The father has left the house. The mother is upstairs in her room; their younger brother, 10, is at a friend's house and doesn't know yet what's happening. The news gives the brother a sense of relief and the sister a deep sadness.

13. A man in his late forties confronts his seriously ailing father with the news that the elderly man must leave the house he's lived in for forty-five years and enter a nursing home. The father refuses to consider this, asserting he'd rather die first. The son, who's always been intimidated by his father, holds his ground and insist the move be

made. The cost of the nursing home will put a definite strain on family finances, but circumstances rule out the possibility of the father moving in with the son.

14. A boy, 17, is working the night shift at a filling station. At 3 A.M. another boy, 17, arrives to challenge him about dating his former girlfriend. He is physically bigger, angry, and looking for a fight because he's warned the attendant several times to stop seeing her. The attendant, not the type to be bullied around, really loves the girl and has no intention of breaking it off, especially because he's being ordered to do so.

15. In the kitchen of her home, a woman, 45, confronts her son, 27, who has just told her he has decided to leave the family business run by his father. The business is failing miserably, and the son, who's stayed this long out of loyalty to the father, desperately needs to get out on his own. The mother knows this news will break her husband's spirit, for he has poured his whole life into the business and is stubbornly trying to keep it alive. It's early evening on the father's birthday.

16. Two couples, all high school seniors, are sitting in a car in a county park late at night. They've been there for some time trying to deal with the news that two boys, close friends of all four, have been killed in a car crash earlier that evening. The impact of the tragedy is just starting to hit.

17. A brother and sister are alone together in their parents' living room after the funeral of their father that day. All the guests have left, and their mother is upstairs in her bedroom. The brother never got along with the father and has been estranged from the family for years. The sister, bitter at her brother for abandoning the family, loved the father and was close to him through his final, drawn-out illness. The brother now, for the first time, regrets never having reconciled with the father.

18. A young husband and wife, both 25 and talented actors, encounter each other at 4 a.m. in their New York apartment as he arrives home from his job driving a cab—a job he's been doing nearly two years while making the rounds of auditions. He's tired and discouraged. She's also been making the rounds while working as a waitress. This week she has been called back twice for a lead role in an Off-Broadway show. She's kept this news from her husband because of his

growing depression. But earlier this evening she learned that she has landed the part and now has to tell him the news.

19. A single mother waits up for her daughter, 18, to get home from a date with a 25-year-old man whom she's been seeing for several weeks. The mother has made no secret that she doesn't trust the man and is convinced the relationship will be a disaster for her child. The daughter, who is falling in love, arrives home. The mother confronts her.

20. In a bus depot at 2 A.M., a boy, 17, finds his younger brother, 15, in the process of running away from home. The younger brother has had an increasingly difficult time living under his father's authority; earlier this night he and the father have had a bitter argument. The older brother, who's always had a good relationship with the father, tries to talk his younger brother into coming back home. It's important to him that his brother and father reconcile, but the younger brother is convinced it's hopeless.

21. A woman presents her live-in boyfriend with an ultimatum: Either commit to marriage or get out of her life. Although he says he loves her, he refuses to commit to anything permanent, insisting that what they have now is the best of all possible arrangements. This is an old issue between them and, although a part of her still loves him, she's convinced that only marriage or separation can resolve her doubts about her future.

22. A girl, 15, who is moving from a small town in upstate New York to California with her family, comes to say goodbye to her best friend, another 15-year-old girl. It is the morning of her departure. Neither wants this to happen or knows what to say. The scene takes place in the room of the girl staying behind, a place where the two of them have spent countless hours together.

23. In the kitchen of their apartment, a divorced, single woman, 38, confronts her son, 16, as he arrives home late from a week-night wrestling practice and announces he must go see his girlfriend. The woman is preparing an important dinner party for the following evening with her boss and other professional colleagues, and her son has promised to help her clean the apartment. The boy is upset because he's had a fight with his girlfriend and needs to work things

out. The mother, tired and behind schedule, needs his help or she'll be up all night. She expects him to keep his promise.

24. In the sunroom of their large, well-appointed home, a young woman, 18, announces to her wealthy, conservative mother that she's decided she's not going to college in the fall but wants to spend the next year travelling alone through Europe. The mother insists the daughter start college as planned but the daughter doesn't give up on her plan, even if it means having to finance the trip on her own.

25. Two 15-year-old boys, long-time best friends, say goodbye to each other on the day one of them is leaving with his family for Europe, where the father has taken a job with a multinational company. They've both been upset about this for some time, but have put off the moment of truth. Now, on the front porch of the boy who's not leaving, his friend returns a baseball glove and two bats. They try to remain stoic and in control, while inside they're feeling a tremendous sense of loss and a genuine fear that they'll never see each other again.

26. Two sisters (or brothers), 18 and 16, on the pier of the family yacht club, have been waiting for hours for their parents to return from a day's sailing. There has been a severe sudden storm earlier that afternoon and the parents are long overdue. The Coast Guard has been out searching but there's no trace of the boat, although reports have come in about several capsizings. The two are just starting to realize what they may be facing.

27. Two young American soldiers, both 18 and wounded, find themselves in a bombed-out church after a bloody battle. Having escaped after the enemy routed the rest of their company in hand-to-hand combat, they don't like each other but are aware that a mop-up operation is in progress and that if they're found, they'll be shot. Now, almost beyond fear, they try to deal with their situation and each other.

28. A man and a woman (choose the ages) who have been dating for three months are having dinner together (choose the place). The woman realizes she has to end the relationship because his feelings for her are far more serious than her feelings for him. In fact, he's fallen hopelessly in love with her, and although she likes him as a friend, she has no interest in getting in any deeper. He feels he needs

her in his life and can't imagine living without her. In the scene she tells him it's over, but he refuses to believe it.

29. In the kitchen of their home, a husband and wife, both in their forties and with two children in grade-school, struggle with the man's intensifying need to quit his job as a bank executive—a job he's hated for years—and pursue a writing career for which he has proven talent. He wants them to move from their suburban life near a large city to a small family farm in Vermont. Because of a recent inheritance, they can afford the move, but the wife loves her work as a successful lawyer and isn't ready to leave her job. This is not the first time this issue has come up, but the man has reached the end of his patience with his current career and life-style.

30. On the backyard deck of her home, a woman in her mid-forties confides in a close woman friend that she and her husband are separating after twenty years of marriage because she has fallen in love with another man. The friend is devastated by the news and, risking their friendship, challenges the woman to rethink her decision. The woman is hurt, offended, and angered by the challenge, but the friend, sincerely thinking the woman is making a grave mistake, refuses to tell her what she wants to hear.

This gives you an idea of the kinds of situations that make for good practice scenes. All of these have been thoroughly field-tested and often the results have been quite wonderful. Obviously, in many cases the sexes and ages of the characters can be changed. Reading through these, however, should make it clear that the possibilities are endless.

The important thing at this point is to pick a few juicy situations you relate to and start writing. That's the only way you're going to learn how to use the tools of the trade and develop the touch for good dialogue writing. Think of yourself as an athlete-in-training: You need to get yourself in shape, and the only way you can do that is by working your muscles over and over again—"no pain, no gain," as they say.

So push yourself. There's really no way to cut corners in matters of craft. In giving your writing the breath of life, you can only get better.

10

YOUR FIRST DRAFT

It's scary, and I want it to be scary. It can be healing, and I want it to be healing. It can be hurtful, and I want it to be hurtful. Those things you want. It's a wrenching process.

—ROMULUS LINNEY

When I asked **Arthur Miller** to describe what it's like for him to write his first drafts, he thought for a moment and said: "It's a bit like trying to cross a crevasse, and you have an anchor you throw across the empty space and hope it'll catch onto something on the other side. And then you can build a bridge across on that rope."

If you've been working through the process as presented in this book, you've already procured your anchor, thrown it across the crevasse, and managed to have it catch onto something. You're now about as ready as you're ever going to be to begin building that bridge. The time is at hand to commence with the actual writing and see what happens. As in all aspects of creating a play, this phase continues to be an ongoing process, an evolution.

We'll now consider what you need to keep in mind as you tackle your first rough draft. In succeeding chapters we'll examine the rewriting process, and look at how you can continue developing your play out there in the world at large.

Most people who set out to write plays start at this point in the process. That's the conclusion I've drawn after years of reading new play manuscripts. There's little or no time spent developing and shaping an idea into a workable structural design or getting to know well the characters who *are* the play. And more often than not there's little evidence of some mastery of the tools and techniques of getting everything down on paper in a potent and professional manner. People are in much too much of a hurry to get that finished script in their hands.

If you've focussed your idea dramatically in terms of central character, dominant need, conflict, resolution, and premise; if you've thoroughly explored your characters' external and internal lives, both past and present; if you've given your idea structure and shape, then you've already started writing your play. In fact, you're somewhere in the middle of it.

I'm not suggesting that this next step is going to be easy. First drafts are rarely that. There are no magic formulas. You simply have to sit down and write the damn thing. However, you should definitely take comfort in the fact that you've prepared yourself to deal with just about any situation you might stumble upon along the way.

Let's look at the various aspects involved in actually writing the first draft and how best to get through it.

A Title That Works

Now's a good time to reexamine your working title. Ask yourself if it's the best you can come up with. Does it convey the essence of what you want to deal with in the play? Or has your thinking adjusted significantly enough in the process of exploring and developing your idea and characters that it no longer reflects the basic tone or feel that you're after?

You might be lucky and conclude that your current title still works perfectly, maybe even better than it did earlier. If this is the case, consider it a little gift from the Muse. Most likely, however, you'll find you're not entirely pleased with what you've been using and probably never have been. As a label it's inaccurate or just too generic. It sits on the page without punch or sparkle. It's not a title that would get you interested in the play behind it. When this is the case, you owe it to yourself and your play to come up with something better. And now's the time to do it. These literally are the first words of your first draft.

What you want to come up with, of course, is something provocative and alluring. Something that will stop people in their tracks and make them want to devour the play then and there. Something that captures perfectly the idea you're dealing with and that will resonate loudly in the reader's mind after the play has been experienced. Titles are a critical part of the writing. A good title does not a good play make, of course, but a weak title can threaten the potential life of a good play. It's a label for what's waiting to be read between those covers (and, later on, for what's running in that theater), and it should reflect the life and passion to be found in it. In other words, settle for nothing less than the perfect title.

Here's a simple title-search exercise to use when you haven't stumbled onto the one you think the play deserves. It usually produces great results. First, carefully reread your latest and most accurate idea worksheet and plot treatment. Then, keeping your dramatic premise in mind, think about how you want your audience to feel at the end of the play as the lights fade to black. What's the essence of that feeling? Try to feel it yourself. Now write down as quickly as you can a list of every word or phrase that describes or connects to it. Put down anything that comes to mind through free association, keeping each item as short as possible.

Don't think about coming up with a title when you do this. Just make a list of words or phrases that in some way captures the essence of your play emotionally, intellectually, or both. And don't judge anything you put down. If some of these words or phrases sound silly or stupid, put them down anyway. Just let these descriptions flow out of you. Don't stop and dwell on any of them. Concentrate only on that feeling you want the play to leave the audience with. Force yourself to make as long a list as you possibly can. Stop only when you have at least fifty items.

When you've run completely dry, put the list away without looking back over it for at least a couple of hours. Better yet, set it aside until tomorrow. Engage in something else in the meantime. Write a practice scene or, better yet, go see someone else's play. The important thing here is to not go back over this list immediately, but rather to give your mind distance from it. The exercise is largely worthless if you ignore this step because the distancing factor is critical. Your goal is to come back to the list fresh, as disengaged and objective as possible.

When you do return to the list, read it over carefully, putting check marks next to the items that trigger even the slightest positive response.

Don't necessarily be looking for the title yet. Then look back over the checked words or phrases. Determine which are the strongest. See if any can be combined into something interesting. If so, put them together. Then look at the list again.

Usually by this time a title has jumped out at you. All of a sudden you see it sitting there in that list. You may have to create it by putting together words from two or more items on the list, but it'll be there. I realize this sounds too good to be true, but it almost always works. Hundreds of my students have had greats results using this exercise. The two keys to success are: First, focusing clearly on what you want to leave your audience with at the end of the play; and second, giving your mind free rein when composing the initial list. If you can manage these two things, chances are you'll find your perfect title.

Why dwell so long now on finding a good title? Because if you're excited about what you're calling your play, it helps generate excitement for the play as a whole. And you need all the enthusiasm you can muster as you move into the draft stage. The title you come up with here, of course, still may not be what you finally end up with. You need to test it again after you've written the play. Then you might find that a line or part of a line says it even better. More often than not, however, it's this exercise done now that produces the one that sticks.

Starting Out

You're now about to head off on a long run. You know your route, you have a good pair of shoes, and you're eager to get started. As you step outside you can either set off immediately or take time to warm up your leg muscles by doing a few stretches. There's no hard and fast rule here, but it's generally recommended that you do a little warm-up before heading off.

As a suggested warm-up, write a short scene or two not from the play involving your characters. These don't have to be long. Maybe four or five pages or even less. Draw the situations from episodes in their shared backstory or from appropriate milestones from the long-form bios. Or invent something. The goal here is to get them talking, to get your ear tuned to their distinct voices, to bring them into clear focus. This is sometimes a help in getting you over the hurdle of beginning that first page of the play itself.

There are two ways to position yourself. One is to spread out all the work you've done on the play so far: play idea worksheet, character bios, backstory timelines, plot treatment, and anything else that might be of help. Look them all over carefully one more time and then, leaving them handy for reference, simply start writing the words "As the lights come up," and you're off.

The other way is to file all this prep work away and never look at it at all, the theory being that you've done the work so it's up there in your head somewhere. Your brain will dish it out to you when and if you need it. In turn, this allows your characters more freedom to do and say what they want and reduces the temptation to force them into a predetermined mold.

There is no one best way to get started. You simply have to discover a procedure that you feel comfortable with, that puts you at ease. If all your prep work makes you nervous, get it off the table. If it gives you a sense of security, keep it there.

I find I work best keeping the index cards or the treatment available as a sort of rough guide, but days will go by without my referring to them. I file the rest of the material. The day usually comes during rewrites when I find it useful to take another look at the bios, backstories, and so on, but in most cases this doesn't happen during the writing of the first draft, which has a way of taking on a life of its own very quickly.

Ultimately, of course, no one but you really cares how you write your play. People are only interested in how good the finished product is. So do what you're most comfortable with and get started. As **Romulus Linney** says about getting started with his first draft: "I have mulled it over and thought about it this way and that way, and there is always a moment when you say, 'Okay, for better or worse, here we go.'"

The Computer versus Longhand

In talking with many playwrights in recent years, I've detected no clearly favored way of working. Writing directly into a computer works for some because it allows for a clean copy as the work proceeds and at the end of each day. **Romulus Linney** states:

> You can do wonderful things with a computer, God bless
> them. They can't write the play for you, but they can sure help.
> You used to have to paste things together, and if you changed

one line, you had to rewrite all the pages, and you'd go crazy. Now with computers that's done for you. So, very often when I've done some work on a play, I'll just run the whole thing out again and look at it. I love using the technology.

On the other hand, some writers work in longhand so they can make quick marginal notes as they proceed and keep all their thinking out on the page in front of them. **David Ives** explains:

> I write everything longhand. I don't write on a keyboard. I find that whatever I write on a keyboard ends up very superficial and on the surface. When I'm writing longhand, it's so easy to write notes in the margins and at the top of the page about what's going to happen. So as I'm writing I may realize that this character is going to say such and such to that character at a certain point, and I scribble that in and sort of box it off. And tomorrow when I go back to these pages, I'll see all the things I've written and the whole process of writing this. It's like I'm rethinking along the way. I find that there's a process to writing with my hand that is like the speed and process of my thoughts.

Obviously, you have to come up with what works best for you. If you're just starting out I suggest you experiment with both methods or a combination of them. The right one will quickly surface.

Writing In or Out of Order

Most playwrights say they write their first drafts from beginning to end. It only makes sense the first time out that you start at the beginning and work your way through, one step after another. Because significant discoveries are always made along the way, the writing has an accumulative, one-thing-leads-to-another order to it. The first draft builds on itself as the pages pile up.

Of course, there's nothing to stop you from writing out of sequence. Again, the playwrights I interviewed make clear that there isn't only one way to write a play. In some cases, jumping around to different scenes may be exactly what you need initially to get close to your characters, to capture the tone you're after, or to get a feel for what you're really trying to accomplish with the play overall.

If you do try this, however, be careful not to fall too deeply in love with what you've written; always consider such forays to be preliminary explorations. Keep in mind the four precautions discussed in Chapter 3 concerning exploratory writing. A case in point is **Edward Albee**'s experience while working on *Who's Afraid of Virginia Woolf?*:

> I was writing the first act . . . and I got an idea for a scene for the third act . . . which I wrote down. It was about seven pages, and I thought it was pretty good. Then I went back and finished the first act, wrote the second act, and got into the third act and remembered I'd written these seven pages for the third act. I found them and read them, and I still thought they were pretty good. And I tried to put them in the play, but I discovered that the characters wouldn't say them. They no longer fit into the play because I'd written them too soon. They were perfectly valid. It was good dialogue; it was not extraneous. The characters could have said them, but I clearly didn't want the characters to say them anymore because I'd written them too damn soon.

If you do attempt writing scenes out of sequence, keep an open mind, or you'll risk short-circuiting fantastic discoveries because you're clinging to something you've written early on. Everything that comes before in some way has to conform to that wonderful scene. Albee had the discipline to reject his seven pages, but this is often very difficult to do. I strongly recommend, at least for your first few efforts as a playwright, that you not open yourself to this potential pitfall. It's always safer starting a first draft at the beginning and pushing your way through, one step at a time.

Staying Loose

Always approach the writing of your first draft as an exploration. You know basically where you plan to end up and how you're going to get there, but, as **Terrence McNally** says: "There are a lot of surprises and things that happen along the way." And to keep yourself open for these surprises you have to guard yourself from becoming too fixed as to the exact route.

As discussed in Chapter 7, your plot treatment is a useful guide, but don't let it dictate what happens every step of the way. **Horton Foote** cautions: "Sometimes you get so driven and you want so badly to work things out, and sometimes you just have to relax and let it go."

As we've seen, this means to stay sensitive to your characters' whims and fancies, and when they do something surprising or unpredictable, go along with them. Let them play out new moments or actions that may marvelously inform the play or help you see how to reshape a scene into something more significant and exciting. And if your people suddenly take a major detour and begin wandering down unexplored backroads, getting further and further away from what you thought you were heading for, let them go. At some point one of two things will happen: Your characters will go hopelessly off the track and you'll need to revert to your planned route, or they'll stumble into a wonderful new landscape and go on a different journey. If you like what they've discovered and decide to keep pushing ahead in this new direction, at some point you'll have to reassess what you're trying to accomplish with your play.

And that's okay. That's what it means to explore in this first draft. If reassessing is called for, coach yourself to be neither rigid nor anxious. You have the tools to do that reassessing.

You've never been through this territory before. How do you know your preplanned route is the best one? How do you know that your prior hunch about a final destination is really the only satisfying place to end up? You'll only make these determinations conclusively once you're "out there," living in the reality of your play as it unfolds. As **Romulus Linney** says:

> There's a lot of giving yourself up to it and being not so much
> in command of anything. It's like giving yourself up to
> something that's going to take you with it and that you're going
> to go with, wherever it goes. It may work out, it may not, but
> you're going to go ahead and go there.

First drafts, then, should be an adventure, and you have to remember you're simply in the process of discovering your play. The last thing you want to do is charge through this first pass at your material with blinders on. You might march right by a pathway which, if taken, would have led you to a stunning discovery, possibly even to a different and much more interesting destination.

Those First Few Pages

As you start out, there are several things to keep in mind about openings of plays that always hold true. First, an audience demands to know very quickly who and what the play is about. Even in your first draft you should present the main issue promptly or at least give a strong hint as to what's in store for the central character in terms of his or her major dilemma. The set-up of Act I (as discussed in Chapter 7) should begin to be addressed as soon as the play starts unfolding.

Study the openings of some successful plays. Consistently, the hook is set right away. In *Death of a Salesman,* the opening scene brings Willy home unexpectedly because he's no longer able to function normally. In *The Crucible,* we're immediately presented with John Proctor's relationship with Abigail Williams in the very place where the witchcraft hysteria begins. In *'night, Mother,* Jesse announces her intention to kill herself in the first few minutes of the play. Rarely will you find a successful play where some direct indication of the main character and dilemma isn't offered up in the first few pages. Even when it is subtle and indirect, the hook is set nevertheless.

The audience has to know how to engage with the play before they can know how to listen to it. A relentless stream of words comes at them rapidly, and until they're given something to focus on they have nothing to latch onto, no way to process what they're hearing. Nothing starts making dramatic sense until you've provided these essentials, and then, indeed, the audience hooks itself. They want to engage with the play—that's what they came for. So allow them to as soon as you possibly can. As **John Guare** explains it, your job is "to let the audience know what the rules are so they can then go on this voyage with you."

Lanford Wilson, referring to the writing of *Talley's Folly,* recalls: "I wrote the entire introduction to say, 'This is going to be about time; this is going to be a comedy; this is going to be a love story—sit back and enjoy it. Nothing bad is going to happen.'"

Another requirement of the opening pages is to establish the tone of the play. Again, audiences have to know right away how they're supposed to relate to the unfolding events onstage. Usually this setting of tone happens automatically as you begin writing, but not always. So if you're writing a comedy, let them know within the first few lines that they have permission to laugh. If your play is serious, let them know within a minute or two that they're being asked to engage with it seriously. If it's some combination of serious and comic, inform them that they're going to be expected to balance themselves between the two. If it's a way-out fantasy, let them in on it as the lights come up or very soon after. The audience is waiting for the play to tell them how to engage. You must have their instructions clearly embedded in that first scene.

Also keep in mind that successful plays rarely shift in tone. Once an audience sets its orientation to a play, it's difficult to initiate an adjustment. There's a give-and-take that's established, an intimate and delicate relationship between play and audience that grows increasingly secure as the play unwinds. To change this once it's established is like asking the audience to start over with the play—and that's asking the impossible. Instead, they'll more than likely get angry and tune out or walk out. If it becomes tricky, as sometimes happens, to settle up front on the correct tone for a play, you may find it necessary to experiment and test different attacks on the material. At some point relatively early on, however, the right tone will present itself. You'll feel it when it's right.

Finally, concerning first-draft openings, get some action going right away. Without forcing the situation, attempt on page one to begin raising a series of questions for the audience that makes them want to listen for answers. Make them play "catch up" for a few pages. Make them work at figuring out what's being talked about. In other words, don't waste any time getting that carrot dangling. Keep in mind that right from the start your audience should be leaning into your play. **Emily Mann** observes:

> I always feel that people are coming in off the street. You don't know what their day has been like, and somehow, right there, you have to get them into the world of the play. You have to seduce them to it, whatever that is, and then keep them there. You've got to do that.

A related benefit of a strong opening is that it can help you reconnect with the draft-in-progress as you sit down to write each day. **Wendy Wasserstein**, for example, spends a lot of time on her openings: "I will sometimes almost polish up the first scene or the second scene too much." She does this to feel secure before continuing, explaining: "I feel like I've got something; I'm on the road to a play."

The danger here is spending so much time on the opening scene that it becomes permanently installed in your brain. This can be a serious problem later on if you discover that the rest of the play wants to go in a new direction. First-draft openings should be as strong as possible, but should never be carved in stone. Eventually the play may best be served by totally rewriting those first few pages.

Discipline

Up until now your work has all been a preliminary thinking-through of the play. Now you have to shift gears and enter into a phase which is going to tap more demandingly into your sensitivity and emotional life as an artist. You have to live in the world of the play itself for the first time, and over a period of days or weeks capture that world on paper in all it's richness and nuances. It's a precious, elusive world to which you'll find easy access some days and little or no access on others. And when you do manage to get inside it and are able to record accurately what you see and hear there, it's a gift.

The only way to position yourself for this phase of the work is to make a serious commitment to the task at hand. You need to set up a regular, consistent work schedule and stick to it. Try to write every day of the work week if possible, even if you can only snatch an hour or two per session. You'll have to discover for yourself what your limits are per day. I personally can go about four hours tops. Usually, after three hours, I start to fade. Some writers I know can work for six hours or more—some even eight or ten. I don't know how they do it, but more power to them!

Find what works for you and fits into your life and keep plugging away at it on a daily basis. **Athol Fugard**, when he's ready to start his first draft, plans as follows:

> I always see to it that I've got a good period of time ahead of me, because if I am going to try to write, I am going to need to be at that desk without any interruption seven days a week for four months. I will have organized my life so that I am free to sit down at that desk—and sometimes just do nothing for four hours, just sit looking at blank paper.

Discipline is the operative word here. Discipline comes naturally to some and is a constant struggle for others. But it's worth stating the obvious: One way or another all successful playwrights have found a way to sit themselves down on a regular basis and turn out pages day after day, week after week, and year after year.

It may be painful, even agonizing, to order your body into your writing space and force your mind and fingers to crank up yet again, but this is the only way plays get written. You've got to produce actual pages, lots of them. One at a time. Steadily, stubbornly. With determination. Sometimes with gritted teeth. And sometimes with great pleasure. Page after page after page . . . day after day after day. . . . There's no other way.

Fugard goes on to say:

> Having decided that you're going to write a play, and having put a stack of paper and pens and pencils on the table in front of you, how do you actually start? My advice sounds like a joke, but it's a very good piece of advice: I say, don't sit down until you know the paper isn't looking at you. And when you can catch that paper off-guard, have the temerity to put down "page number one" and open your first bracket for your first stage direction.

Wendy Wasserstein admits she has a struggle with discipline, but she has an approach:

> I'm innately a very undisciplined writer. I'll be distracted by anything, basically. I take phone calls, I speak too many places. But finally, when I think, "This is too much, I can't do this any more, I must write," I set aside time and say, "Wendy, every day for x amount of hours you'll be in a room writing—no telephone. You must do this or you're going to go mad." So that's what happens. It really takes discipline.

And **Terrence McNally** says:

> I have to sit at my desk to work. I'd love to pretend that while I'm shopping or driving, I'm working. I'm not. I'm shopping, I'm driving. I have to sit there and look at that computer screen. And not talk on the phone. You have to be really grown-up, put the answering machine on monitor, and turn the volume down. And when friends say "I have tickets for. . . ." say "No." Once you start a play, it's an enormous emotional, physical, spiritual commitment. It's a big thing to write a play.

John Patrick Shanley made an early-morning habit of writing:

> At a certain point I had a job, so I had to get up at five o'clock every morning and write for three hours, and then I would go to work. That went on for a year, and during that year I learned the discipline of being a writer. Because there's nothing

else going on at five o'clock in the morning. . . . My only rule was that I had to be sitting at that typewriter. I didn't care if I wrote anything or, if I did, what it was. Just so long as I was sitting at the typewriter, then I was writing. So I created a space and habit in my life with that.

One of my biggest ongoing disappointments as a teacher of playwriting is recognizing genuine talent in someone and then discovering that the commitment isn't there. Without self-discipline, even a towering gift lies dormant.

Battling that Negative Voice

Two-thirds of the way through writing *'night, Mother,* **Marsha Norman** heard an inner voice saying: "I don't know what this is. I'm in real trouble here. I mean, nobody's going to want to do this, right? It's going to be real embarrassing." Luckily, she managed to dismiss such thoughts. If she hadn't, she may not have finished her Pulitzer Prize–winning play.

All writers deal with the negative voice to some degree. It usually takes the form of a persistent whisper in your ear: "Who are you trying to kid? Give this up before you make a fool of yourself. This is garbage. You're wasting your time."

Terrence McNally has days when he asks himself: "Why can't I just get a job at a bank and be an honest worker?" He remarked that the day before my interview with him he had had a terrible time working on the first draft of a new play: "I wanted to kill myself, burn the play, quit the Dramatists Guild, resign from being their vice president, quit teaching at Juilliard. How can I teach playwriting? I don't know what I'm doing."

Wendy Wasserstein says: "I start writing, and then I call people and say, 'It's terrible, I know it's terrible.'"

Athol Fugard relates:

There is always a mortifying moment when, having pushed through that first draft without going back and checking anything—just working, just driving, just trying to create that arc on paper using the scraps that you've accumulated—there is always that moment when you say, "All right, that's finished, now I've got to read this." And then you read it, and it's an awful experience. . . . I have never experienced anything but the most appalling, sinking feeling on reading the first draft of a play.

Every time! And I should know by now that it's going to happen, but there is no way I can avoid an engulfing wave of despair.

And **Emily Mann** captures it nicely when she simply says: "There are crazy days when you lose all belief."

When you hear such a voice, it's imperative that you find some way to tune it out and push on—especially when writing your first draft. You're in the most vulnerable phase of the work, when it's easy to get seduced into giving up. First drafts are tough largely because they don't have that polished and professional authority you sense when reading successful, published plays. The initial pages you're turning out simply don't measure up. What's important is that you keep reminding yourself that every one of these successful, published plays were brought into existence in the same way your play is. Any given play on your bookshelf may be a fifth, or tenth, or twentieth reworking of a tentative first version. It's quite possible that very little, if any, of the very first draft may still be contained in the play you admire most.

So push through those inevitable moments of uncertainty and doubt. **John Guare** says that he can get lost in his first draft. His solution is "to let it sit. . . . It's not writer's block. It's just that inside, down deep, you're trying to figure it out. And it's just saying, 'Leave me alone for a bit. Just go away and do something else, because I'm trying to figure this out. Come back in a couple of days.' And I trust that process."

Terrence McNally tells us: "You should write with confidence and courage and boldness and be grown-up enough when you have the bad day to just go out and get some ice cream and say, in the immortal words of Scarlett O'Hara, 'I'll think about it tomorrow.'"

John Patrick Shanley puts it this way: "You look at it and say, 'I don't know what to do,' and then you tell yourself. 'Well, you haven't known what to do before, and someday you will know what to do. Put it away and go on with whatever else you're doing.'"

Keeping It to Yourself

As you start into the draft, you'll feel an urge to share what you're writing, or at least to talk about it. It's natural to be excited about what you're coming up with. Writers write to communicate with others. However, this is one of the biggest mistakes you can make at this stage. My advice: Do not, under any circumstances, show your work or talk about it to anyone while you're working on your first draft. Keep it totally to yourself. This is your private world, your virgin soil. It should be written as a personal and solo experience.

As **Marsha Norman** observes: "Plays are not written by committee. They are written by single voices. They are products of a single vision."

And **David Ives** says he never shows his early forays into a draft "until I'm baffled by it and I don't know what else I can do to it—until it's as much as I can think about. And sometimes that can be months."

It's imperative that you protect this private world from all outside influence. Think of it as contamination, even if it comes from a friend. Indeed, nothing can destroy a first draft faster than to show pages to the well-meaning people in your life. They'll want to and even feel obligated to give you feedback. As Norman goes on to say: "People love to get in and tell you what to do. Isn't that true of life and of writing? Everybody knows what you ought to do."

The moment people give you input, you won't be able to get it out of your head, whether it's positive or negative. It's contamination either way. You've let others into a place where they should never be allowed to enter. **Wendy Wasserstein** says emphatically: "I would never show anybody an unpolished draft of mine. I just wouldn't." And the reason is that she knows it's crucial to get it down as *she* hears it first.

Resisting this urge to share your first-draft discoveries helps build an increasingly stronger and more intimate connection between you and your material. It's as if your relationship with your characters were taking on the deeper sense of trust and mutual confidence that you would have with real people. What's happening in the play becomes yours and your characters' own secret and your unique source of strength. This, in turn, produces an energy which helps propel you through to the end. Even when you're stuck on something and go through a few days or even weeks of feeling lost, the experience remains a private one, shared only with the people inside the play.

The time will come soon enough when it's necessary and useful to share your play with others and hear what they have to say. Now, however, it's just as critical that you don't.

Pushing Through

Once you get rolling, it's important to keep up the momentum and push through as quickly as you can. Just get it out of you. **Michael Weller** has an interesting slant on it:

Half of getting through a first draft is just being too stupid to know how bad it is and to just keep going and going and push through to the end. Then you go back and you say, "Okay, how can I persuade myself that this thing really happened?"

And **Romulus Linney** says it this way:

You try to go right through. You want to write that first draft as fast as you can. Faulkner called it the tightrope. On a tightrope you don't want to look down and question yourself, "Is this really a good idea?" You just walk across.

Once you get started, there's always the tendency to go back through what you've already written and start fixing. Of course, some of this can't be avoided. The rewriting process begins as soon as you've written your first line and immediately think of another way to word it. Some writers, such as Wasserstein, do a lot of rewriting as they move through their first drafts, especially in the first scene or two. **David Ives** also shares how he uses early revision to push him forward:

Every day I go back over what I wrote the day before, fixing yesterday's dialogue to get a kind of momentum. This also reminds me of things I may have forgotten. John O'Hara used to stop writing every day in the middle of a sentence so that the next day he could continue that sentence and have a springboard, a way in. Hemingway said you should always stop when you know where you're going—and never stop when you don't know what's next, because you'll be lost.

It's only after the first draft is finished, however, that most of the necessary changes become obvious. Inevitably, many of the lines or pages you've slaved over will have to be thrown out or considerably changed. But for now, as **Marsha Norman** says: "It's a mistake to go back and revise too much until you see what you have."

Lanford Wilson views revising this way:

I'm writing *pages*, I'm not writing a play. I'm writing 90 or 102 pages, that's all I'm trying to do. I'm just trying to stack up work—in other words, to keep going. I edit only the previous day's work and make a few changes there, and that helps me to get on to this day's work. If something comes up and I realize, "Oh, that character shouldn't be a man, it should be a woman," I'll just make a note and go on as though I've changed all of the first part. And then, as soon as I finish, I go back and change all that. When I get finished with a play, and I have it there, that's when I say: "What in hell is this now?"

When you do find it necessary to rework things as you go, keep telling yourself that everything is still in flux and not to become too attached to specific moments or lines. The serious rewriting starts when you have a completed draft to work with, clumsy as it may be. Again, **Lanford Wilson** explains:

> The first draft is a creative process, and I'm the artist or the writer at that point. When I finish, I become an editor—it's a little schizophrenic—and the editor doesn't have nearly the fun the writer has.

Setting a Time Frame

Set up a goal for finishing the first draft as quickly as possible and avoid letting it drag on for months and months. Projects have a way of losing their vitality when first drafts take an inordinately long time to get through, because the play is a reflection of who you are at this point in your life. A year, even six months, from now, you're going to be a different person who would write a somewhat different version of the play. **Marsha Norman** says she thinks you have about a two-year window for a play, from start to finish:

> In two years you change as a human being and you're no longer the person to finish it; you're not the person you were when you started. And it's very difficult to keep working on a play for a long time because you tend to keep changing what the central problem is. You try to get it to be more like what you're worried about now than what you were worried about two years ago.

Whatever your time frame, it's especially important that first drafts capture the consistent and passionate voice of the *you* that you are now. And the only way to do that is to set up a disciplined schedule and honor it. Your job now is to turn out the pages and keep on turning them out until you've finished.

Getting Some Distance

A finished first draft is like a freshly baked pie. When you first take it out of the oven, you have to put it on the rack to cool. If you try cutting a piece hot, it falls apart, the insides oozing out, as you attempt putting the piece on a plate. If you try tasting it, your tongue gets burned.

It's mysterious how this works, but distancing yourself from a finished first draft is essential. The degree of objectivity gained with even a few days of "cooling off" helps enormously as you go back to appraise what you've come up with. As **Romulus Linney** accurately says: "It's awfully hard to be objective about something that you've just poured your guts into."

More often than not, when you finish writing the final page, that negative voice will have grown from a whisper to a shout. However loud it may be, resist concluding that what you've written is terrible. Realize that these feelings are normal.

There's the outside chance that the opposite may happen, that you'll be so excited about what you've written that you can barely contain yourself. Or you may be somewhere in the middle, uncertain as to its merits. Whatever your feelings toward that stack of pages, to start immediately reworking them is a mistake. You need, instead, to put your newborn play away and totally forget about it for a while. Two weeks to a month will permit you to gain some distance, but some people may need much more time. **Wendy Wasserstein** takes breaks during the writing process itself: "When I finish the first act, I'll take a break for three weeks, or when I finish a scene that's very hard for me, I'll rest and put that down. I'll just rest from it."

During this time, try to engage yourself in some other all-consuming project, perhaps even starting work on another play. Or, as **Marsha Norman** suggests: "You should just find wonderful things to read between the time you put the play away and the next time you pick it up. You should fill your mind up with other language, other characters' concerns."

Romulus Linney reminds us:

> Playwrights who really work at this often have works around in many states of completion, in various stages. So when you're working on one and you hit a stone wall or you need some distance, you put that aside and you say, "All right, what else is around here?" And you can pick something else up. It's a never-ending process.

I also highly recommend that you continue to keep your work private, even though the urge to share your completed draft with someone is often compelling. During this "down time" your play is still incubating. It should remain *your* process only. Getting input from others now could forever destroy that special, intimate relationship you've been nurturing with your work and that you still have a use for.

Usually what happens when you return to your draft after such a distancing period is that it surprises you. If you hated it when you put it away, now it'll most likely read better than you thought it would. If you loved it, now it'll probably be obvious that it needs more work. The point here is that your ability to judge its merits can only really be trusted if you've allowed yourself to gain some objectivity, and the only way you can achieve that is to put it on the rack for a while. I've never encountered an exception to this.

Now the task is before you. Make a commitment to it and don't stop until you've finished. Find some way to stagger through this virgin territory. Be tough on yourself and you'll get through. Don't, under any circumstances, give up. **Emily Mann** makes the case for perseverance this way: "You just pray for breakthrough, for inspiration. If you work long enough and hard enough, eventually, I believe, it comes. But you never know when."

Realize that in the playwriting process, the first draft is just one of the steps along the way—a big and arduous one, to be sure—and in the majority of cases far from the last.

So go for it.

11

BEGINNING THE REWRITING PROCESS

It's a struggle, and you resent it, and you want to throw it out the window or stomp on it. But you just have to do it.

—HORTON FOOTE

The hardest thing about writing may indeed be getting from nothing to the first draft, but no one said it gets much easier after that. In almost all cases, it's the rewriting that makes or breaks a play. And making it right is rarely an easy task.

From the outset, it's important to realize that the process of rewriting will include many phases. It starts now with your initial reworking of the first, rough draft and any subsequent early "private" drafts. It continues as you begin sharing the play with others and as you eventually move into the development phase, actually testing and retesting your script's stageworthiness with other theater artists. In an ideal playwright's world, the rewriting process finally draws to a close when the play receives its first professional production.

Through each of these phases the rewriting may be extensive or minor. Rest assured, however, if your script takes the typical new-play journey, it will be in an ongoing refinement process. **Romulus Linney** says:

I think you should think about revision in the same way that you think about writing the first draft: Revision is not so much a mechanical process of hammering something out, although sweat is a part of it—it is hard work—but revision should have to it the same mysterious searching that that first draft did. It can be as creative.

As **Tina Howe** puts it:

So much of writing is about rewriting—going through those endless, humiliating drafts. I never get it right the first few times. It takes me at least eight or nine drafts. I'm of the school that it's in the rewrites that the play is born. It's a refiner's craft.

Most successful playwrights place themselves in this school and agree with the adage that "the art of writing is the art of rewriting." This chapter looks at the first critical steps in this process.

As you proceed, think of yourself as a potter at the wheel. Your first draft is your raw clay, and your job now is to work and rework the clay in your hands as it spins on the wheel. You may have to work through it over and over until it has the exact texture, thickness, and shape you want. Like a potter, you only produce a finished piece of quality in this way, one pass-through after another. Slowly your play responds to your steady, gentle coaxing.

There is real craft involved here, of course. But success also depends on attitude, on patience as you take it one step at a time, on getting in there and working through it again and again. Eventually a piece will emerge that you can take off the wheel, glaze, and fire in the kiln.

Re-establishing Contact

When you *honestly* think enough time has gone by for you to read your first draft with an objective eye, pull it out again. I stress the word "honestly" because, if gaining emotional distance were ever absolutely essential, it's here. You're at perhaps the most critical and delicate phase in the entire creation process. You're about to begin passing judgment on this vulnerable first pass-through, throwing things out, revising and altering, reworking and reshaping. So don't let your eagerness get the best of you. Revisit your play only when you know you can look at it with level-headed, unbiased, and constructively critical eyes.

It's worth repeating that, as you enter into this first phase of rewriting, you should continue to resist the urge to share the play with others. Now more than ever as you examine the draft, you need to protect that private relationship between you and the play. *Your* impressions at this point, *your* reactions, *your* ideas for changes, are the important ones. As **Terrence McNally** advises: "It's so public the minute you let someone put a finger on it, so keep it one-on-one as long as you possibly can."

The urge to share, to get the opinions of trusted friends can be almost overpowering at this point. You want to know how others respond, what they think, what they understand and don't understand. But my plea is: Be patient. Just keep thinking you owe it to yourself and your play to go back through it "privately" at least one time.

It's crucial you become as confident and convinced as possible about what's on those pages before soliciting reactions from others. Believe me, the process changes radically and irrevocably as soon as you've exposed your "child" to the world. This is your last opportunity to get it right as you see it. Once you've let even one other person into the process, you can't retrieve what you had before.

Successful rewriting will depend at least in part on your ability to grasp and hold a sense of the entire work as you attempt fixing pieces of it. I therefore suggest that this first encounter with your "cooled-off" draft be a nonstop read-through from beginning to end. Make pencil marks in the margins if you must, but force yourself to get through the whole play in one sitting. It's important you establish contact with the entire draft, not just up to where you start having problems. You need to absorb and retain a sense of the whole as you begin the rewriting process.

From now on, what you do on page three will affect what happens on page thirty-three and vice versa. Something late in the draft may be so right, so on-target in terms of what you want the play to accomplish that it will help determine how you adjust everything that comes before. Therefore, you should try to avoid having blinders on as you begin fixing a specific scene.

This initial reconnection with the play is often aided by reading it aloud to yourself. Although you're still alone and it's a private experience, reading it aloud will let your ears literally hear the play. Character voices will start to be felt. You'll begin to get at least a sense of pace and flow. The play becomes one step removed from that silent mental experience you had when you first wrote it. It starts taking on a life of its own. Obviously, this is only a small step compared to that moment when actors will first read the play, but it can be useful here when you're still not sharing it with anyone else.

Primary Adjustments

If your first draft took a major turn in direction and doesn't really resemble what you thought you were going to write when you started out, let this be a cause for excitement, not panic. Your characters have taken over the play, and you've been honest enough in your writing to let them take the lead. More than likely you've tapped into something that in the end will make for a much better play.

If this has happened it's important to make the necessary readjustments now in your thinking about what the play's trying to do. The best way to do this is to fill out a new play-idea worksheet. This will help you analyze what you came up with and give you a clearer structural sense of the play you're going to be working with from this point on.

It may be necessary to do some substantial rethinking of who your central character is and/or what the dominant conflict/dilemma is. If the resolution has turned out different from what you'd planned, what does this mean in terms of your dramatic premise? Is your play now communicating something different? If so, determine what it says now—or attempts to say—to the audience. No rewrites can really start until you've reassessed how the basic dramatic ingredients are operating.

If what you've written has altered what you thought you were writing about, just look honestly at what you've come up with and decide if you like it better. If you don't, you'll have to work the play back to a point where you do. If you decide you like the new direction, proceed with your rewrites accordingly. If, for example, a different central character has emerged, the front end of the draft will probably need major reworking, for you started out with a different focus. However, none of this should daunt you. Just trust your subconscious and go with what it's telling you.

You may also discover that the characters who appear in your first draft are not exactly the personalities you thought they'd be. Perhaps your carefully worked out, shared backstory and personal milestones no longer fit. If this is the case, I strongly suggest you explore these people more thoroughly now, before plunging into any significant rewriting. Try working through some new milestone experiences that come to mind and rethink the shared backstory so it makes sense with the new information revealed in your first draft. Become very knowledgeable about these different characters who have emerged.

Basic Rewriting Principles

When you've finished making any necessary primary adjustments, the following basic principles will guide you as you plunge into rewriting your actual pages.

The Tyranny of the Written

The biggest rewriting hurdle for many writers is freeing themselves from words already written. You can repeat the phrase "words are cheap" a thousand times, but when it comes down to tossing out a scene, a page, or even a single line of dialogue, a protective wall will usually rise and a threatening voice will say: "Don't you dare touch this!" or "This is clearly an essential part of the play!" or "This was written with great pain and it stays!"

Prying loose material that's been set in concrete is almost impossible. That's why you have to develop an attitude that doesn't allow your mix of words to harden too quickly. Later on, when a professional production of the play is in its last week of rehearsals, the hardening process can accelerate, but before then you're more likely to make your play as good as it can be if you convince yourself that, indeed, words are cheap.

As **Romulus Linney** reminds us: "Faulkner said, 'Kill all your darlings.' You want to suspect things that you love a lot. Because that's usually betraying some self-indulgence on your part."

I've discovered that all the established playwrights I know have found a way to do this. A striking example is **Edward Albee**'s experience with his 1975 Pulitzer Prize–winning play *Seascape*. He discovered at the first rehearsal that what he thought was a play in three acts (with two intermissions) was really a play in two acts (with one intermission), so he dropped his second act completely. One day the play had three acts, and the next morning it had two. And he tells this story with no regrets whatsoever. Hearing the actors' first read-through of the play told him the second act didn't belong, so he cut it. The work as a whole was served, and that's what counted. (Don't forget that the use of the term "acts" here should not be confused with the three structural parts or "acts" of any well-constructed play.) Albee discovered that the play was structurally sound without the material between the first and second intermission breaks.

Horton Foote says:

> You have to divorce yourself emotionally. . . . There's a point where I just calm down and cool it and become as objective as I can. I find those moments that are really essential, and I find those that are nonessential, and sometimes it kills me; I've cut some of the best writing that I've ever done.

The basic rule is: If the play as a whole is served, you have to be willing and able to let things go.

If you can't abide by this rule, your play will suffer. Ultimately you're the one to determine if the play as a whole is served by removing a part of it; you stay in the driver's seat. However, the implied warning here is not to become your own worst enemy and insist on keeping material that weakens the play. It's an easy trap to fall into, and I've seen it happen many times, both with my own plays and while working as a dramaturg with other playwrights. The tyranny of the written can easily dim the potential brilliance of any play-in-the-making.

If in Doubt, Cut It Out

This is another way of saying the same thing, of course. But don't be fooled by the cuteness of this little writer's cliché. It's almost always true. You may not fully understand your doubt about a line or exchange, but if you feel at all uneasy about it, trust that probably there's something wrong with it. And usually the problem turns out to be that the material in question isn't really needed and in fact slows down the forward movement of the play. Train yourself to become sensitive to this built-in sensor and not to ignore its warning buzzer when it sounds, quiet as it may be at times.

Edward Albee says: "The difference between writing a good play and a lousy play is the difference between the arbitrary and the inevitable. Everything in a good play should be inevitable, no matter how outrageous or unexpected it is."

This is a good test to apply when doubts appear. Ask yourself: Does this have to be in the play? Does the story I'm telling and the character I've created dictate that this material must stay, at least in some form? Does it have a dramatic purpose? Does it directly or indirectly push the play forward toward its destination?

The easiest way to answer these questions is simply to cut out the material and see what happens. This may sound ruthless, but you'll be surprised how often you'll discover that the scene works better without it. Of course, sometimes you'll have to struggle to rework the altered scene until the difficulty disappears. Often some version of the line or lines in question must remain for the proper unfolding of the story. However, try to make a habit of testing troublesome material by taking it out of the play and seeing if you really miss it. If you do, then you know it serves some purpose and you need it. And because you've already gone through the motions of cutting out the doubtful material, you'll inevitably find it easier to try something new in its place, instead of simply putting the old material back in.

One of the common traits among established playwrights I've worked with or interviewed is that they all have the same attitude about this. They're ruthless when it comes to cutting material that isn't exactly right. Most have said in one way or another that it's when they finally disciplined themselves and developed the ability to cut that their playwriting started to take off. They've found it liberating and exciting.

Tina Howe has at times carried the practice to the extreme by throwing out her only copy of an entire early draft. She explains:

> I throw it in the garbage. Literally. Cram it in the bag with the
> egg shells and coffee grounds. Down the toilet! Goodbye!
> Gone! I tried, but it didn't work! So you mustn't look back.
> Destroy the outlines, tear up the notes . . . then see if you want
> to start again.

This kind of drastic move takes a special kind of courage and may or may not be something you can muster. But Howe communicates powerfully the importance of not allowing yourself to be saddled with material that isn't working. One way or another you have to get rid of it.

Romulus Linney sums it up nicely:

> What you want to do is go back through your draft and keep
> working over it until you discard everything that's superfluous,
> until finally the only thing that's left is that which is absolutely
> necessary. That, it seems to me, is basically the act of revision.

This ability to discard has been a major factor in the success of all great playwrights. It's one of those elements of the craft that they've mastered, and its application has played a role in lifting their work into a league of its own.

Less Is More

Another cliché, another basic truth. Especially in writing for the theater. You should make a continuous loop tape of this three-word sentence and have it running in your head whenever you work on rewrites.

First drafts are notorious for overexplaining and forcing information. On a first pass-through, you are exploring and discovering as you go, at least to some degree. A certain amount of overwriting is normal and inevitable.

Now, with the finished draft in your hands, you know where your play ends up and the initial route it took to get there. This allows you to apply the "less is more" principle with a good measure of confidence as you work your way through the script again.

In explaining his rewriting process, **Horton Foote** says:

> I am merciless about it, and I say to myself "Is this scene too long, or have we lost the *wants* here? Are they talking too much? . . . Is there too much exposition? How can I do this more simply?" I believe in elimination. I always ask myself, "What can I do without?"

Remember, there's no faster way to get audiences and readers to engage with your play than if they have to fill in the blanks and make connections the characters only allude to. In other words, your job now is to get everything out of the script that the audience can discover for themselves. So in your rewriting strive to put as much between the lines as you have in the lines. That's when less really becomes more.

Keeping in mind the above basic principles and having made any essential structural adjustments and additional character explorations, try to determine how well your script measures up to the characteristics of good dialogue and stage directions explained in Chapter 9. Everything you need for testing your draft is there. If this is your first play, focus on your draft *point by point,* working carefully through it as many times as it takes. With each pass-through, concentrate on making the adjustments dictated by the principle you're focusing on. This approach will help give you a sense of control in the rewriting process. It applies some methodology to what can seem like an arbitrary, never-ending task and allows you to appraise what you've written—and then rewritten—with more clarity.

Between Screen and Page

Whether you write your first draft longhand or on a computer, the rewriting process has become generally more pleasant with the advent of word processing, compared to how one used to work in the days of the typewriter, with its tedious retyping and cutting and pasting—I know, I've made the transition. I declare unabashedly that the second greatest invention in the history of writing (just below the printing press) is the computer keyboard's "print" button. And the "block" and "move" buttons are near the top of the list as well. Anyone who writes on a computer quickly gains a keen appreciation of these tools as rewriting commences.

If you work on a word processor or computer, I suggest that when you've finished rewriting a scene you print out and take a look at it on the page, making pencil edits and deletions. Then, before you appraise the rewrite, put the changes in, print out a clean copy of the new version, and look at that. This is extremely helpful, even if the changes are minor, because then you're always seeing it fresh with all the edits included and the new material inserted. You're able to assess the new version without the clutter of the pencil edits and rewrites.

Of course, computers do not good plays make. Those writers among you who are "hold-outs," with your legal pads or typewriters, don't despair. Although it may take you a bit longer to come up with your new, clean drafts, rest assured you have equal potential to write brilliant plays. And there is one advantage: You can write your masterpiece in a wilderness cottage miles away from the nearest power line.

However you work, be careful that you don't wait too long before looking at your rewrites cleanly printed or typed out. Mysteriously, your pages always read differently when they get one step removed from your own handwriting, marginal scribbles, and drawn arrows. If you write exclusively on a computer, it's wise every so often to experience your developing script as actual pages you can hold in your hands. Again, it will read differently on the page compared with the screen.

Another Look at Your Title

At one or more points in the rewriting process you should look again at your title. Is it still working as well as it did earlier? Has the writing of the first draft and/or your reworking of it opened up any new possibilities? Are there any specific references or turns of phrase in the dialogue that now pop out at you? Does anything hold a double or triple meaning, working on several levels at once? Don't be afraid to try a new title on for size and live with it for a while. You can always go back to your earlier one. If you think you might have found something, go so far as to make up a new title page. Then wait and see if it grows on you.

Keep searching and testing until you're absolutely convinced you've found the perfect title. Don't lock in too early or become so rigid that you pass right over a brilliant title lying there in, or between, the lines. Keep challenging yourself to find something better. It may happen early or far into the rewriting process, but you'll know when you've hit gold—you'll feel it. So don't settle for something you've simply grown used to.

Scanning

After you think you've made all the necessary revisions and the play works for you from beginning to end, I suggest you take this initial rewrite one step further. Put the play away for a few days, still not showing it to anyone. When you pull it out again, try to "reprogram" your mind to become an ultrasensitive scanning machine that you're going to feed each page into. Make yourself into a hypercritical, word-sensitive, fine-tuning device that can pick up even the slightest static of doubt or nag of uncertainty. With this machine nothing gets through that isn't absolutely right. Feed in the first page and begin scanning each stage direction and line word by word. When anything stops you, a word choice, the smallest whisper—"This isn't perfect, but it's good enough" or "Do I really need this?" and so on—have the beeper in your mind go off and stop and fix it. Don't move on until you can scan back over the same material and no longer hear that beeper.

Make this "scanner" a frequently used tool as you move through the rewriting process. When you come across difficult problems that you can't get by the scanner no matter how hard you try, you know you're probably not ready to begin sharing the play with others. Of course, some problem areas may be completely solved only after you've heard the play read by actors and seen how an audience responds to it. But at least you will have identified where and what they are. You'll be aware of what to watch and listen for, what questions to begin asking.

The point here is to make your script as good as you can before you offer it for others to respond to. That's the only way you're going to make genuine progress with it from here on out. If you're not happy with what you're asking others to respond to, why waste their time?

The simple fact is that in the art of playwriting there's no room for sloppiness or laziness. Anything less than your absolute best effort just doesn't "cut it"—in the end, you never get away with it. True professionalism means more than extraordinary talent. It means patience and hard work and being honest with yourself as to how good your writing really is.

John Patrick Shanley, in describing a problem he was having with a play, said:

> I kept writing, over and over, ten pages for six weeks, seven days a week. I kept writing the same ten pages over and over again, and I just kept saying, "This isn't true enough, this isn't true enough." And I kept on trying to write it more truly. It was one of the most grueling things I've ever done. A horribly painful thing to do.

Every playwright who has consistent success in the profession takes this as a matter of course. Becoming your own scanning machine (or whatever you want to call it), therefore, is simply one of the essential requirements.

Which Draft Is This?

A good rule of thumb in this "pre-sharing" phase of the rewriting process is to keep combing through the play until you're comfortable with the thought of letting your most astute reader take a look at it. Regardless of how many times you've worked through it, however, the version you finally share with others for the first time is the one generally referred to as the first draft. So think of all the rewriting work you've done up to this point as just getting the script presentable for its initial release to the world.

As suggested in Chapter 8, it's best to identify your various drafts of a play by date rather than by number (as in "first draft," "second draft," and so on). You'll always be working on the latest draft of the play, regardless of which "number" it is, and dating each draft identifies it for you and anybody else who may need to know what version they're working with. But it doesn't broadcast how many drafts you've been through—information that's really nobody else's business. It's probably best if even you don't keep an actual count.

As **Romulus Linney** said when I asked if he thought in terms of first, second, or third draft: "I don't care. I lose track. It just feels better."

Also, for future reference, be sure to keep a copy of both your very first rough draft and your privately reworked version(s) and file them away somewhere. The day may well arrive when you need to go back and rediscover what you thought this play was about when you first wrote it and before you showed it to anybody else.

Releasing Your Child for the First Time

I advise you to finish at the very minimum one complete rewrite before sharing the play with anyone, but my strongest recommendation is to keep working beyond that if necessary to produce the best version you can free of outside input. **John Guare** keeps working until he can just say to himself, "I think this is it":

> I can tell when I can't do any more writing on it. . . . You have a sense of completion, of feeling that all the elements are in place. I know where the play started, where it's ended, I know what I want it to feel like, what I want it to look like. I'm ready to show it. I have a sense of completion where I feel, "Ah, maybe it's not right, but I'm ready to let somebody into it." But I won't let anybody into it until I feel I'm ready, that I can't write anymore on it.

As **Marsha Norman** puts it:

> It's better to wait until you at least have hold of what you have. So when you get an opinion from someone, you have something to hold up against it and say, "No, that wasn't what I was trying to do."

You'll only "have hold" of it when you've gone back through the entire script as many times as it takes to get it right.

I can't stress enough how important the first sharing of your work is. You're about to cross a line in the life of the project that you can't ever cross back over. Outside input will now enter your creative process for the first time. And it's going to have an impact, positive or negative or both. It's going to reshape how you think about your play. **Lanford Wilson** reminds us:

> It's such a mysterous and delicate process . . . as all of this is filtered through some sort of machine that we call "the Muse" and down onto the paper. And you don't know where half of

that comes from. And you don't know what's going to stop it or what's going to impede that flow.

The initial feedback you get, therefore, should be from carefully selected sources and needs to be tightly controlled. Many of the playwrights I've worked with rely on one or two trusted people who have become invaluable as early readers of their work. In some cases, it took a long time to find these people. Once located, however, the playwrights consider them a wonderful asset and an important part of the writing process—or, perhaps more accurately, of the birthing process. These friends are, indeed, like midwives at the birth of children; they help guide each play into the world. They often continue in the role of godparents as the child "grows." You, the writer, have to go through the labor, give birth, and care for each child's development, but these people often play a crucial role. **Wendy Wasserstein** observes:

> You're very, very vulnerable when you write a play, and you want input—it's like you're *dying* for it—the way actors want input. But you have to be very careful in choosing whom you listen to—that's the best advice I could give you. Because there are extremely brilliant people who could give you advice that's just not right for you.

The initial readers of your play should be people who have three basic qualities: a perceptive mind, a generous spirit, and a good working knowledge of the theater. Wasserstein further explains:

> When you've just finished something, you're so delicate that the last thing you need is for someone to say, "Well, there's second-act trouble. . . ." Whatever it is, I think you need somebody who says, "You're wonderful," and then has criticism and leads you in a very good way.

Marsha Norman agrees:

> Clearly, there come to be people whose opinions you value above all others, and you trust them. You trust not only what they think but the way they will talk to you about it. . . . People need to come into it very carefully and speak with not all the candor in the world but very respectful of your process and "where you are."

So be very careful in choosing those people who will first read your play. I suggest two people whom you respect a great deal, who know something about the theater, and who won't be afraid to tell you what they really think. Two is usually better than one for this initial feedback, because the second person will tend to reinforce or give some balance to the first person's responses.

Once you've located your readers and they've agreed to the task, expect to wait a while before hearing from them. For most people, reading a first draft of a friend's play is a big order. They'll take this very seriously and wait until they can clear a morning, afternoon, or evening for the task—something that, for almost all of us, takes time to pull off.

After they've read your script, set up separate, one-on-one sessions with each of them. The last thing you want is for them to hear each other's reactions as they're attempting to tell you their own.

While you're waiting for them to read the play, be thinking about the questions you'll ask. You want to find out the following from your readers:

- How did the play work for them personally?

- What did the play ultimately say to them?

- Can they identify a central character and describe his or her dominant need?

- Did they care about the people?

- Were there any places they lost interest or thought the play sagged in its forward momentum?

The questions should always focus on what they got out of the script they read. Never formulate questions that identify problems you're having with the play. **Marsha Norman** suggests, for example, that if you're having difficulty with the end of your first act, ask them, "How did you feel at the end of the first act?" and don't let on that you're not sure about it. Just get their impressions. This kind of "pure" feedback is always the most valuable.

You'll be able to maintain control of the discussion throughout by asking all the questions yourself and never allowing your readers to question you. Develop the skill of turning every question directed at you back at them. When they ask you what you meant by something, simply say that what's important are their impressions. Ask them what they thought it meant. Don't let them trap you into explaining what you were after in the play or, worse, force you to start defending what you've written. That's a waste of everyone's time. You know what you intended, so your job is just to listen to what they got out of the script. This is the only feedback that will help you assess what's working and what isn't.

I'm assuming these people will indeed be your close friends and will therefore be motivated to help you as much as they can. Because of this, be prepared for two things. First, they'll almost always attempt to encourage you and make you feel good about the work you've done. They'll admire the fact that you've actually finished a draft of a play and be flattered that you trusted and respected them enough to share it with them first. The last thing they'll want to do is hurt your feelings with negative comments. Your job, of course, is to graciously accept any praise and then coax them into telling you what they really thought.

To help with this, **John Guare** suggests that these initial readers be given a focus when they read:

> You've got to protect yourself by giving your first reader a task, because otherwise all bets are off and anything goes. You've got to do some sort of steering—not to control, but to say, "Did it make you laugh? Do you think this is funny?"—to make the discussion easier, to give some theme to the discussion. That way, I think, you get a more honest response.

The second thing that often happens is that your initial readers will start suggesting how you should rewrite the play. Again, they're just trying to help. You've flattered them and they want to return the compliment with their well-meaning advice. It's absolutely essential that you never let them do this. Under no circumstances should you allow them to start telling you what you should do to make the play better. If they try, politely stop them and explain that you only need their reactions to what you've written, not their version of the next rewrite. That's your job to come up with, not theirs.

At the end of these readers' sessions, make a point of writing down what you've been told about your play. Be as detailed as possible. I've found that these notes are valuable to have on file, especially as more and more people read subsequent drafts and you can start to compare reactions. Certain similar comments from different people can keep coming up over and over. Slowly, you begin to understand how something has to be adjusted to deal with a persistent problem. People's reactions have a way of being rather quickly forgotten, so train yourself to take notes on what you're told at the time of the telling, starting with this very first exposure.

Dealing with the Initial Feedback

As you think through these first reactions to your work, always remember that you're still the one in control. Regardless of what you've been told, you make the decisions as to what your play should be and the future changes it will undergo. If your first readers confirm that you've written what you set out to write, or that you came close, the confidence it will engender will help as you continue developing the play.

If, at the other extreme, both readers indicate that they thought the play was saying something quite different from what you'd intended, then, obviously, you need to take a hard look at what you've written. Something led these readers off track. You have to figure out what caused this and then decide if you want to make the adjustments necessary to prevent such a derailing in the future. It may be that the play is indeed trying to say something different from what you thought it would and that your readers are picking up on this. One way or another, you'll have important choices to make before you can proceed.

Usually, if you've chosen your initial readers carefully—and that's a big if—you're wise to listen to what they've told you. Guard yourself from going into some sort of long-term denial. At first, rejecting negative feedback, because your readers have not given you the answers you want to hear, is natural: Who wants to be told he or she has failed? However, once the sting is gone, you owe it to your play to identify the problem areas and try to solve them.

Tina Howe knows how important it is not to dismiss valid criticism:

> It's very hard to find smart critics and honest critics.
> Playwrights need them desperately. So if you find them, and
> they're creative and on your wavelength, listen to them. As
> territorial as we are, it's important to be challenged.

For some writers it's possible to go back to work on the script immediately after obtaining these initial reactions. For others, another cooling-off period is necessary. My own possessiveness toward my writing is so strong that the only way I can ultimately be fair to the play, when it comes to considering this early response, is once again to put it away for a while.

If this sounds familiar—and I know I'm not alone here—now more than ever is a good time to start a new play, something you can get genuinely excited about and can pour your energy into. When you discover you need a breather from that play, too, you'll more than likely be far enough removed from your previous play to begin dealing honestly with what people told you about it. By then, usually, what needs to be adjusted is more clearly perceivable and choices can begin to be made. Most often, a new—and stronger—draft is the result.

Hearing It Read

After you've attempted another draft of the play based on your first readers' responses, it's useful to pull together a group of your friends—preferably actors with genuine talent—to read the play aloud. **David Ives** says:

> The way I read a play for the first time is to get a bunch of friends in my living room. I give them beer and pretzels, and they read the script cold. If they're good actors they'll know when something has gone wrong, when a character is doing something that doesn't make sense. They read it through, and I ask them what they think. I ask them to be honest, and usually you know more at that point, far more, than you started out with.

People who are not in the theater can often serve your purpose as long as they have skill at reading dialogue. **Emily Mann** explains: "I don't necessarily need great actors. I need to literally hear it. So they can't be terrible, obviously, but they don't have to be the people who are going to do it in a production."

On the other hand, many people are dreadful at this, and you should not include them, at all costs, even if they're close friends. You should perhaps invite them to the reading, but don't have them be a part of it.

The purpose here is for you to hear the play, and your only hope of accomplishing this lies in casting people with a flair for this sort of thing who come as close as possible to fitting the age and type of each character. **Terrence McNally** remarks:

> This first reading is really for me. And with good actors you can tell if it's alive. That's the only really important question about any play—does it live or not live?

Again, **Emily Mann** expresses it this way:

> I need to hear it. I do not have a perfect ear. I have to hear it,
> and then I hear what it has to be. I can't see it on the page and
> know that it's going to resonate. And it has to resonate like
> music or poetry. If it doesn't, and it lies there, then I have to do
> something about it.

Without question, the degree of reliability of this first real test of your
play will largely be determined by the cast you've assembled. If even a
single actor is seriously miscast in an important role, the project can easily malfunction. The entire reading can quickly become distorted and
might not sound at all like what you heard in your head while writing it.
And this can be disastrous. **John Patrick Shanley** relates:

> I thought one of my plays was a dead loss on the basis of a
> reading. It was *Danny and the Deep Blue Sea.* I heard the
> reading, and I said, "Well, I guess I was wrong. I thought it
> was good." Then I did another reading, and I thought, "Well,
> it's better." And then I got some good people, and I thought,
> "All right, now we're talking!" So you have to be very careful
> not to write off a play on the basis of a bad reading.

Emily Mann recalls a similar experience:

> I thought a full character wasn't going to work because an
> actress—truly, a brilliant actress—had not a clue to what this
> woman was about. I thought, "It won't work." And I really had
> to try to erase that voice, that tape in my head, because it
> would have been deadly, destructive to the play.

The message is clear: Make every effort to get the best possible actors
available to you. It's really not worth the effort to put a reading together
if you don't.

Most writers resist the urge to read a role themselves or be immediately
involved in the actual reading. The normal procedure is to go through the
script carefully and mark the essential stage directions that need to be
read, eliminating those the actors will execute automatically in their reading of the lines. Then assign someone else to read the stage directions.
Your goal should be to keep yourself as unencumbered as possible during
the reading so you can concentrate solely on listening to your work.

A different approach to the first reading is offered by **John Patrick Shanley**:

> What I did for many years was a sit-down reading and then a staged reading of each play. Now, whenever I finish something, I meet with a group of playwrights, and we all read our work. I read my play aloud, performing it to the best of my ability. I don't distance myself or protect myself from it, I jump in and try to make it work. And if I bomb, then I know that something's wrong. And you can feel yourself bombing. The thing is, if you're going to read something aloud to other people, you read it to yourself with an entirely different eye. And you say, "Well, I'm not saying that," and you cross it out.

Obviously, this approach will be most beneficial when the writer is also an actor of some skill. Shanley, however, makes a good point about activating your internal editor during the reading of the draft or during the writing of it, because you know you'll soon have to read the material aloud in front of other people.

Regardless of approach, this first reading usually works best if it's kept informal, with no real "audience" listening to "actors" on a "stage." Do it in someone's living room (yours, most likely). Even if a theater is available to you, it's usually best at this point not to conduct this first reading there. Theater settings have a way of automatically raising expectations. Now you're simply trying to get a sense of the play in its delicate infancy, and the less weight placed on the occasion the better. "It's really scary, the first reading of a play," **Wendy Wasserstein** says. "I can't think of anything more scary."

As **Lanford Wilson** puts it: "It's an alarming thing to hear something for the first time. And also when you're so vulnerable."

Most playwrights agree with this assessment. There's normally no rehearsal (or very little), and the actors reading are usually not perfect for their roles. So it's important to keep this initial reading as simple and unadorned as possible.

Guiding the Response

After the reading, once again make sure you control any discussion of the play—that is, if you decide you want to get any feedback at all. I've led hundreds of discussions with audiences after readings, and there's one rule I always announce before starting: "Don't tell the playwright how to rewrite the play." Nevertheless, someone will invariably launch into how he or she thinks the story should be changed to make it work better. When this starts, I politely cut such people off. I suggest you do the same. Remember, you don't want their ideas for rewrites. You want them to describe the experience they've just had with your play. It's your job to determine what adjustments, if any, should be made, based on what they've told you. Insist on this or you'll run the risk of suddenly having a half-dozen collaborators.

Lanford Wilson explains how the guided audience response period would serve him at the Circle Repertory Playwrights' Lab:

> They were not allowed to ask you any questions. You were sort of hearing the dinner-table discussion of people who'd seen that play that night. And if someone said, "Well, why has she got only one arm?" someone else answered that, you didn't. From the discussion you'd realize they didn't have a clue, you hadn't said what you'd intended to say. And by that time you kind of knew what you intended to say, whether you could put it into words or not. With *The Fifth of July* I said that if their description of the play begins either with "It's about this Vietnam veteran" or "It's about this English teacher," one or the other, then I've done it right. If it starts out with "They're going to sell this house" or something like that, then I've screwed up.

John Patrick Shanley is also discriminating about what responses help:

> I don't need, "On page 23, why does she walk across the room?" That doesn't help me. But if you can tell me how you felt when you saw it, where you felt exhilarated and where you felt down, then I know what to do eventually. If you can just tell me what part doesn't work, I can do something.

Romulus Linney sums it up well:

> Somebody can say, "I didn't believe this, I didn't believe that, I was confused here, I didn't know about that, I don't buy the whole thing." Or "I really saw what you were trying to do here. I didn't think you did it, but I thought this was good." Just very simple things like that. If I start getting a lecture from somebody, I smile and go away.

The Rewriting Cycle

After your first reading, you'll most likely go back to your writing room and work on yet another draft. (Notice why numbering drafts quickly becomes meaningless?) And then you'll want to hear it again. So you'll have another reading and then produce yet another draft. Of course, at some point, for better or worse, this cycle has to come to an end. **Romulus Linney** says: "There comes a time when you have to let a play go and move on to the next thing."

And as **John Guare** aptly points out:

> One lesson I learned involved a play I'd written a draft of and then another draft of. We then did a production of it, and I did another draft, and then another a year later. And in the process I changed my ideas about the play. I think the play went through fifteen drafts altogether. And what I learned was that there are times you have to say goodbye to a play. That you can't write fifteen drafts of a play. That the work you're doing on it belongs to the next play. You have to trust that original impulse and, for better or for worse, you have to say, "Failed or not, that is as much as I can do on that play." There's no such thing as a perfect play. If you are rewriting a play so much that you keep having to go back to change this character and change this element and that element, what happens is that your insides finally say "Move on. All this work you're doing belongs to another play."

Of course, not all professional playwrights work this way. **Edward Albee** and **Michael Weller**, for example, don't feel the need to test what they've written and, therefore, they keep rewriting to a minimum. In Albee's case, it's practically nonexistent:

> I don't think there should be much difference between the play that an author hears and sees when he writes it and the play he hears and sees in a good production. I think a playwright must be able to wield his craft to the point that there won't be much difference in the two. It's a question of how you listen and how you see.

I say "more power to him." Albee's success as a playwright testifies that he's found what works for him. However, most playwrights—especially in

America—find the repeated cycle of testing and reworking an important part of the process of getting their plays "wright."

Your finished script by this point may or may not be close to completion, but it's definitely evolving. And what starts to happen is that the line begins to blur between working in relative isolation on rewrites, with the occasional help of some friends, and the beginning of the development phase of the play where other theater artists get involved. You sense the need to hear the play read by real actors and to have time to work with them on the script in rehearsal. The thought arises of bringing the talents of a director into the picture to help give the play pace, shape, and focus. And then, very quickly, you'll want to feel how the play works on an actual set in a real theater before a real audience.

This next phase is really a part of the rewriting process, but it's also more than that. Your play is inevitably moving from a personal writing project you've generated in the quiet of your writing room into a more public and communal work for the theater world at large. It's time to look at how to maneuver your script through the many steps of this often difficult final phase on its journey to production.

12

THE ONGOING DEVELOPMENT PROCESS

Learning to write for the theater is learning to be a human being,
because the theater by its very nature makes you deal with other
human beings.

—DAVID IVES

There comes a time in the creation of any new play when you realize it's necessary to offer up your work to other theater artists and see how well it fares in front of an audience. **John Guare** explains:

> You write it, and then you want to see that mysterious thing
> that happens. Every play is written and rehearsed with one of
> its main characters missing—the audience. And the play is only
> completed when it connects to an audience. And that is the
> mysterious thing that in no way can you predict.

Exactly when this happens varies greatly from writer to writer and even from play to play, but the moment of truth always arrives. Rewriting can go on only so long without the input of good actors and a good director, artists who are sensitive to the needs of a new work and familiar with the exploratory nature of the development process. Entering into collaboration with them requires a major shift in your orientation to your work—from the writer working in isolation to one of the players on an artistic team. **Horton Foote** puts it well:

> It is a collaborative medium. We have to face that fact. We are not novelists, we are not poets. We are dependent, and this is what I hope our theater can finally learn: We are not enemies. The actors and the writer and the director are a unit, really, and I am no good without good acting and good directing, and I don't think actors and directors are so good without good plays.

Your work on the script never stops, of course. What changes is your relationship to the material. You must assess what happens when other artists step inside the play, try it on for size, and then attempt to bring it to life in front of an audience. Echoing Foote, **Terrence McNally** explains:

> To me, playwriting is so hands-on. It's bodies bumping into other bodies. It is the exact opposite of what I assume it must be like to write a novel or a poem, where you can be in an ivory tower and, maybe, you deal with one editor. The theater is so involved with personalities, real estate, ticket sales, actors' schedules—I mean, it's real hands-on *process.*

This chapter looks at what you can expect, what you should watch out for, and how to maneuver through these exciting but always potentially dangerous waters.

An Initial Warning

In most cases, theater people who work in play development do so because they love helping playwrights realize their vision on the stage. The dedication I've personally witnessed by directors and actors working with new plays has been extraordinary. People who work in this arena are generally caring, selfless artists who genuinely enjoy the challenge of putting before an audience what the playwright had in mind and seeing how well it plays. They want to help make the play work better. They get excited by the process and give of themselves and their talent inexhaustibly. In the majority of development projects, regardless of complexity, the collaborative process is productive, insightful, and extremely helpful to the playwright.

At the same time, be aware that play development is not without risks and potential pitfalls. Plays have been known to be mutilated or eaten alive by well-meaning people intent on "helping" a script. I've seen this happen also—and many times, unfortunately. Sometimes writers are conned out of their plays, seduced into thinking that what they really wanted to write was actually very different from what they thought before sharing their work with a team. They enter into a collaboration that takes their work away from them and leaves them with a stack of pages they no longer feel connected to.

John Patrick Shanley reminds us: "The point of doing this kind of work is that you're trying to have a more deeply singular point of view, because the more deeply you have that, the more powerfully you'll have a style."

For this and other reasons, some established writers don't believe in "play development" as it has evolved. They think it does more damage than good and that playwrights should stay away from it entirely. **Athol Fugard**, for example, told me he finds the American development process something he could never be a part of. He says he knows what he wants his plays to be when he writes them and doesn't need to put his work through such "testing":

> My process is very, very different on the score of privacy from that of the American process. I stay at that desk until I have written the play. The first time I hear it is when the actors I have cast read it through on the first day on rehearsals. . . . I'm able to remain subjectively involved in the actual process of putting words down on paper and, at the same time, to have this halfway sitting-back objectivity, saying, "Am I getting it? Am I getting it?" And that is what I have placed my reliance on in the course of my thirty years of playwriting—being able to do that double act.
>
> Now, it seems to me that a lot of American playwriting has not developed that. It says, "Let's have a reading and see if, at this stage, my play is getting through to this special little group that has been invited and see what their responses are going to be and what their questions are going to be.". . . I do all that myself. I go through the same process, but I use myself.

Michael Weller agrees:

> I think the move toward developing plays . . . has developed
> bad habits in playwrights. They take a draft and say, "Well, I
> don't know what to do, so I'm going to have a reading of it."
> No, if you don't know what to do, put it away and go to
> medical school or something. But when you're sure you're
> ready to get in front of a thousand people booing, then you're a
> playwright. Then put it on.

Many playwrights have found the development process—or at least aspects of it—to be useful, even invaluable, in ultimately getting their plays "wright." And as this chapter makes clear, play development has become widely established in America. For all but the most successful playwrights, therefore, it's difficult to avoid becoming involved with it on some level somewhere. With the proliferation of the so-called *regional* and *resident* theaters in this country, when highly professional stage companies appeared in many cities besides New York and Chicago, play development programs have been designed to help develop new scripts for the theaters' seasons. If you work in such a program, ultimately only experience will tell you how the process—or what parts of it—will be useful for you. Realize, however, that if your play takes the normal route to production, it will probably be subject to developmental practices of some kind.

So, as you first enter this arena, rule number one for you, the playwright, is to make sure the other artists becoming involved have read the same play that you've written. Again, ask lots of questions and listen carefully to the answers. **Marsha Norman** advises:

> It's critical to ask directors what they like about a piece, why
> they want to do this piece. I mean, question them really quite
> seriously, as seriously as you would question someone who
> said, "I would like to take your child around the world." You'd
> ask some pretty serious questions of that person, wouldn't you?
> You might want your child to go around the world, but you'd
> have to know some things first.

Directors may say they love your play, but the possibility exists that what they're really excited about is what they hope they'll be able to turn your play into. Don't be naive about this. Again, Norman warns:

> There are a lot of people who wish they could write plays, and
> they will try to do it over your dead body—on *your* piece of

paper. And you've got to try to stop them from that. When somebody says "I want to do your play," you have to figure out if they really want to do your play or if they want to do their play that's sort of like yours. Because if they want to do their play that's sort of like yours, you're going to be in trouble and there's nothing you can do about it. If the director or an actor has a different idea than you do and you give the play over to them, it's their idea that's going to end up on the stage, not yours.

The worst thing you can do is give your new play away to people who don't understand what you're trying to accomplish with it. If, in your initial discussions, you don't hear them tell you what sounds at least close to what you were after in writing the play, think twice before handing it over. You may be bursting at the seams to have the play worked on by actors, but if the director or producer or whoever is in charge of the project isn't "on beam" with what you intend, especially at this early juncture, you're opening yourself up for frustration and potentially a great deal of pain. **John Guare** relates:

> I worked on a play with a director, and I realized that the rewrites he was asking me to do were getting the play into areas I had no interest in. . . . And I said. "I really don't want to work with you anymore on this play," because I realized that this was the wrong director for the play. We didn't speak for many years. But that's the way it goes. You have to be very careful if somebody says, "I wish this were the play." You have to say, "Okay, if that's what you want it to be, write your own play. Just tell me about what my play is saying to you—not what you want my play to be, but what my play is saying to you."

This is often a difficult call for playwrights. You don't want to be overly protective and shield your play from any and all interpretations that vary from your own. Challenges to your vision and intent can be positive and can actually help to clarify what the play attempts to accomplish. Your understanding of the play can be deepened, and this can help you with further rewriting. When all goes well, you can end up with a much better play that presents your premise with more punch and lasting effectiveness.

What it all comes down to is two things: trust, and the ability to communicate. By trust I mean that you feel good about the people you're going to be working with: There's mutual respect for each other's talents and a sense that the play is going to be genuinely served. Good communication involves both speaking and listening clearly. Both you and those involved have to feel free to say whatever comes to mind without worrying about hurting feelings or being misunderstood. Everyone should be speaking the same language and heading in the same direction as the work proceeds. If things get off track, a little straight, honest talk—awkward as this can be at times—usually gets the process righted again.

The Buck Stops with You

To arm yourself for the work ahead, always remember that, in the theater, the playwright has the final word. "The burden of our work is always with us," **John Guare** reminds us. "We have to make the decisions." And this is not only a long tradition, it's written into the Dramatists Guild's standard production contract, and has been since the 1920s. When you've signed this standard agreement to have your play professionally produced, literally not a word of your script can be changed without your approval. If a producer or director makes even tiny changes against your wishes, you have the right to withdraw your play. In most cases, the playwright also has final approval over choice of director, casting, and designers.

In other words, overall artistic control ultimately rests with you, the author. This is generally accepted as a given in all tiers of the theater profession, and most people behave accordingly. Respect for the written word is traditionally held above all other considerations. Without a doubt, this fact is what keeps most good playwrights writing plays.

The opposite is true for the writer in films and television. Here all rights to a script are sold to the producer, and all artistic control passes out of the writer's hands (unless producer and writer are the same person). Once their work is sold, screenwriters and teleplay writers have no artistic say over rewrites and no power to stop their scripts from being changed beyond recognition. Their work becomes the exclusive property of the producers, and it's understood that if they stay with the project, they've been hired to do any and all rewrites as ordered. If they object, they are replaced by other writers.

The tradeoff, of course, is that film and television writers generally make more money than writers for the stage. Provided that one can break into these fields, one can actually make a living writing in them—something playwrights rarely pull off. What is forfeited, however, is that power to protect the artistic integrity of your work from the whims and fancies of those who bought it.

Many playwrights write for television and film to pay the bills and write for the theater to express themselves as artists. And, relatively speaking, the gulf between the two is as great as the three thousand miles separating New York and Los Angeles. The lure of Hollywood is strong, but new plays continue to be written, for in the theater the playwright is, in a very real sense, the supreme artist: What gets up there on the boards is properly his or her personal vision. And when playwrights see their work realized onstage and affecting an audience, that's a form of payment in itself. In fact, for most, it's an experience money can't buy.

The Shift from New York

Since the early 1970s playwrights have had steadily increasing opportunities for testing their new plays in the professional theater *before* submitting them for production consideration. It used to be that a writer of a new script would polish it as well as possible at home and submit it for immediate production consideration, or he or she would pull some actor friends together privately to hear it read. There was no system or generally accepted procedure to follow in the profession for "developing" a play, except in the case of the well-financed Broadway play, which had its out-of-town tryout production. However, the Broadway playwright had already signed a contract. Pre-production development opportunities hadn't been invented yet.

As already noted, play development activity proliferated in the intervening years, and a large number of theater companies and other organizations interested in fostering new plays committed themselves—in varying ways depending on artistic mission and budgets—to helping playwrights test and promote their new works. Consequently, even with national economic fluctuations and their effect on theater budgets, playwrights today have vastly more opportunities available to them than a generation ago.

As **Marsha Norman** attests: "The regional theaters really are the American theater now. . . . Probably, the really significant work we're doing gets done outside of New York."

Lee Blessing, whose plays have been developed almost entirely at regional theaters, agrees: "I have to hope that people stay conscious that that is where new plays get developed in this country now." Jeanne Blake, who is Blessing's wife and serves as the dramaturg and director of many of his plays adds:

It's been exciting to see what a welcome you're given, what a beautiful job they do in the regionals. For a long time, certainly, we'd had the prejudice that if it weren't going to happen for us in New York, where was our career going to be? And it's been just the opposite.

Terrence McNally gives this advice to young playwrights:

If I were starting all over again, right out of college, in my twenties, I'd probably move to a city like Seattle or Chicago, where I think theater is really exciting. And I'd say, "This is where I'm going to live and be the best playwright in Seattle," and I'd get actors and create a theater. Theater is local, it's regional, and New York is finally just a stop on the regional theater circuit.

This shift in "where the action is" in play development doesn't mean that New York no longer plays a potentially significant role—it does. Most of the upper tier of theatrical talent still makes New York its home base and, as a result, the amount of new play activity there is greater than in any other metropolitan center in the country. And the quality of the work is very high. However, even in New York, two significant shifts have taken place since the 1950s: First, most commercial productions of straight plays have moved from Broadway to the more intimate and lower-budget off-Broadway venues, and second, most new play production has shifted from the commercial to the not-for-profit theaters.

This latter change, more than anything else, has served as the great equalizing factor between play development in New York and in the regional companies, where virtually all production organizations are not-for-profit resident theaters. There may still be some added prestige if a play is developed and produced at a not-for-profit theater in New York, but this has grown less and less the case in recent years. More and more frequently, highly successful plays start, and often sustain, their professional lives far from New York. Many never have a life in New York at all. **Romulus Linney** speaks for many playwrights when he relates:

I've had wonderful experiences at resident theaters. You're not going to get the kind of huge, pyrotechnic blast-you-out-of-your-seat performances that you can get on Broadway with dazzling stars and so forth, but on the other hand the audience is closer to the play; there's more of an intimacy. The theater can be a little more relaxed and doesn't have to be gangbusters every minute. We tend to think it's got to blow you apart every ten minutes like a Hollywood movie. So I can't praise the resident theater movement highly enough. They fund new plays; they care about playwrights. They're not all angels— there are problems there, as in a lot of theater. But they have done more for American playwrights than anything else in the last twenty-five years.

Where to Start

So let's assume you have a play you think is ready for the development pipeline. Now what? As mentioned in Chapter 11, if you have a group of theater friends, preferably actors, you may want to produce a reading yourself with an invited audience. This is often the best way to start because you can stay in complete control of the project and design it to fit your needs exactly.

Lots of playwrights do this to begin the development process relatively quickly and initially test the play before exposing it to the world at large. As **Horton Foote** wisely suggests: "Instead of writers and actors and directors sitting around waiting for the phone to ring, it's better to try to find some companionable people and, in a house, in a living room, no matter where, to start generating something."

Beyond putting together your own reading, if you know people in the field of play development, by all means let them know you have a new unproduced play. As in most professions, whom you know can make an enormous difference as to how fast your work is read and how eager a theater will be to work with it.

However, if you don't know anyone at all in the profession, don't despair. If your work is good and you follow a few basic procedures, you'll most likely make a positive connection sooner or later.

Let's assume you know no one and have decided your play is ready for serious development. Without question the best way to begin is to pick up a current copy of *Dramatists Sourcebook*, published by Theater Communications Group (TCG), 355 Lexington Avenue, New York, New York 10017, or of *The Playwright's Companion*, Feedback Theatrebooks, P.O. Box 174, Brooklin, Maine 04616. These annual publications come out every fall and list hundreds of opportunities for playwrights throughout the country, as well as advice and information. Script opportunity entries are divided into several categories: production, prizes, publication, and development. Other sections list agents, grant and residency opportunities, and playwright service organizations. They're carefully put together, up-to-date, and accurate. My advice: Don't proceed without at least one or the other.

Another useful publication, also published by TCG, is *Theater Profiles*, a biennial reference on over two hundred and fifty professional theaters in America. Familiarity with theaters that produce new plays is an essential part of being an informed, working playwright, and the latest edition of this book will give you a detailed overview of what's out there. There are other reference guides useful to playwrights, all of which are listed and annotated in *Dramatists Sourcebook* and *The Playwright's Companion*.

Look through the development section of either of the latter two references and, difficult as it may be, select a number of programs you think might be right for your play. You'll discover a wide variety, ranging from theaters' play development workshops to special festivals, national conferences, and contests focusing exclusively on new plays.

What they hold in common is a concern for the playwright and a support of new work. They want to find writers to work with, to help them test their plays, and to launch new works into the mainstream. If you know people in the profession, ask them about opportunities they know of that may be promising. Much of this will be random shooting in the dark, but you have to start somewhere. You'll begin to learn who likes your work and who doesn't.

Starting out, you'll probably have to pass over the numerous programs requiring that a professional recommend or that an agent submit your work. However, there are numerous opportunities open to everyone, so don't be discouraged by the closed doors that read "no unsolicited manuscripts."

One of the best opportunities for unestablished writers is the various playwriting contests held around the country every year. An ever-increasing number of competitions are being offered for full-lengths, one-acts, specific theme-related plays, plays for and about women, for and about specific ethnic groups, and so on. And they all have an open submission policy. The prizes, of course, are generally awarded to plays that show little or no need for further work, yet many organizations sponsor contests looking for plays to put into their development programs. You may not win or place in a contest, but you just might hear from a theater anyway because they like your "voice" and the subject matter of your play. This happens often.

As you start submitting your work, keep in mind that, in most cases, you have one chance at each theater or program. In other words, don't start sending something out unless you're certain it's ready. I realize this sounds like a "Catch-22" situation, and in a sense it is: You need to put your play into development to get it perfected, and the only way to get into a development program is to have a brilliant play. But that's the business. Be forewarned: The competition is fierce.

My point here is that writers often jump the gun with submissions. While serving on selection committees for new play conferences and contests, I've seen it happen over and over again. Judging from the poor quality of most of the plays received for consideration, I've concluded that way too many people submit way too soon. They clearly haven't taken the time to go through the early rewrite process or do any early testing with friends. They haven't had the patience to put the play away a while and then pull it out later for another revision. They're satisfied to send it out still unpolished.

Once a play is considered by an organization and rejected, that's it. In almost all cases, you've blown it with that particular group. Resubmissions sometimes get taken seriously, but the play now comes in with a negative history. It's hard to shake that off. So, again, my advice is: Fight your impatience and be sure you've done absolutely everything you possibly can to make your play work before sending it out.

As **Michael Weller** puts it: "Be ready to do seven rewrites before it's ready to go, but don't show it until you can't think of anything that could be made better now."

How to Submit

As you research development in the *Sourcebook* or the *Companion,* note that theaters and other organizations that work with new plays vary greatly in submission requirements. Some are open to direct, unsolicited script submissions. Others only want to see a synopsis of the play and ten pages of dialogue. A number of theaters will only consider scripts that come with a professional recommendation or an agent submission. Still others ask for a completed application and a small reader's fee along with the script.

Once you've selected where you want to send your play, follow the submission requirements, whatever they may be. Pay close attention to the specified time of year that submissions will be accepted or to the submission deadline, if there is one. Theaters have legitimate reasons for posting their requirements and procedures. If you ignore them, more than likely your play will either be returned unread or simply tossed in the circular file. Harsh as it may sound, theaters simply don't have the staff hours—in other words, the funds—to deal with ill-timed or incompletely prepared submissions.

If there aren't specific submission requirements listed, always include a brief cover letter including a short one-paragraph biography on yourself. "Brief" is the operative word here. And take great care in composing this. You're presenting yourself as a writer, so this first introductory page should strongly hint that you are one. Attempts at being cute or clever should definitely be avoided.

If a synopsis of the play is requested, be especially careful in composing this as well. Make it short and to the point, never more than one page. Don't describe every turn of the plot but, rather, present the story so that in the telling you give a clear sense of what the play attempts to communicate. Don't ever submit a synopsis where you have to state the theme explicitly; it should be clear in how you summarize the action of the play.

If you want your script returned, include a self-addressed, stamped envelope (SASE) for that purpose. Mail your submission first class to ensure prompt and safe delivery. Put fourth-class "book rate" postage on the SASE—there's no logical reason to have your rejected script rushed home to you, so save your money. If you have access to cheap or free photocopying, you may opt not to include an SASE for return of the script. In that case, always mention this in your cover letter and, instead, include a letter-sized SASE for any communication the theater might send you about your submission.

I suggest submitting to several theaters or programs simultaneously, keeping careful records as to where you've sent your work and when. Index cards work well for this. And always have a list prepared of other places you'll send your play to when the inevitable rejections start coming in. When you get a return, send the play out again right away to the next theater on the list.

Most theaters list a response time. As a general rule, if you haven't heard from a theater two months after their own stated response time, a follow-up letter is warranted. If no response time is listed, you should give the theater six months to respond before sending a short and polite follow-up letter asking about your submission. Also keep a record of when you send these.

This may seem like an inordinately long time to hear about a theater's possible interest in your work, but that's the reality. As we'll discuss shortly, almost all theaters struggle to stay current with submissions. They're understaffed and overextended, and you have no choice but to be patient.

After you've sent out your first batch of submissions, the best thing to do is to sit down and start a new play. In other words, forget all about having sent your play out. Your only thoughts should be on the next one.

What Happens at the Other End

In most situations, when your script arrives at its destination, it is first logged in by the literary department, which is usually run by the literary manager. Normally a staff member, the literary manager processes all submissions and tries to help locate new scripts that the artistic director of the theater might be interested in developing or producing. If you've submitted your play to a playwrights' conference or new play contest, roughly the same procedure is followed. The only real difference is that a selection committee put together by the sponsoring organization usually replaces the role of the artistic director in choosing the scripts.

The literary manager assigns your script to a reader, one of several trusted people who read submissions, usually for a small per-script fee. The reader, having a general idea of the kinds of plays the theater is interested in, writes up a report on the play and returns the script and the report to the literary manager.

If the reader's report is positive, the literary manager will either take a look at the script or send it out to a second reader. If it's sent out again and the second report is also positive, the literary manager will definitely take a look at the play. If the initial reader's report is negative, your script may or may not be sent out to a second reader. This usually depends on how negative the first report is and how much the literary manager respects the opinion of the reader.

If the first report is very negative, the script will most likely be returned to you at this point with a simple form letter saying that your play "isn't what we're looking for at this time" or something similar. If it's sent out to another reader and the first reader's report is contradicted by a positive second report, the literary manager will usually take a look personally in order to make the decision. However, if the second report is also negative, the script will definitely be returned.

Assuming the best for your play, you should be prepared for a wait of at least six months before it's read by the literary manager. As you enter into this process with your play, keep in mind that most theaters working with new plays receive hundreds of scripts every year. Managing this volume of paper in a responsible, professional manner is a big job. That is why the profession of literary manager exists in the first place. Keeping track of so many submissions and where they all are in the reading process is complicated and much more involved than most playwrights realize. Everything has to be read and considered carefully. From the literary manager's perspective, at times the daily mail delivery begins to take on the likes of an endless paper stream with no cut-off valve.

If you're fortunate enough to get a positive response from the literary manager, your play will next find itself on the desk of the artistic director. I say "desk" because that's where it will typically stay for at least several more weeks (if not months). Artistic directors are extremely busy people, and carving out time to read new scripts, even with daily nudges from the literary manager, is sometimes next to impossible.

Eventually, of course, it will get looked at, and this is the critical read in terms of your script's future with that theater. With very few exceptions, the artistic director has the final say on script selection. If he or she likes it, great. If not, you'll get it back in the mail, this time most likely with a slightly different and more friendly rejection letter saying something like "This play isn't right for us at this time, but we'd be interested in seeing your future work." Admittedly, this is still a rejection, but don't overlook the fact that it's also an invitation to submit your next play. Remember, what has most commonly taken place is that the literary manager liked your play enough to give it to the boss to read. Be encouraged.

If the artistic director likes your play, either he or she or the literary manager will write or call you with this good news. And it is, indeed, amazingly good news. Even the largest theaters working with new plays can't possibly put more than a handful of new projects into development in any one season—perhaps one or two percent of the plays submitted.

If you've submitted your play to a playwrights' conference (a developmental "lab" of some sort) or to a contest, usually it is assigned two readers. If both readers' reports are positive, the script is read by a preliminary selection committee charged with choosing finalists. The finalists are passed on to another selection committee that chooses the "winner(s)" for that year's program or contest. Usually, conferences select a number of plays to be worked on.

What follows is the typical journey your play will go on once it gets accepted into a play development program. Obviously, the process varies from program to program, but the phases discussed below are what you'll most likely find in one form or another.

The Table Reading

This is usually the first phase. Rarely is it open to the public. Those in attendance include the playwright (if he or she is within easy travel distance), the actors reading the script, theater staff members, and, most likely, a handful of others whose opinions are highly valued by the artistic director or whomever else is in charge of the new play program.

Some care is taken to cast actors who come close to fitting the roles. Often this is a cold reading, meaning that actors are given scripts beforehand and have had the opportunity to examine the play singly but not to rehearse it. Other times, one rehearsal is scheduled with or without the playwright, usually on the day of the reading. A stage manager might be assigned to the project if there's a rehearsal, but typically there is no director involved.

Most often, the reading takes place around a large table, hence the name. The mood is informal and relaxed, and there's a conscious effort made to avoid any sense of a performance. The only purpose is to hear the play read aloud. There's almost always a feedback session with the playwright immediately following. If the playwright is too far away or otherwise unable to attend, the reading and the ensuing discussion are often taped and sent on to the playwright.

This early reading can be useful to get an initial feel for how well the play might work once on its feet. You can start to get a sense of how well character personalities play off each other, how successfully the play sustains forward movement, and whether it builds in tension as you intended. The feedback, if properly directed, can also be useful. Again, you should come armed with the questions you want to ask about what everyone has just heard.

The biggest drawback to this type of reading, of course, is that the actors haven't had a chance to discover their characters, to work with each other, or, in most cases, to even hear you explain your ideas. Everything is hit or miss. When there is no rehearsal, an actor can take a wrong approach to a key character, and as a result the emotional tone of the entire reading can be thrown off. If you face the situation of a cold reading, and if it's at all appropriate, I suggest you politely request a little time with the actors beforehand, when you can explain what you're after for each character and the whole play and answer questions. Doing this can protect you from a disaster.

The other possible drawback with this type of reading is that you may not have much or any input into casting the roles. Assigning actors who are at least close to what you envision for the characters is critical, even in this simple first reading. But for the table reading, auditioning is out of the question. In most cases, the theater will invite actors familiar to them to participate. If you're fortunate enough to be asked to suggest actors, by all means jump at the opportunity if you know of people you think would be perfect and available.

Chances are, the theater will put some talented actors at the table. And as **Wendy Wasserstein** says:

> The luckiest thing is when, in that first reading, even if you
> don't use the person eventually, you find somebody whose
> voice is right for your play. Because then that voice enters into
> you for that character and for rewriting that character.

Wasserstein goes on, however, to give this warning:

> If a reading is miscast, it's just so horrifying, because there goes
> the birth of the play. It's unbelievable . . . it's just not there. . . .
> This has happened to me, and it's awful. You feel like you're
> losing your hearing.

Or, as **John Guare** puts it:

> If it's the first time a play's being done, I don't want it done by
> actors I don't know. Since I'm a stranger to the theatrical,
> public life of the play, I want to make sure I'm working with

actors I trust. Because it's very, very hard to say, "My god, is it me or him?"—it's a nightmare. And that's part of our lives as playwrights, learning how we protect ourselves.

In most situations, theaters will at least consult with you about casting. If it appears that they're not going to, take the initiative and inquire as to how they plan to cast the reading. The general rule here and throughout the development process is to *be involved in the selection of actors* as much as you can be. If and when you're able to establish a relationship with a theater (it is to be hoped that you will once they've worked with one of your plays), it's usually much easier to become a part of the casting process.

Actors' Equity Association (AEA), the professional actors' and stage managers' union in this country, has a standard agreement with professional theaters for readings. At this level, actors receive no remuneration, but all travel expenses must be paid by the theater. The more established and committed theaters make every effort to use first-class actors and often pay a small fee as well as travel expenses. Rehearsal time, if any, is restricted by Actors' Equity to a few hours. (The union has shown flexibility in these agreements for readings, and this has helped engender play development activity.)

It can't be stressed enough the enormous debt playwrights owe the actors who help develop their plays. And there seems to be an endless supply. From my experience of putting my own and dozens of other writers' plays into development, I can guarantee you'll be amazed at the generosity of these artists and the devotion they bring to helping writers get their plays "wright."

David Ives offers this view:

> The theater is actors. Directors are nice, designers are wonderful, playwrights have their virtues, but without actors they are out of jobs. I admire actors and love to see them work. And in rehearsal actors always put their fingers on exactly what the play needs.

Actors are, by nature, giving people. And, of course, we playwrights couldn't complete our work without them. Take every opportunity to let the actors you work with know you appreciate that fact.

Always keep in mind that this first table reading—when you manage to get one—is as far as most plays go along the development path at any one theater. Theaters can't continue working with every play they put into development but must constantly narrow their choices to fit the few slots budgeted for further exploration. Unpleasant as the image may be from the playwright's perspective, this initial phase is like a giant sieve with irregular openings: Only a very few plays make it through. However, also remember that what one theater is passing up, another is looking for, in terms of theme or style.

If a decision is made not to continue developing your play, don't succumb to discouragement, but be grateful for the interest the theater has shown in you as a playwright. Even though a part of you feels abandoned midstream, you've heard actors read the play; the theater now knows you as a person, not just a name on a title page; and the waiting game with the next play you send them will undoubtedly be shorter. Never underestimate the importance of these accomplishments.

Consider, also, that you will have learned some positive things (I hope) about what works and what doesn't work at your initial reading. This should motivate you to go back into the play to make some necessary adjustments. Then resume the submission cycle. Keep searching for a theater that relates to your work and to what you're trying to say—until that giant sieve lets your play progress to the next phase.

Of course, the most difficult part of being cut off so early is that you basically have to start over in your search for a theater interested in developing your script. And you need to realize that it often takes years to connect with the theater that will make a significant commitment to your play.

The Public Sit-Down Reading

At a growing number of theaters, the next step is to schedule a simple public reading of the play. Some theaters call this a "concert reading" to differentiate it from the non-public reading around the table. It takes place in an actual theater setting, and if a table reading preceded it, the same actors might be used. Usually, there is at least one rehearsal scheduled for either the day of the reading or a day or two just before.

Because the actors will rehearse and the reading will be public, a director is normally assigned to this kind of project. Although time is obviously limited, his or her task is to begin to shape the reading as much as possible to the playwright's vision. Given the time constraints, the director can do little more than lay out broad concepts and interpretive ideas about the play and then give basic adjustments to the actors after hearing it read.

It's normal for directors on this type of project to let you, the playwright, do much of the talking at rehearsals. However, with the appearance of a director you have to begin contending with another artist whose job is to be "in charge" of the actors. What's important is that you thoroughly discuss the script with him or her before meeting with the actors. You want to be sure you're working on the same wavelength—that is, in agreement about what the play's trying to say and what *you* want the play to say.

At this phase the actors are still only reading the script. Sometimes two rows of chairs are arranged, one downstage of the other. The actors remain onstage throughout the reading but move from the upstage to the downstage chairs when they "enter" a scene, and they reseat themselves upstage when they make an "exit." There's no other blocking or staging of any part of the play. Again, a feedback session with the audience is often scheduled so that, immediately after the reading, you, the director, and/or the literary manager can solicit responses.

As before, the purpose is to hear the play, to listen to the voices of the characters, but the presentation before a public audience in a theater allows the playwright to get a keener sense of how the play might work in performance. It's always a bit mysterious, when the play is read this way in front of an audience, how problems in the script often jump out at you. This public "airing" of the play somehow allows you to confront the play anew, as if you were hearing it for the first time. You go on the journey with the audience and experience it with them. The objectivity this can give you is invaluable.

Three bits of advice at this point. First, if the director doesn't have a clue as to what your play is about, and you perceive he or she isn't willing to strive to give you what you want—even under the time constraints—don't proceed with the project. It'll be a waste of time. This doesn't happen often, but the possibility always exists. Now is not the time to be lured into a new interpretation of your play. This is when you need to experience your vision for the piece. Don't even listen to a director's alternative ideas, or anybody else's, until you've adequately tested your own and heard your play read as you intended it.

Second, I strongly urge you to refuse any offer of a *public* reading unless at least one substantial rehearsal can be scheduled with you present. There is nothing more risky and potentially painful than to expose your work to an outside audience when you've had no opportunity to hear the cast read it beforehand and—with or without a director's involvement—to make basic acting adjustments where needed.

It can do you and the play great harm to experience the audience's response to a reading which is wholly or partially out of step with what you intended. The script may sound like it doesn't work at all, when in fact it's the cast that isn't working. (And take note: The actors may be brilliant. They're just wrong for their parts or have the wrong take on their roles.)

I've heard many horror stories from seasoned playwrights who have learned the hard way, and I've had my own unpleasant situations. Just remember that you're perfectly within your rights to insist on enough time with your actors to go through it once and give notes. It's your play and the reading is for your benefit. Don't work with people who don't agree with this simple fact.

Third, it's worth repeating that, in the feedback session, never get coaxed into explaining what you meant—not even in a line. Listen instead to what the people who have just heard your play think it means and what problems they had. Let them describe their experience with the play and give their explanations of what it said. For as soon as *you* explain, all comments become tainted. From that point on you'll only get opinions about how well you accomplished what you set out to do and what you need to change to do it better. Truly valuable responses will no longer be forthcoming. It is no one's job but yours to figure out what needs to be changed.

The Staged Reading

This next step in the development process is used extensively. For professional companies, staged readings normally involve fifteen to twenty hours of rehearsal, depending on whether the theater hires actors who belong to Actors' Equity Association. If it does, usually the rehearsal follows the union's limit of twenty hours, inclusive of performances. Non-Equity theaters generally take a bit more time, but not much.

Because Actors' Equity does not require that actors get paid for readings, it does not allow the theater to collect admission fees for the event. The union does require that actors be reimbursed for travel expenses. In practice, most theaters do pay actors a small fee plus travel expenses. For non-Equity projects, every effort is usually made to avoid having actors pay even simple expenses out of their own pockets.

Staged readings always involve a director, who schedules about three or four substantial rehearsals with actors he or she has cast especially for the roles. On rare occasions auditions are held. Playwrights are usually consulted on casting choices, as they should be. The amount of movement or blocking involved varies greatly from director to director. Typically, the actors are on their feet, making entrances and exits and executing at least the essential physical actions as called for in the script. A simply improvised floor plan is laid out on the stage, with key furniture pieces and other special set requirements suggested. Theaters which produce staged readings regularly often use modular set elements, such as cubes, simple tables and chairs, door units, and so on. Props are kept to a bare minimum because the actors still have their scripts in hand. Simple lighting effects might be incorporated, but these usually involve little more than fades at the ends of scenes.

Sometimes actors remain onstage throughout the reading, sitting off to the side or upstage when not in a scene. Selected stage directions are read if the requirements of the set or a specific physical action are critical to the understanding of a scene, yet are too complicated to stage with actors holding scripts.

The Playwright–Director Relationship

The director—for better or for worse—will become your artistic partner for the staged reading and any more advanced work on the play. Be prepared to enter into a creative collaboration with him or her as the project unfolds. The director will serve as a liaison between you and the actors, offering (after consulting with you first) his or her own interpretive ideas along the way.

Always keep in mind that although you may still have overall control of your play, the director is in charge of the immediate project and, working with the actors, is responsible for bringing the script to life onstage. If he or she understands your play and what you're trying to accomplish with it, this can be a wonderful collaboration. Without that understanding there's a high probability the project will short-circuit, at least for you.

In describing the best directors he's worked with in his long career, **Arthur Miller** says: "They always perceived what the underlying thrust was in the play and didn't get lost in the details." From this point on in the development process, this is the only kind of director you want to work with. **Tina Howe** sums it up well:

> What a playwright needs most is a director, because a good
> director lifts the play off the page into radiant life. The
> playwrights who've succeeded have had that director. To my
> mind, it's the most important collaboration in the theater.

The key here is careful and frequent communication. It's absolutely essential that you and your director agree on just about everything in the script, having worked through any perceived differences before the first rehearsal. Make it your goal to eliminate any surprises once actors get involved, at least in terms of what your director is telling them. You don't want to suddenly hear your director say something in rehearsal that you know will skew the play or twist a relationship between two characters into the very thing you went to great pains to avoid. Of course, there will be surprises. Things will come up that will need clarification by you, the author. But the more you and your director can be in sync, the more positive will be the work you accomplish in the limited rehearsal time available.

Directing Your Own Work

This brings up the question of whether or not you should ever consider directing your plays yourself. It is generally considered wise not to attempt serving in both capacities because of the way it changes your relationship to the script. As director, your primary responsibility is to bring the play to life with the cast you have to work with. Your primary focus is on your actors and their problems, on what they're giving you. Your work centers on how you can shape their work into performances that mesh with each other and, together, make the most sense of the play as a whole.

John Patrick Shanley, who directs the first production of most of his plays, admits:

> When you direct your own work, you know that you're going to
> be in big trouble if there are serious problems with the play,
> because you're going to be too busy directing it to fix it. You
> can fix things, but you can't fix *structure*—you can't fix big, big
> things and direct the play. You don't have time.

And **Romulus Linney** says:

> In most cases, I don't think it's such a good idea to direct your
> plays. You really need a whole other set of nerves and blood

and bones to come in there and give it life. You usually very much need for somebody else to direct.

What often happens, if you're functioning as a director should function, is that your objectivity as a playwright greatly diminishes. You become so tied up with the cast and production that you lose that precious distance you need to see if your crafting of the play works as well as it could. It's no longer possible to step back and concentrate solely on the effectiveness of the words you've written, watching how the staging and performances aid or abet the communication that you, the author, wanted. For most playwrights—especially those just starting out—losing this objective eye is a serious hindrance. In the end, the play usually suffers.

Of course, every developmental project presents its own set of circumstances, and serving as director may very well be the wisest plan of action. Usually, if you're working with a theater on a project, you won't have this choice open to you. However, if you've put together a project yourself and can't find a good director—one that you feel truly understands your play and has had considerable experience with the kind of project you're developing—you'll have to function as your own director. Sometimes rehearsal and time limitations dictate that you serve in both capacities.

On the positive side, when you do take on the dual role, you eliminate the possibility for misinterpretation and distortion of your play. You can communicate your ideas directly to your actors, without working through another person—a clear, unobstructed channel from writer to performer. You stay in control throughout.

As **John Patrick Shanley** has discovered, directing his own work has also put pressure on him to work harder than ever to have the play ready by the first rehearsal: "I used to think, 'Well, we've got four weeks, I can tinker with this.' But I don't feel that way anymore."

In the final analysis, it's usually best for your play—your primary consideration—that you enter into a partnership with a talented director, someone who understands and believes in your play and who knows his or her own craft very well. On average, the end result is stronger.

Enter the Dramaturg

In more sophisticated play development programs, a *dramaturg* may also appear on the scene at the staged reading level. Ideally, this person is well-versed in dramatic structure and functions as an adviser to the playwright, objectively helping to identify what is or is not working in the script and offering suggestions on how to strengthen the play. Although the director often pulls double duty and serves in this role, the dramaturg, as an independent member of the collaborative team, has become a common participant.

As a third set of eyes and ears, the dramaturg doesn't have to deal with actors and the task of putting the script on its feet, so instead he or she can concentrate exclusively on the play's dramatic construction. In some cases, dramaturgs also do research into topics relevant to the play that might be useful for the playwright in rewrites, but this is a luxury usually reserved for established writers with a record of success.

In the best dramaturg–playwright relationships, the dramaturg becomes a sort of silent, temporary writing partner, helping you the playwright reinforce the play structurally, especially by asking you valuable questions that get you thinking about, or rethinking, the specific detailing of scenes. Obviously, he or she does not actually rewrite pages of script, but the dramaturg does become an extension of your brain as you both focus in on the play. Needless to say, such a collaborator should sit in on all script discussions you have with your director.

Know What You Want

You, your director, and your dramaturg, if there is one, should spend considerable time discussing not only the play but also what you hope to accomplish, for the time allotted the typical staged reading is much too limited for you to deal with everything you'd like to. That is, determine at this point in the life of the play what are the most important things for you to get a sense of. It might be the degree of intensity in a relationship, or how fast the piece should play, or what trimming, if any, needs to be done, or where the play might fall flat, causing all forward movement to grind to a halt.

If you go into the project expecting to solve everything, usually nothing very productive gets accomplished, no specific problem gets dealt with effectively. The staged reading is just another single step in the process of getting the play wrought perfectly. It's one of many tests of the material. You and your collaborators need to keep this in mind from the start of the project.

Staged Reading Pitfalls

If handled properly, the staged reading can be an extremely valuable test for a play. The work is on its feet for the first time, and you can begin to get a feel for how it might work in full production. At best, it will give you a taste of the real thing.

Often theaters will offer two and sometimes three performances of the project, so that playwrights have the opportunity to look closely at how the script plays in front of different audiences. Although rehearsals are limited in scope, actors have had more time to explore characterizations and discover how their roles function in the play as a whole. The director has been able to give some definition to the piece in terms of rhythm and pacing. Audiences then quickly forget that the actors are reading from scripts, and when everything works, the staged reading can have surprising power.

Again, however, there are potential pitfalls. The most common danger is that a director will try to accomplish too much in too little time. For example, asking actors to execute the major blocking and physical actions for an entire play while still reading the words on the page is a big order. There's also a natural tendency in good actors to make the reading a real performance in spite of limited rehearsal. They're going to be out in front of an audience, and all their instincts are telling them to perform. They may push themselves beyond what can reasonably be expected at this point, and their work may suffer. The entire project can become stressful and the results uneven.

If a director is not experienced with the staged reading format and tries to do too much, what usually happens is that the opening scenes get most of the attention and, as time runs out, the last half of the play remains relatively unexplored. This, obviously, will tend to distort what you learn from the audience's response during the reading or in feedback sessions afterwards.

A related problem arises when too much rehearsal time has been allotted. Good actors quickly reach a point where they start getting "off the page." When given enough time, they inevitably begin making the transition from reading to performance. In a public presentation, their eyes start leaving the page for too long, half-memorized lines start to be paraphrased, and cadences and internal rhythms you've struggled to write into speeches are lost. This is normal and expected in the rehearsal process for a full production, in which case the actors eventually pass through a transition period and the play reappears in the late rehearsals with greater precision and clarity than ever. However, if rehearsals for a staged reading are extensive enough to reach this transition from reading to performance, the project will suffer. The time simply isn't there to carry the work *farther*, so that it's once more serving the text as it should.

Along these lines, **John Patrick Shanley** says that the staged reading doesn't always work for him:

> It becomes a middle ground, with just enough rehearsal for the spontaneity to have gone out of it. The actors are not playing "I love you"—they're playing "I think I walk over here on that line." So you end up in this gray world that's kind of horrible. Sometimes the readings work, and that's great. But I wouldn't bank on it.

Romulus Linney agrees:

> A staged reading is halfway between a production and a reading. It's not spontaneous. The actors are looking at the script while they're trying to indicate. . . . It's like a half-born creature, not one thing or the other.

This problem rarely occurs in Equity theaters because of mandated rehearsal-hour limits for staged readings, except perhaps when the time allotment for a full-length play is given to a short play. In some non-Equity situations, rehearsals can go on too long and spontaneity can be lost. I've found that a good general rule for staged readings is that over fifteen to twenty hours rehearsal for a full-length play brings you into the danger zone.

The basic rule for staged readings, then, is to keep everything very simple. In a scene involving difficult action, for example, such as a physical fight, it's better to have the actors concentrate on reading the lines rather than to stage the moment. A modest suggestion of the physical action is usually a wiser choice, or, if the action is complicated and interwoven with the lines, it's preferable to have someone read the stage directions so the actors are free to concentrate on the script.

Constantly remind yourself (and your director if necessary) that this is not a production of the play, as much as everyone involved may wish it were. Just lay down some very clear ground rules in your initial discussions with your director that safeguard the project from becoming overly ambitious from a physical-action standpoint.

Rewriting During Rehearsals

With the staged reading, you enter a new phase in the development process. During rehearsals, you often learn wonderful things about your characters from the actors, and you may discover how a scene needs to be rewritten to work exactly as you want it to. You should feel free to make line adjustments or to cut material that the actors are clearly communicating through their presence onstage or their physical relationships. Because it's a reading, the actors should be able to make adjustments almost up to performance time. Nothing ever gets set in stone. The whole project is being done to test and experiment with the script, so take advantage of it.

Actors are usually excited to see that you're learning things about the play through working with them. They're there to help you do just that and are happy when their playwright is making discoveries.

At the same time, be careful that you don't let your collaborators talk you into doing too much reworking in rehearsal. It's a matter of balance, for you still need to experience the play you wrote getting on its feet in front of an audience. Except for obvious and relatively minor adjustments, I suggest you politely insist on leaving in any questionable scenes and see how they play first. You need to witness the flow of the whole piece in front of an audience, how it unfolds from beginning to end with no interruptions.

Like the public sit-down reading, when you sit in the audience experiencing your play as other people do for the first time, the staged reading will give you a marvelous sense of hearing the piece differently. All of a sudden certain lines will have new meaning, ideas will come to you that you've never thought of, feelings will emerge that you've never felt. Because the insights gained are often unexpected, you may be surprised at how you find yourself responding. Designed to help you identify problem areas and give you insights as to how you might fix them, the staged reading at its best serves as the most important pre-production test of your play's stageworthiness.

How Many Readings?

Established playwrights will often groan that their plays are "read to death." What they mean is that they keep getting offers for sit-down or staged readings but can't get a theater to mount productions of their work. This, of course, is a fact of life for all but a small group of playwrights in this country. Production opportunities are few and far between, compared to the opportunities for readings. A ratio of a thousand to one is probably close.

Wonderful as readings are, there comes a point when these groans are justified. You can only hear your play read so many times before there's nothing more to learn, even when the readings involve entirely different casts, different directors, different stages, and different audiences. Obviously, the number and type of reading opportunities any one play can be put through and still have productive results will vary. If rewriting is extensive from draft to draft, continued testing is important and can be very helpful. However, most plays in development eventually reach a point where the "law of diminishing returns" sets in and another reading of any type simply will not be worth the effort.

The fact is, a play desperately needs to move on to the next step in the process.

The Workshop Production

The next rung up the developmental ladder is the workshop production. Although in recent years the lines have begun to blur between a well-rehearsed, ambitiously mounted staged reading and a workshop, generally a "workshop" signifies that the actors have memorized their lines, so that the performance is totally off-book. Usually a two- or three-week rehearsal period is allotted, depending on the dimensions of the play, and it's fully mounted in terms of blocking, stage business, and use of props. Designers normally become involved in the project; sets, lighting, and costumes, although dealt with simply, are given enough serious attention so that these elements begin to have theatrical impact in performance.

What mainly separates a workshop from a full production is the size of the budget for the project. Costs are kept to a bare minimum, and most of the available dollars go toward giving the actors enough rehearsal time for substantial explorations into subtext and character. Thus, the foremost goal is the actors' concentration on delving deeply into the material, rather than on design and other production elements.

As a result, the typical workshop has a rather "bare bones" look to it. Even so, most workshops are scheduled for a run of several public performances. Larger theaters often have an entire second season of workshop productions of new plays with its own subscription series.

To make it to this point with your play means that you've arrived at a level of work on your material that the most ambitious of readings can never provide. At long last your script pages are transformed before your eyes and ears into a work of live theater in performance. Participating in rehearsals as your play takes shape with a gifted director and a talented cast makes all your lonely weeks of writing and long months (or years) of waiting worthwhile. And when the actors have struggled through memorization of your lines and start to live their roles fully, interacting naturally with each other and their onstage environment, it's a thrill few artists ever experience. You've entered the ranks of that rare breed in the theater called the "produced playwright."

Of course, things can still go wrong and often do. Your director may suddenly no longer understand your play the way you thought and may decide to take it places you don't want it to go. An actor may not be connecting with a role and start distorting what you intended. Or maybe time hasn't been budgeted properly and the final days are spent in panic wondering how an audience can be brought in to see something so incoherent. As **Terrence McNally** rightly points out:

> Those three weeks go by so fast. The actors will give you two weeks, make it all about you and your script—not quite two weeks. The third week is about them: Their asses are on the line, they're the ones performing. . . . Don't ever put off anything you can do to make the play better before rehearsal and think, "Oh, I'll fix it then." You'll find a million things to do in rehearsal as it is, even with a "perfect" script.

In the theater you're always open to dangers. That's the nature of the beast. My advice is to think positively and be cautiously optimistic. Insist on being there when the critical casting and design decisions are made and for the important rehearsals: the first read-throughs, the first run-throughs once it's on its feet, and the final week. Never be afraid to say what you think, but speak up right away when you sense a problem. Strive to stay always in close, open communication with your director. Most importantly, always have your script as ready as it possibly can be before going into rehearsals. Other than that, you can only hope for the best and ride out any storms with as much dignity as possible.

Continuing with Rewrites

Expect that your relationship to your play will go through a rather unique shift during rehearsals. As performance values begin to appear, you'll find yourself oddly distanced and removed from your own creation, and the play will increasingly take on a life of its own. Or, rather, your script will now be in the hands of other talented artists and they'll make it their own.

As **Athol Fugard** explains, this is as it should be:

> Certain of my plays that exist now in published form owe quite a lot to the rehearsal process, where actors have helped me understand what I've written . . . see areas which needed to be fleshed out just a little bit more and made me conscious of redundancies.

Accordingly, as you make new discoveries during rehearsals, especially when scripts are out of the actors' hands, it's important that you feel free to put in changes, at least up to the final week or so. After that, incorporating rewrites becomes increasingly difficult.

Sometimes there's a tendency to back off from making adjustments during rehearsals as the director and actors "take over," especially when they seem to be making something work which you suddenly realize could have been written better. There's also the problem of the director or cast who do not want to go back into a scene they've struggled to bring to life. Try not to be intimidated when you sense this resistance. Always remind yourself of the ultimate purpose of the workshop, and, with as much grace as you can muster, politely insist that your changes be put in.

Also be careful not to fall into the classic playwright's trap of blaming actors for something that isn't working. Of course, it may be you have an actor problem. However, As **Terrence McNally** advises us:

> I used to blame everything on the actors: "Well, they're playing it wrong." No. I really take full responsibility for the writing now, and I leave the acting to the actors. That may sound flip, and I don't mean it that way. The simple fact is that it all comes home to roost. If something's not right in the play, it's going to be right back in your face when it's up there on the stage.

Keeping this in mind, the only other real danger with rewriting during workshop rehearsals—assuming you and your director and/or dramaturg are all on the same wavelength—is not to overadjust your work to fit the particular talents of specific actors. You can thereby subtly, or not so subtly, distort your play. Such changes may work wonderfully with this cast, and indeed some reworking may be necessary, but you risk throwing the script out of balance when it once again has to stand on its own without this set of workshop actors.

The Full Production

This, of course, is the final phase, the home port, the ultimate destination. Again, it differs from the workshop mainly in terms of the sheer size of the project, which the budget reflects. The extra dollars buy more rehearsal time, more fully realized sets, lights, and costumes, more publicity, more performances. The production is usually part of a theater's mainstage season, so it normally occurs in a larger theater than a workshop space. Your play is given as lavish a treatment as any show the theater presents.

When a play makes it this far in the professional theater, it will have been through many readings and, most likely, at least one workshop. Throughout all this developmental work, a refinement process has been going on. By the time rehearsals begin for the first full production, the script should be about as solid as it's going to get. Changes, even substantial rewrites, are possible at this point. But the typical journey for a new play in today's professional theater has allowed for such substantial testing that your primary job now will be to watchdog the proceedings to protect your creation from eleventh-hour distortions. You've slaved over this material so long and been through so much with it that you've earned the right to watch over it closely—and you'd be a fool not to.

For the vast majority of American playwrights, landing a full production of a play in the main season of a respected regional, or resident, theater is a major career accomplishment. As mentioned earlier, there was a day when only a New York production could solidly establish a playwright's career. Of course, such an event still has tremendous impact in terms of publicity and reputation building. But it is definitely no longer the way most writers for the theater launch themselves. Increasingly, successful productions in the regionals open the door for New York productions to follow—and a complete reversal of a long-established pattern occurs. Most dramatists first workshop their new plays far out of town, and even the most consistently produced of them have shifted their focus from New York to the regional theaters.

When your play makes it to a full professional production at a reputable theater, you automatically enter a new league as a playwright. And, depending on the size and significance of the presenting theater, the reception your play receives will have a profound effect on its future life. If it's a hit with the local audiences and critics, more than likely it will be picked up by other theaters around the country. The networking between professional theaters is extensive, and many plays have a long and happy production history playing in regional theaters. This even happens independent of any plans for a future New York production. If New York theater producers get interested, all the better. Rest assured, they keep their eyes on the new work being presented around the country. Also, when a play is received positively in the regionals, publishers of plays, such as Samuel French or Dramatists Play Service, will also become interested.

Do You Need an Agent?

It's only when a first-class professional production is within your reach that the question of representation really needs to become a serious consideration. The idea that you need an agent before then is often suggested in various books and articles, but don't be misled. Only you can effectively guide your play along the developmental road. Most agents don't have the time or inclination to stay on top of a script's progress through this maze.

However, when the play starts receiving consistently positive praise at the workshop level and beyond, good agents definitely will become interested in your script. Conveniently, it's only at this point that you're going to need the services a good agent can provide.

My point here is that an agent doesn't "place" your play. You do. And it's only when you've managed to maneuver and nurse your script to the brink of a professional mainstage production that an agent becomes useful. In fact, you'd then be foolish not to have a good agent representing you, because the agent's primary job is to protect you in contract negotiations and generally look out for your financial interests regarding the script.

Before any real money is in the offing, you're probably better off without an agent, because then you won't be forced to constantly work through an intermediary when dealing with theaters. You also won't fall into the often disastrous trap of convincing yourself that your agent is faithfully sending your script out to theater after theater, playing the game of artful persuasion with literary managers and artistic directors. The fact is, agents don't do that very well. You may hear or read that Agent X brilliantly handled a script, landing a first-class production at a premier regional theater. But, except in extremely rare cases, the client was one of a handful of already established playwrights, someone whose name alone opened the door that needed to be opened.

As **Michael Weller** relates:

> I had an agent for fifteen years, and there was not a single production I got because of that agent, not one. And yet he was a very, very good agent—excellent. Once you had a theater, he was a great negotiator: Terrific at contracts, understood what's a good placement and a bad placement, and all that. But I knew as much about all these theaters as he did. I was left to do it myself. And I don't think there are too many exceptions to that.

Granted, without an agent you're forced to maneuver your way around the "no unsolicited submissions" door at many theaters. At times this will seem like another "Catch-22" situation: You can't get a theater to consider a play without an agent, but you can't get an agent unless a theater has first taken a serious interest in your play.

Unfortunately, this is a fact of life for all theater artists, not just playwrights. Actors just starting out, for example, have a similar dilemma. And their only strategy is to find work wherever they can and then struggle to get directors and agents to come see their work. At times the obstacles seem overwhelming and insurmountable. However, somehow new and previously "unknown" theater artists of all persuasions arrive on the scene every season. People are constantly breaking down the barriers by tenacity, perseverance, hard work, and talent (usually in that order). In other words, you simply have to make it happen in whatever way you can and find the energy and the faith in your work to keep you going until you do.

On the positive side, once you manage to start down the developmental road with a new play that has genuine potential, doors that at first seemed rusted shut tend to swing open. You meet people and people become interested in you and your work. I'm not saying it's an easy road, but it certainly is not impassable without representation. For a playwright just starting out in the profession it's a struggle, to be sure, but an agent, even if you manage to land one of the best, isn't going to get you where you want to go any faster than your own efforts will.

How to Get an Agent

Even when you're ready, finding a good agent—the right agent for you— is rarely easy. Oddly, getting a representative interested in your work, even if you have been offered a contract by a reputable theater, is often very difficult. Agents are always busy, overworked, and engaged with more clients than even they think they can handle. Coaxing one of the better agents to see a play being mounted in New York is a herculean task; getting one to see an out-of-town production is simply not a reasonable expectation.

The most reliable way to get agents familiar with your work is to send a carefully written query letter asking if they would be interested in reading your play, highlighting the production history, noting any upcoming productions or other developmental work being done with it, and a bit of information about you. Some will be interested in taking a look, and some won't. If agents respond positively, the reading of your play may take some time, but if they request it, it'll get read.

If, after reading the play, an agent calls and is interested, he or she will most likely suggest that the two of you meet. If not, politely suggest it yourself. The point here is that you must be able to relate to and feel you can communicate with this person. A meeting "in the flesh" is almost essential to find this out. As much as you want representation, there's no point to working with anyone you feel uneasy with or are seriously intimidated by.

Any agent who agrees to represent you is working for you, not the other way around. I've known many writers who don't like their agents and don't feel comfortable even calling them on the phone. To be sure, there are often basic personality differences between writers and agents, but finding and maintaining a workable relationship shouldn't be an impossibility. Why enter into any sort of relationship, professional or otherwise, with someone you don't want to talk to? Life's too short to set yourself up for that kind of frustration.

Of course, you do want the agent to serve you well in negotiations, and that takes a special kind of energy and push. What's critical, however, is that the two of you can communicate comfortably and that you trust this individual to serve your needs, not his or her own. You should definitely feel that your agent respects and understands your work and genuinely wants to serve your career. As obvious as this may sound, I state it here because of the many horror stories I've heard from playwrights with agents who are not serving them well at all.

If you think you're at a point in your career where you definitely need representation, I suggest you try to make contact with at least two or three potential agents before making a decision. Again, the *Dramatists Sourcebook* and *Playwright's Companion* always have up-to-date listings of the most reputable theatrical agencies. Ask around, too. Compare notes with writers, directors, and producers. Agents have definite reputations.

Unless you have a major first-class production pending in New York or at a major regional theater, you should focus on the reputable smaller agencies, rather than mega-talent stockyards such as William Morris or International Creative Management. There is nothing wrong with the big agencies, but they spend most of their time on clients who have big names or a big hit. The odds are that you'll consistently get lost in the shuffle on some assistant's desk if you're not "where the money is." The smaller agencies are more apt to give you serious attention and be willing to make a more long-term commitment to representing you and your work.

Developing and Maintaining Contacts

Without question, most plays get into development and are eventually produced because of "who you know." The theater business is an extended network of working professionals throughout the country, and one way or another you must plug into it. This can start simply enough by volunteering your time at a theater you admire and getting to know some of the staff. As often as you possibly can, go to readings and workshops of new plays and make a point of meeting the writers and directors. Do some research and locate the organizations within striking distance that are working on new plays. Get on their mailing lists and go to see their projects. It shouldn't take you long to accumulate a list of acquaintances in the field of play development.

The danger in this approach is that many writers come in the door with an agenda written all over their faces—and their scripts hidden under their coats! For theater staff people there's no bigger turnoff than the calculating, maneuvering playwright. As you enter into this game, make a point of leaving your own ambition on the shelf next to the copies of your scripts, at least until you've established a genuine relationship with a theater. This will give you credibility as a person first. Then, perhaps weeks, months, or a year or more later, they will accept you as a playwright. Long-term, productive artistic relationships are always forged this way. Self-serving and self-centered people aren't fun to work with for long, even if they write brilliant plays. The veterans in this business know this and have learned it the hard way.

Once you've made some connections, it's important to maintain them over time. Theater people are frenetically busy most of the year, and if you don't make the effort to stay in touch, you'll soon be forgotten. It's not that they're being unfriendly or that you made a bad first impression. They're simply too preoccupied to keep up with playwrights. So make it a point to reconnect on a regular basis with the people who might one day be interested in your work. If you have a reading of a new play, by all means send a postcard announcing it to everyone you can think of in the business. Few people will actually come, but they'll read the card and be reminded that you're still around and active.

The Art of Waiting

It bears repeating that patience is the operative word when you're at the beginning of the development process with a new play. Every script presents a different set of circumstances but, generally speaking, it is three to four years—and sometimes much longer—from the time a play is first released into the developmental process to the day it (possibly) opens as a mainstage production. I realize that sounds like an absurdly long time, but let's put your play through a typical development sequence.

As mentioned above, expect at least a six-month wait before first hearing from a theater. If the literary manager likes the play and passes it on to the artistic director, typically it'll be at least another two to three months before he or she reads the script. So now you're eight or nine months into your wait. And if a positive response comes mid-season from the artistic director, chances are that nothing can really start, not even a simple reading, until the following season. That's another six months or more. Total wait so far: at least a year and most likely more.

If the response to the first reading of your play is positive, most likely it will be slotted into the next phase of the development program—a public sit-down reading or a staged reading—when a director is assigned to the project.

By the time this decision has been made, however, the play development schedule for that season—and, possibly, for the next season also—will have already been determined and announced. This means that if the theater likes what it hears at the reading, it may promote your play to the staged reading or workshop phase to test it further the *following* season.

Then, if this happens, and the theater still loves your play, they might decide to slot it into their production schedule the season following that.

I count three years so far from when you first decided it was time to test your play. And that's if everything goes beautifully. If the play doesn't get beyond the first reading, you have to try again at another theater, which usually means another "initial" reading. A fact of life in this profession is that, in the vast majority of cases, the opening of a "new play" really means the opening of a play that has been working its way through the developmental gauntlet for a very long time.

Creating a Body of Work

The most productive way to deal with the slowness of the process is this: Always be working on a new play. Given the above scenario, it'll take at least three years of writing on various projects before you can hope for production consideration on the earliest of them. You can take comfort in the fact that you're creating a body of work—an ever-growing "family" of scripts, one or more of which may attract serious professional interest someday.

Indeed, your job and your true reward as a playwright is to keep creating new work. It's the *process,* not the end result, that is the dramatist's *raison d'etre.* **Romulus Linney** has this to say about the completion of a new play:

> I want to go on to the next thing. Because to me writing is a
> way of life, rather than a creation of one or two or three things.
> It's an ongoing process.

In other words: You must simply love to write. Then, when there's interest in one of your plays, it's always a bonus.

This steady focus on your writing—and what you want to communicate in your work—is the key to continued, long-term sanity in this business. And it's the only way to establish your career over time. One of the problems today is that so many people want instant success. In the theater that rarely happens. The so-called "new face" with a hit play in New York has more than likely been writing plays for years and struggling through the developmental maze like everybody else. So you have to keep sending your work out there and keep promoting it and nursing it along wherever you can. You need to keep looking for opportunities to meet people who might be interested in your plays. But at the same time, you need to keep working on that next play and the next—all the while developing a mastery of the craft.

If you're going to become a playwright, you have to write plays. Many plays. And the way you do that is to keep at it. **David Ives** offers a warning along with good counsel:

> If you get away from writing for too long, the rationalizations
> get to be too easy. You say, "Well, I really don't feel like it
> today, so I won't write"—and three years later you still haven't
> sat down to write something. That's why a schedule is so
> important—writing at the same time of day every day.

Edward Albee says his goal is to write one play every year, and he's done it for over a quarter of a century now. And **Horton Foote** says:

> The main thing is to get a body of work. It's hard when you
> feel unwanted. You feel there's no place for you. But don't
> "stick" on one play. This is one thing I am sure of. When it's
> done, and it's the best you can do at that moment in your life,
> then go on to something else. You can always come back to
> that one, and you might come back to it three years, ten years
> later.

As you write, you grow as a writer. Your plays build on each other. You find your voice over time, and if you have a God-given gift for writing for the theater, sooner or later your work will get produced and you'll experience your completion as a playwright.

The Dramatists Guild

No matter what your current level of achievement, if you're at all serious about your future as a playwright, I urge you to join the New York–based Dramatists Guild, an organization of like-minded people who are writing for the theater and striving to get their work produced. Formed in 1919, the Guild is the only professional association of playwrights, composers, and lyricists in existence, and as an organization it has much to offer. To quote from their statement of purpose:

> The Guild was founded to protect and promote the professional interest of authors of dramatic and dramatico-musical works, to protect their rights in such works, to improve the conditions under which their works are created and produced and to formulate types of production contracts with respect to such works. A fair royalty, maintenance of subsidiary rights, artistic control, and ownership of copyright have remained of paramount importance since the Guild was established.

In addition to this emphasis on the business/production side of the profession, the Guild publishes *The Dramatists Guild Quarterly,* a monthly newsletter, and an annual directory that lists agents, festivals, fellowships, play contests, producers, and so on. It also holds numerous special events and symposia in major U.S. cities each year. Every Guild activity, of course, focuses on the playwright's interests and concerns.

There are three levels of membership:

Active member: To qualify you must have had a first-class professional production (Broadway), an off-Broadway production, or a mainstage regional theater production.

Associate member: Open to any playwright, produced or unproduced.

Student member: Open to anyone currently enrolled in a college writing program leading to a degree.

All membership categories receive the Guild's publications and business advice, and the annual dues are modest. For more information, and an application for membership, write or call:

The Dramatists Guild
1501 Broadway, Suite 701
New York, NY 10036
Phone (212) 398-9366

There is no better way to stay informed and to get a sense of the profession than to join this organization.

A Final Word

This book was written to help you write plays with power and impact, plays that are finely wrought and that work beautifully when up and running on the stage. The process you've been introduced to in these pages gives you a solid, basic approach to accomplishing those ends, but obviously, it is not the only way to go about this mysterious business. The excerpts from my interviews with numerous dramatists make that clear. However, what these successful writers have to say about how they work also makes it clear that, different as their approaches may be, certain elements, certain basic ingredients, are always present in their work in some combination.

As you continue writing, over time you'll automatically develop your own approach to this process, an approach that works for you regardless of what anyone else advises. But rest assured, this won't happen with just one play. Think of your playwriting as an ongoing mission, something that will never stop. When you finish the draft of one play you should be already taking notes on the next one. If you get stuck on one, put it aside for a time and go on to another one for a while. Eventually you'll discover your own way of thinking and working. And as long as you incorporate the basic ingredients common to all good plays, you just might write something exciting.

As you proceed in creating your own body of work, make every effort to avoid the trap of writing for "success," or "making it" in the business. This is not your most important goal. Instead, struggle to stay true to what you believe to be true, and write about ideas that genuinely come from your heart. Disregard whatever ideas and themes might be popular socially, politically, or intellectually at the time. The theater is filled with stories of important playwrights who have written powerful, significant plays which have not always found instant success in the marketplace. Trace, for example, the long careers of Arthur Miller, Horton Foote, and Edward Albee. Their work has fallen in and out of favor, but they have never written a play that they didn't totally believe in.

By contrast, many who compromise and calculate to fit the tastes of the times in their writing often do find easier and faster acceptance. These writers, however, tend to appear and disappear from the scene rather quickly, and their work has fleeting popularity. The point here is that acceptance doesn't always equal "success" in the long run. What really counts is to write what you believe most deeply and to express your unique vision of the world. My plea is that you never compromise that.

Finally, always remember that the only way plays get written is to sit down and grind out those pages. Without the discipline of tackling the work on a regular basis, the scripts will never materialize. You may talk and think like a playwright, but you won't be taking the action necessary to become one unless you start putting those words down, one after another. So be tough on yourself and get to it.

I extend to you my best wishes for a long and happy career.

ABOUT THE PLAYWRIGHTS

The interview series from which almost all the excerpts in the book are drawn began in the fall of 1992, with Horton Foote, at the Dramatists Guild's headquarters in New York City. The two exceptions to this are Athol Fugard and David Ives, who were interviewed at McCarter Theatre and Drew University, respectively. All the Guild sessions have been either published in full or summarized in issues of the *Dramatists Guild Quarterly* between 1993 and 1996.

The following entries about the sixteen playwrights must necessarily include only a representative sampling of their achievements.

Edward Albee is the author of many plays, including *The Zoo Story, The Death of Bessie Smith, The Sandbox, The American Dream, Who's Afraid of Virginia Woolf?* (1963 New York Drama Critics Circle Award), *Tiny Alice, A Delicate Balance* (1967 Pulitzer Prize), *All Over, Seascape* (1976 Pulitzer Prize), *The Man Who Had Three Arms, Marriage Play,* and *Three Tall Women* (1994 Pulitzer Prize). He is a member of the Dramatists Guild Council, P.E.N. American, and the American Academy and Institute of Arts and Letters, which also awarded him its Gold Medal in Drama.

Lee Blessing's numerous plays include *A Walk in the Woods, Down the Road, Fortinbras, Two Rooms, Eleemosynary, Nice People Dancing to Good Country Music, Lake Street Extension,* and *Patient A.* In New York, the entire 1992–93 Signature Theatre Company season consisted of productions of his plays. A recipient of grants from the National Endowment for the Arts and the Guggenheim, McKnight, and Jerome Foundations, he has had plays developed at the Eugene O'Neill National Playwrights Conference, the Sundance Institute, New Dramatists, and the Playwrights' Center, Minneapolis.

Horton Foote has written plays for both Broadway and off-Broadway, including *The Trip to Bountiful, The Chase, The Roads to Home, The Traveling Lady,* and *The Young Man from Atlanta* (1995 Pulitzer Prize). His screenplays include *To Kill a Mockingbird* (1963 Academy Award), *Tender Mercies* (1983 Academy Award), *The Chase, The Trip to Bountiful, Baby, the Rain Must Fall, Valentine's Day, 1918, Courtship, Of Mice and Men,* and *Old Man.*

Athol Fugard is acclaimed as the leading South African dramatist of his generation. His plays include *Sizwe Bansi Is Dead, The Island, The Blood Knot, Hello and Goodbye, Boesman and Lena, A Lesson from Aloes, Master Harold . . . and the boys, Playland, A Place with the Pigs, The Road to Mecca, My Children! My Africa, Valley Song,* and *The Captain's Tiger*—all originally produced in South Africa and subsequently produced worldwide.

John Guare's plays include *The House of Blue Leaves* (1971 New York Drama Critics Circle Award), *Rich and Famous, Marco Polo Sings a Solo, Landscape of the Body, Bosoms and Neglect,* the book for *Two Gentlemen of Verona* (1972 Tony Award), *Women and Water, Gardenia, Lydie Breeze, Six Degrees of Separation* (1990 New York Drama Critics Circle Award; Obie Award), and *Four Baboons Adoring the Sun.* He is a member of the Dramatists Guild Council.

Tina Howe is the author of *The Nest, Birth and After Birth, Museum, The Art of Dining, Painting Churches, Coastal Disburbances, Approaching Zanzibar, One Shoe Off,* and *Pride's Crossing.* She is the recipient of a 1983 Obie Award for Distinguished Playwriting, an Outer Critics Circle Award, and an American Academy and Institute of Arts and Letters Award in Literature. A member of the Dramatists Guild Council, she has held fellowships from the National Endowment for the Arts, the Rockefeller Foundation, and the Guggenheim Foundation.

David Ives has written numerous one-act plays, including "Sure Thing," "Philip Glass Buys a Loaf of Bread," "Foreplay, or the Art of the Fugue," and "Universal Language." An evening of his one-acts, *All in the Timing,* won the Outer Critics Circle Award and the John Gassner Playwriting Award. His full-length plays include *Lives and Death of the Great Harry Houdini, Ancient History, Don Juan in Chicago,* and *The Red Address.* He is the recipient of a Guggenheim fellowship.

Romulus Linney is the author of over thirty plays, including *The Sorrows of Frederick, Holy Ghosts, Child Byron, Heathen Valley, April Snow, F.M., The Love Suicide at Scholfield Barracks, 2,* and *True Crimes.* His awards include the 1992 Obie for Sustained Excellence in Playwriting, a 1980 Obie for *Tennessee,* and the 1984 Award in Literature from the American Academy and Institute of Arts and Letters. He is a member of the Dramatists Guild Council.

Emily Mann is the artistic director of McCarter Theatre, in Princeton, N.J., and the author of *Annulla, An Autobiography, Still Life* (1981 Obie Award), *Execution of Justice, Having Our Say,* and *Greensboro: A Requiem.* A member of the Dramatists Guild Council, she is the recipient of the Helen Hayes Award and fellowships from the National Endowment for the Arts and the Guggenheim Foundation.

Terrence McNally's numerous plays include *Corpus Christi, Master Class* (1995 Tony Award), *Love! Valour! Compassion!* (1994 Tony Award), *A Perfect Ganesh, Lips Together, Teeth Apart, The Lisbon Traviata, Frankie and Johnny in the Clair de Lune, It's Only a Play, The Ritz, Bad Habits,* and *Where Has Tommy Flowers Gone?* He was librettist for *The Ritz, Kiss of the Spider Woman* (1993 Tony Award), and *Ragtime.* A recipient of two Guggenheim fellowships, a CBS fellowship, and a citation from the American Academy and Institute of Arts and Letters, he has been the vice president of the Dramatists Guild since 1981.

Arthur Miller is the author of many now-classic plays, including *The Man Who Had All the Luck, All My Sons* (1947 New York Drama Critics Circle Award), *Death of a Salesman* (1949 Pulitzer Prize; New York Drama Critics Circle Award), *The Crucible, A View from the Bridge, Incident at Vichy, After the Fall, The Price, The Creation of the World and Other Business, The American Clock, The Ride Down Mount Morgan, The Last Yankee,* and *Broken Glass.* His screenplays include *The Misfits, Everybody Wins, Playing for Time,* and *The Crucible.* He has written short stories, several novels, and an autobiography, *Timebends.*

Marsha Norman is the author of *'night, Mother* (1983 Pulitzer Prize), *Getting Out, Third and Oak, The Laundromat, The Pool Hall, The Holdup, Traveler in the Dark, Sarah and Abraham,* and *Loving Daniel Boone.* She is the librettist of *The Secret Garden* (1991 Tony Award) and *The Red Shoes.* The recipient of grants from the National Endowment, the Rockefeller Foundation, and the American Academy and Institute of Arts and Letters, she is a member of the Dramatists Guild Council.

John Patrick Shanley's numerous plays include *The Big Funk, Savage in Limbo, Beggars in the House of Plenty, Danny and the Deep Blue Sea, Italian-American Reconciliation, Welcome to the Moon, Four Dogs and a Bone,* and *Psychopathia Sexualis.* His screenplays include *Moonstruck* (1987 Academy Award; Writers Guild Award) and *Joe Versus the Volcano.* He is a member of the Dramatists Guild Council.

Wendy Wasserstein is the author of *An American Daughter, The Sisters Rosensweig, The Heidi Chronicles* (1989 Pulitzer Prize; Tony Award; New York Drama Critics Circle Award), *Uncommon Women and Others, Isn't It Romantic?*, and the book for the musical *Miami*. Her other awards include the Susan Smith Blackburn Prize, Drama Desk Award, and Outer Critics Circle Awards. She is a member of the Dramatists Guild Council.

Michael Weller's plays include *Now There's Just the Three of Us, Moonchildren* (1971 Drama Desk Award), *Fishing, 23 Years Later, Loose Ends* (1976 Outer Critics' Circle Award), *Dwarfman, Master of a Million Shapes, Ghost on Fire, Spoils of War, Lake No Bottom, !Help!*, and *Buying Time*. His screenplays include *Hair, Ragtime, Lost Angels*, and *Getting Rid of Alex*. He is the recipient of a grant from the Rockefeller Foundation and serves on the Council of both the Dramatists Guild and Theatre Communications Group.

Lanford Wilson's plays include *Redwood Curtain, Burn This, Balm in Gilead, The Rimers of Eldritch, Lemon Sky, Serenading Louie, The Hot L Baltimore* (1973 New York Drama Critics Circle Award), *The Mound Builders, Angels Fall*, and the Talley cycle: *Talley's Folly* (1980 Pulitzer Prize; New York Drama Critics Circle Award), *Talley & Son*, and *Fifth of July*. He is the recipient of the American Academy and Institute of Arts and Letters Award, the Vernon Rice Award, and three Obie Awards, and is a member of the Dramatists Guild Council.

INDEX

Buzz McLaughlin is founding director and former artistic director of Playwrights Theatre of New Jersey, a professional (AEA) theatre dedicated to the development of new plays, and a professor of Theatre Arts at Drew University, where he teaches playwriting. His plays, which include *Sister Calling My Name, Spirit on the Plains, Absent Without Leave, Limits,* and *Wings* (a musical adaptation of Aristophanes' *The Birds*), have been produced regionally and in New York and have garnered him numerous national awards. With his wife Kris he has written several screenplays and teleplays. For many years he has served on the advisory board and script selection committee for the New Harmony Project, a national playwrights' and screenwriters' conference held annually in New Harmony, Indiana. He holds a doctorate in theater and dramatic literature from the University of Wisconsin and is a member of the Dramatists Guild and the Writers Guild of America.